THE
FORBIDDEN
ZONE

THE
FORBIDDEN
ZONE

MICHAEL LESY

Farrar, Straus and Giroux

NEW YORK

For my father, Max, and my mother, Sadie
And for Warren, my teacher

FIRST EDITION, 1987

A portion of the 'Pathologists' chapter appeared originally in *Journal: A Contemporary Art Magazine* under the title "If You Die in the University Hospital," 1986

Library of Congress Cataloging-in-Publication Data
Lesy, Michael.
The forbidden zone.

    1. Death—Social aspects—United States.   I. Title.
HQ1073.5.U6L47   1987   306.9   87-7446

CONTENTS

Preface / 3

The Skull and the Letter / 19

Pathologists / 25

Detectives / 43

A Slaughterhouse / 71

A Murder / 91

Shochets / 115

Death Row / 135

A Man-killer / 161

AIDS / 189

Undertakers / 225

To Roger Straus III and Carl Brandt for seeing things through. To Robert Lifton for his understanding. To Liza Nelson, Susan Rosenberg, Ilene Segalove, and Jeremy Zwelling for their insights. To Ari Caratzas, John Fleming, Nancy Joseph, Nick Lemann, Susan Lofton, Karen Peterson, and Kent Stephens for their friendship. And to Liz, Nadia, and Alex for being alive.

PREFACE

*T*here is a forbidden zone marked on the map of twentieth-century American culture, a place every citizen knows but fears to enter. It is a place whose borders are open but never willingly trespassed, a place guarded by dread but surrounded by fascination. It is the zone of death, the modern American Hades. All of us know we must die, but as much as we fear it, we want to know about it. Some of us want to know in order to prepare ourselves; others to discover some way, if not to avoid it, then at least to choose the time and place. Most of us want to know only just enough to experience it imaginatively and then live to tell the tale, like Lazarus returned to the light. Our curiosity makes those who pretend to reveal death's secrets rich and famous. Critically acclaimed best-sellers are written about pathological killers; television programs are punctuated with murder, every death followed by commercials that, like antidotes, promise health, happiness, and unencumbered freedom; crowds of ticket holders wait in line to see films of massacre and dismemberment, homicidal spectacles equivalent to the ancient Games, whose dramas of carnage reminded their audience that they were alive. Our culture is permeated by images and accounts of death, but they are only fictions, works of the imagination, counterfeits. The real thing is carefully hidden. Photographs are cropped; news footage is edited. What finally appears is only a flicker, out of context, reduced to a rectangle of light or printer's ink. Every Hollywood movie, television drama, and executioner's song, no matter how explicit, is only a fabrication, mantled with art, artifice, and commercial interruption. Death's fictions are everywhere available, shrink-wrapped like chicken legs and hamburger meat, but death itself is rarely revealed, only the mirror image of our fear, dread, and fascination with it. Eighty years ago, people died at home and their friends prepared their bodies for burial. In England and America, cemeteries were designed as parks where families strolled for refreshment—landscapes dotted with graves, where the living might contemplate the dead. Today, instead of gazing at death, we watch violence: instead of the long look at the steady state, we switch back and forth from one violent epiphany to the other. Ordinary and inevitable death, death as an actual part of life, has become so rare that when it occurs among us it reverberates like a handclap in an empty auditorium.

Perhaps it's naïve to compare our present with our past, to claim calm and enlightenment for our ancestors and anxious confusion for ourselves. After all, our grandparents had no choice and we do: epidemic death walked among them, and, like it or not, they had to acknowledge it. We don't: medicine has set us free. But medicine hasn't made us immortal. Death still comes to us like sleep, but, unlike our grandparents, few of us believe in the consolations of heaven. We are, as a nation, like that man at the beginning of John O'Hara's *Appointment in Samarra*: one morning, in a crowded bazaar in Baghdad, Death accidentally jostles the man. Death looks at him in surprise: the man looks at Death in horror. The man rushes away, in fear for his life. "I will ride from this city and avoid my fate," he says. He flees to Samarra. Death remains in the bazaar in Baghdad. There, she confesses her surprise at seeing the man so early in the day. According to her calendar, it was to be that evening in Samarra that they were to have their appointment. Like that man, we try to avoid the inevitable, and so our lives are awash with it, sodden with its replicas, soaked with its allusions. We are like the wolves the Eskimos kill with the animals' own appetites: the hunters stick knives in the snow, blades up, smeared with suet; the wolves come and lick. They taste the fat and then they taste their own blood. They lick and lick and lick until they die. Our fascination, our dread, and our denial breed only more fascination, dread, and denial. The fictions we live only famish our craving. The solution, I suggest, is actual knowledge. Not another docudrama whose hero is a pathological killer turned into a fallen angel. Not another sensational novel whose little horrors compound one another like adolescent orgasms. There are actually those among us who deal with death routinely. They enter the forbidden zone not as helpless suicides, or as compulsive killers, or as ordained ministers, but as workers. They deal with death so we can evade it. They do what they do, armored and insulated by any number of rationalizations, both secular and religious, but they do it willingly. They do it as volunteers. It is about these people, what they actually do, why they do it, and what they know about themselves, about us, and about death as a fact of life that I propose to write.

In some cultures, the dead are ritually unclean and those who touch them must be ritually cleansed. In America, those who deal with the dead have social identities that shift back and forth like stationary objects that seem to move from left to right and back again as one eye is opened and the other one closed. Sometimes they look like pariahs and deviants, sometimes like charlatans. Other times they look like heroes or even adepts, initiates, and priests. Those who deal with death work at an intersection of opposites, tainted by the suffering and decay of the body, transfigured by the plight of the self and the destiny of the soul. The world never considers anyone who routinely deals with death to be "pure," but it does place them in a morally conceived hierarchy, their positions determined by how much the world believes they serve either the flesh or the spirit that animates it.

At the base of this hierarchy are those who slaughter animals, since in America, in this part of the century, the soul is considered an exclusively human possession. Egyptians who once worshipped Osiris incarnate in Apis the bull, and Thoth, the god of wisdom, incarnate in an ibis, might differ. So might Buddhists, who believe in the transmigration of souls; so might Hindus; and so might Jews, who still ritually slaughter the animals they eat. But, at present in America, animals are considered creatures of flesh, and those associated with their wholesale deaths are treated like brutes, their minds deadened by endless disassembly lines of carcasses, as inert and identical as ingots or engine blocks. At a considerable distance from them in the hierarchy, considered morally questionable if not reprehensible, are those who serve justice as the professional killers of men. Executioners, police sharpshooters, and mercenary soldiers comprise this group. Above them are homicide detectives, and above them are forensic pathologists and medical pathologists. To protect themselves from what they do, all of these men construct personas whose hands and faces they wear like masks and gloves. Police sharpshooters carry themselves like hunters; mercenaries consider themselves warriors; some homicide detectives behave like cynics, others like avengers; pathologists pretend to be men working on a puzzle. Just as the Germans who exterminated the Jews used language rules in their documents, referring to "transport and resettlement," so these men, speaking through their masks, refer to "posts," targets, and stiffs. Far above them in the hierarchy, as distant from them as Dante's Paradise was from his Inferno, are those who comfort the dying and console the living. If the world brutalizes its slaughterers and shuns its man-killers, it honors and sometimes reveres those who serve the terminally ill and help the living to bear their grief. At the apex of the hierarchy are the hospice workers, the modern advocates of what the fourteenth century called "the good death." At a considerable distance beneath them, honored (but sometimes suspect) for the way they serve the worst fears of the living, are the morticians, who disguise and display the dead as if they were asleep. Long ago, La Rochefoucauld compared death to the sun, a force of nature whose sight no man could endure without glancing away. Of all those who routinely deal with death, it is the hospice workers who bear the "sight" of it most steadily and for their humane resolve are the most honored.

But whether those who deal with death are placed at the base or at the summit of a moral hierarchy, they are subject to the same questions: Why do they do what they do? How do they bear it? What do they know that the rest of us don't? Whether they are shunned or honored, degraded or revered, tolerated or sought out, all of them exist on an edge, at an outer limit. From that lonely place, they not only look at things that the rest of us refuse to see, but they look back at us from a distant, perhaps even a revelatory perspective. For some reason, they have chosen to set up shop on the shores of a gigantic whirlpool, a place where transcendent visions, final truths, ultimate meanings, famous last words, and dying breaths swirl around, mixed with every kind of garbage, both physical and spiritual, every kind of cruelty and pain, every variety of lie and deception, every remnant of false hope and evasion, and all the most pathetic shreds of memory and forgetfulness. The questions remain: Why are they there: how do they bear it: what do they know? The answers will be the subject of this book, its chapters equivalent to a journal kept by a single climber as he struggles from the base to the summit of a mountain that no one has yet climbed. What he sees, you will see; what he hears, you will hear; what touches him will touch you. His voice will run through this book like a safety line up a rock face. A voice, like a rope, made of twisted strands of thought and feeling, observation and projection, description, confession, and analysis.

There is, of course, another set of questions, parallel to the first. Questions about the climber who has offered his services as a guide. Questions about who he is and why he's chosen to make the climb. Is he reckless or prudent? A fool or a hero? A liar who tells tales or an honest man who tells the truth? Is his vision clear or clouded, his touch sure or timid? In fact, can he be trusted? If he were up there all alone, no one would care. But he intends to take people along. How does he know what he's doing? What's his experience, his background, his training? One false move and the rope might break; one false step and he could take everyone over the side. Who, in the name of God, is he?

I am the climber who's offered his services. And who am I? A man who is almost forty, the father of two children who watched them be born. A man old enough, according to Jewish tradition, to ask questions about what is above, what is below, what came before, and what comes after. A man old enough to ask and perhaps even to be answered. A Jew, the son of a remarkable man. A man who was born in Poland in the first year of this century, who came to America, unable to speak English, when he was twenty-one; a man who avoided the Holocaust, became a doctor, and fathered a child, an only son, the child born in 1945, on Thanksgiving, just as the dead were being counted, born into the tribe of Levi, the tribe of scribes, born under the sign of Sagittarius, a mutable sign of spiritual quest, the child named after an archangel, the Archangel Michael, and that child me.

In some families, the child is loved and loves both parents. In mine, I was loved by both, but deeply I loved my father, so that, like a little animal, like a dog, when I heard his voice, the blood beat in me. I listened to him and listened to him as every night, at dinner, he told the stories of his patients as if they were his family, stories of their suffering and stubbornness, their frailties and sickness, their diagnoses and recovery, their misfortunes and death. Every other night, though, he stopped and, instead of telling me their stories, he told and retold the story of himself:

Himself the child of a poor man who lived in a little village until one day, when he was almost forty, he got sick and went to Warsaw and died on the operating table, killed by a cancer in his bowels. A poor man who was buried in my father's sight, a poor man who left his wife to live like a beggar, and his children to live like orphans. My father weeping in the arms of his sister, at night, in a cold, dark house, asking her, "Why don't we have anyone to care for us?" My father, a little boy six years old, left alone to go out before dawn in the winter to say prayers for his father's soul, a little boy who stepped into a snowdrift and was stranded there, too small to escape, crying and freezing, until a man passed by on his way to say his own prayers, and rescued him. My father, chased across the fields by other boys, big boys, Polish boys, yelling, "Kill him! Kill him! Kill the Kike!"

Then, just before the First War, they all fled: my father's sister and her husband to America; my father's brother and mother and my father to London, where he pulled a cart through the streets until one day he stopped near a hospital and watched a lorry being unloaded, a lorry full of wounded and dying men, brought back from the war, men who cried and groaned like cattle, as my father watched and thought, "Is this all there is? Is this what it comes to?" Then, when the war ended, everyone starved. My father wrote and told his sister; his sister pawned everything she owned and paid for my father and his mother to come to America. There, my father worked as a tailor and dreamed of becoming a designer. At night he went to school. All day, he worked and studied, worked and studied. In three years—"Three years!" he said—he learned to read and write and talk and count and graduated from high school. Then he went to college. And there he nearly died. He caught rheumatic fever: he lay in bed for months and months, and when he rose up again, he was changed. He decided he would become a doctor, that nothing in the world would stop him, that he would become a doctor or die. No one believed him. It was impossible; it was a dream; he was a dreamer. Everyone bowed and smiled and called him "Doc" and laughed. He ignored them. He went back to England and enrolled in medical school. A woman he met introduced him to the Chief Rabbi of Dublin. The Chief Rabbi found him a place at Trinity College. There he studied medicine. One summer he returned to America and was introduced to my mother. They were engaged in July, and in September she came to London and they were married. They went on their honeymoon and then, for five years, they never saw each other again. Not once. She worked and sent him what money she could. He studied and studied, and when he'd learned all he could and had gotten his degree, he came back to her.

Perhaps you've read stories like this before. But I was only a child when I heard them and they filled my heart. My father was forty-five and my mother was forty-three when I was born into their middle age. My father said they had waited so long because they hadn't trusted the world. That wait cost my mother her uterus; it cost me any brothers and sisters. By the time I was old enough to notice, I saw it had cost my father his health. All those years of pushing carts and sewing pants, of studying at night and living on twelve cents a day, had ravaged his heart, ruined his teeth, scarred his stomach, and ground down his spine. He was a sick man, in constant pain, who spent his days curing others. At night he came home and told his stories. I was frightened he would die. He had sacrificed everything to be a doctor. One day, it would be my turn.

When I was old enough, my father sent me to the best private school in the city, a school that had had quotas to keep out Jews until the Second War and its aftermath had shamed it into admitting a few more of us. There I studied and was chased, not from field to field, but from corridor to courtyard, by the sons of rich men who yelled the same things at me that the sons of peasants had yelled at my father. There, every morning I went to chapel and sang all the hymns and loved the words and the music of every one of them. Every afternoon, I went to Hebrew school, recited the prayers, and learned the stories of Abraham, Isaac, and Jacob. By the time I was thirteen, I knew the Lord's Prayer as well as the Shema. Above all, I knew that Christ was a Jew who had suffered. Which is what my father had done and what I was learning to do. What friends I had couldn't understand my sadness. Their fathers were cabinet officers; their relatives lived on country estates. "Why are you so gloomy?" they asked. What could I tell them? My father had run for his life? My relatives had been incinerated? I didn't know what to say. I went to chapel, sang the hymns, and was bar mitzvahed.

When I was fourteen, my father decided I was old enough to work in a hospital. He found me a summer job in an experimental animal laboratory. He said it would prepare me for medicine. I believed him, as I always had. The lab where I worked performed open-heart surgery on dogs in the belief that it was best for heart surgeons to make their mistakes on animals before they tried the same thing on humans. Every week a heart surgeon would try to replace a dog's aorta with a piece of plastic and wait to see how long the sutures held. To do this, he bypassed the dog's heart with a heart-lung machine whose reservoir had to be primed with blood. If the patient had been human, the lab would have called the Red Cross and requested twelve units of blood. But there were no blood banks for dogs. To get the blood it needed, the lab kept a large kennel. At 4:00 a.m. on the day of the operation, eight dogs were selected to be sacrificed. One by one, the dogs were anesthetized and strapped to a table. A French resident surgeon opened their femoral arteries, inserted a catheter, and let them pump themselves out into a jar. If they were small dogs with a small blood volume, the resident opened the chest and squeezed the heart like a sponge. I watched. I listened. I smelled. The dogs whined and urinated as they died. The sound of their chests being opened reminded me of my mother cutting apart chicken breasts. When it was over, a big, slow-moving black man named Oscar lifted them off the table by their legs and dropped them, one on top of the other, into an enormous paper bag. Later, he hauled them off to the incinerator. The operation itself took three hours. None of the patients survived. I watched it all and thought. I thought of how Aztec priests had cut open men's chests with obsidian knives. I thought of how the Germans had burnt Jews. I thought of how Abraham had bound Isaac to the altar. I saw doctors and dogs, then I saw Germans and Jews, and then, for some reason, I saw me and my father, his sacrifice and mine. That fall, my father sent me to boarding school. I came home very seldom after that. When I did, we argued. We argued for six years. Then I told my father I'd never be a doctor. I made some excuse about failing a chemistry course. I never told him I was afraid. I never told him I was appalled. I was, and I am, but it didn't do me any good. My father was very gracious about it. He said it was my life, not his. Unfortunately, the world didn't have his manners.

Do I have to remind you of all the people who died in public in the sixties? Real people, not actors. Presidents, prize laureates, former Attorney Generals. Various heads of state, ideologues, activists, entertainers, and writers. Any number of Vietnamese shot and incinerated. One afternoon, during a lull in the fighting, I was looking through a collection of old pictures in a photo archive. I didn't know then that I was about to begin my career as a mountain climber. Ever since I'd broken the news to my father, I had been jumping all over the intellectual landscape. I had studied theoretical sociology and European history. I had read a good deal of nineteenth-century Russian literature and had spent much time teaching myself to be a photographer. The result was that, at the age of twenty-two, I had come to the University of Wisconsin to study with a man whose specialty was the Weimar Republic and the rise of the Nazi Party. Unfortunately, the man had decided that the writings of Martin Luther were important to him. So important that he asked his graduate students to put aside their own work and help him analyze Luther's letters to the German princes. Since the fighting seemed to be getting closer and closer to home, I refused. I declared myself to be an American historian and began to search for something relevant to investigate. I settled on the assassination of Lincoln and the impeachment of President Andrew Johnson as something sufficiently bloody and dramatic. One afternoon, I decided to take a break and look at a collection of photographs made in a small town in Wisconsin at the very end of the nineteenth-century.

It seemed to me that history and photography were more deeply linked than the specialists who practiced them knew. Both enabled their practitioners to enter the river of time, temporarily stop its flow, and scrutinize it. Both disciplines allowed their practitioners to fuse their methods of inquiry with the workings of their imaginations and, by that fusion, to take advantage of coincidences between their own preoccupation and the events that swirled around them—coincidences that enabled the best of historians to find a needle of data in a haystack of facts, and the best of photographers to be at the right place at the right time, camera in hand. What I didn't know, as I sat idly looking at photographs that afternoon, was that history and photography were about to place me at the center of such a set of coincidences, and that, once there, I'd use them not just to stop the flow of time but to drive a set of spikes into the side of a mountain—a mountain I'm still climbing.

What happened was that I saw the face of a young woman, dark-haired, dark-eyed, dressed in a black silk gown, standing behind her mother in a family portrait. Her glance was extraordinary: direct, clear, and luminous, the pupils of her eyes as black and perfect as opals. I stared at her and stared her; she returned my glance so steadily that, as I tried to understand her meaning, I projected myself into her, and as I looked up and out of her face, I realized that her glance had been frozen by astonishment and fear. I pulled away then and looked behind her. Above her head, the emulsion of the negative had so decayed that it looked as if the air around her had ruptured and turned to blood. Of course, this couldn't be: it was only the silver salts of the negative that had come apart and clotted; it was only the length of the original exposure in the photographer's studio that had frozen open her eyes. I asked the curator if there were other pictures in the collection. There were many, he said; thousands, he said, all the work of one man. Could I see them, I asked. He brought them out, box after box. As I looked, I saw the same amazed and fearful glance in the faces of others. And as I looked, I thought of the extraordinary portraits of German peasants made during the Weimar Republic by a photographer named August Sander, who had set himself the task of methodically photographing every human social type as if he were an anthropologist from another planet, making an illustrated catalogue of human society. The Nazis, who had their own ideas about social types, found his to be subversive and, after the first volume of his portraits was published, ordered the printing plates destroyed. I was only halfway through the collection when the curator told me it was closing time. I asked the name of the little town where all the pictures had been made. "Black River Falls," he said. He turned out the lights and I went to dinner.

It was two months later that I asked to see the microfilm copies of the Black River Falls newspaper for 1885, the date of the earliest pictures in the collection. I threaded the microfilm through the slits of a reading machine, found the front page for January 1, and scanned it: nothing unusual, a typical mix of national news and local comings and goings. I unwound some more, until I reached a two-column spread entitled "Local News." I started reading. Without knowing it, I had just stepped into the center of a conjunction of history, photography, and my own inheritance. The column began with a report of a ghost, followed by the story of a woman who had cut her own throat, followed by a public notice about a woman who had been adjudged insane, followed by the report of an old woman who had thrown herself in front of a train and been cut into three pieces, followed by a story about a destitute woman who had been found wandering the streets of a nearby town with a dead baby in her arms. I rewound the microfilm and asked for another reel, this time for 1890. I unwound it, randomly turned to the month of April, located the "Local News," and read the story of a woman who had disappeared on her wedding day and been found the next morning wandering about, dazed, unable to remember what had happened. This, followed by a report of five children in one family killed by the same disease, followed by a report of a woman who had slit her own throat with a case knife, followed by the death notice of a woman whose five children had died of diphtheria the summer before. I read the local news for the rest of the year. It went on like that: epidemic disease, suicide and insanity, interrupted by ghosts, arson, armed troops, murder, exhaustion, window breaking, and lake monsters. I turned off the machine's reading light and stared at the dark rectangle of the screen. "What's going on?" I thought.

I'd like to say that I knew. That I ran upstairs and checked the statistics for the rate of insanity and epidemic disease in the county where Black River Falls was located. Or that I immediately requested the microfilm reel for 1893, the year that marked the onset of the last of the Great Depressions of the nineteenth-century. I'd like to say that, but it didn't happen. The only history I'd ever studied was European. The only Depression I'd ever heard of had begun in 1929. I still couldn't understand why some very important people had wanted Andrew Johnson impeached. Perhaps, if I'd had time that first afternoon to look at all the pictures from Black River Falls and had seen all the dead babies, I might have dropped what I was doing. But I didn't. It took me a year to discover that Andrew Johnson had collided with a child's toy version of the military-industrial complex. It took me another year to learn enough American history to realize that even though Black River Falls was a typical little town, no one but some novelists had ever described what happened to human beings when a series of farm depressions coincided with epidemics of smallpox, typhoid, diphtheria, and dysentery.

Even when I went back to look at all the photographs and read all the newspaper entries and the public health statistics and the mental hospital records and the diaries—I'd like to say that I knew what I was doing and why I was doing it. But I didn't. What I knew was what I felt, and what I felt was that I was descending into darkness. Every day, I walked out of the light and into the cold, dark, quiet room where the microfilm machines were kept. Every day, I began a new day, in a new week, in a new month, in a new year, but that day was eighty years old and it was a chronicle of suffering, madness, and disaster. Around me, the clerks gossiped, the reading machines whined and hummed, the other researchers shifted in their chairs. But, in front of me, the screen was filled with the stories of individual souls alight and aflame, twisting and collapsed, as if I were watching a whole field of wheat catch fire, one stalk at a time. I took careful notes. At the end of the day, I went home. Every night I read and reread *Slaughterhouse-Five*, rocking back and forth to Billy Pilgrim's "So it goes." I'd like to say Vonnegut kept me sane. I'd like to say that I was filled with sorrow and pity. But the truth is, I went mad. Six months later, when I woke up, I was changed, as changed as my father had been when he'd risen up out of his bed after nearly dying of rheumatic fever. My father had decided to be a doctor; I decided to be a writer.

I made my notes and the photographs from the archives into a book. It was called *Wisconsin Death Trip*, which is what some people who used drugs at the time called hallucinations of death and rebirth. Those who read the book couldn't decide if it was poetry or history, a fabrication or a discourse, a hoax or a revelation. The book took on a life of its own. It bred other books; it bred plays and ballets, concertos and an opera. It made me famous and notorious; honored and suspect. I began to watch. Once, when I was invited to speak at a university, I got off the plane expecting to be met, only to be ignored by the greeting committee, who anxiously scanned the faces of my fellow passengers, looking for the wise old man who had written the book they admired. Necrophiliacs wrote me letters. My publisher told me the book had become a cult item on the Riviera and a collector's item in Stockholm. My fellow historians declared I was either a fool or a charlatan. Artists, especially photographers, claimed I was one of them. It took me ten years to realize what I'd done and why.

What I'd done was to discover a massive amount of pain, suffering, and death in the middle of America. In fact, what I'd described was a holocaust without Jews. I did this, I was able to do this, for two reasons. First, because of my father and his stories. And, second, because of my ancestors. I'm sorry to have to refer to them. I know it sounds as suspicious as a politician evoking the honored dead, but Jews have been on intimate terms with the Angel of Death since the Exodus. We've known about fiery furnaces since Shadrach, Meshach, and Abednego. We weren't the first to have been nearly obliterated and we won't be the last, but we've had a lot of practice at it, so much practice that we've learned to take notes and to turn those notes into books—books that bear witness to the mortal predicament we share with everyone else on the planet. Obviously, if we had any choice in the matter, if history or Fate or God hadn't forced us to learn to live in perpetual double jeopardy, we wouldn't be able to see so well in the dark. Like it or not, I inherited that ability.

One consequence was the book called *Death Trip*. Another is this book. In between, my motives haven't changed. Only now I think my father may die any day. His bones are brittle; every joint is inflamed; his heart misses and forgets; his blood pressure plummets and soars; the vessels of his brain threaten to explode. He lies on his back, heavy-lidded. When he rises, he lurches and falls; when he speaks, he slurs and forgets. His house is about to be sold; the furniture about to be auctioned. He and my mother will withdraw to an apartment, where they will watch television and wait. Every evening, the news reports another famine and another battle. The war that everyone has been expecting for forty years grinds closer, like a glacier moving down a fjord. Perhaps none of this matters as much as we think. Perhaps, as the Brahmins believed, we are merely in the final age, an "age of darkness," the last stage of a huge cosmic cycle that will begin again, as it always has, with a new dawn. Or perhaps, as the Cabalists thought, there is no final death, only rebirth and renewal, that the primordial souls of everyone who stood at the foot of Mount Sinai to receive the Ten Commandments are born and reborn in every generation. I don't know about any of this. Perhaps I'm a fool to ask. But I'm going to ask anyway.

THE SKULL
AND THE LETTER

*I*t was in January, the coldest month of the year, that my parents called me to come home. They'd found a buyer for their house, but before they left it, they wanted me to choose what I wanted to keep for myself. For thirty years their house had been a mark of their wealth, a sign of their grace, its address the evidence I gave to strangers to prove my good breeding, the place where I always returned, no matter how long I'd been gone, no matter how far I wandered, no matter what arrangements I'd made elsewhere. My mother was still healthy, but my father was growing weaker. Soon he might die and she'd be all alone. Before anything happened, they wanted to be ready, bags packed, cash in hand, traveling light, prepared to cross the border. For a week I sorted through their books and records, their china and crystal and silver and linens. I moved the furniture to be sold away from the furniture to be kept. Everything I touched and saw made me think of who I was and who I wasn't and who I might have been.

Outside, it was so cold not even cars moved through the streets. The snow blew so thick that the streetlights burned until noon. Inside, the furnace kicked on every half hour, its motor humming through the floors and walls of the house like an engine deep in the hold of a ship. Every day I packed boxes, while my father lay dozing in the library and my mother sat in the kitchen looking out the window, waiting for the mail. One day, on the second floor of the house, I opened the door to an unheated room that had been unused for twenty-five years. Against one wall sat a steamer trunk, its body black, its corners capped with brass, its sides plastered with labels for ocean liners that had left Liverpool for Dublin, and London for New York, fifty years ago. It had been my father's trunk, the one he'd used when he'd studied medicine at Trinity College in Dublin, and sailed back and forth across the Irish Sea and the Atlantic, between his brother in London and his sister in America. The trunk had sat unopened since I was a boy. When I was eight, I'd asked my mother what was in it. She'd said, "Papers." When I was thirteen, I asked and she'd said the same thing. When I was twenty-one, she gave the same answer. When I was thirty, she'd said it again.

Now I was almost forty and I asked my mother for the key. "Why do you want it?" she said. "There's nothing in there. It's empty. It's junk. I'm going to give it away. Someone else can fool with it." "Mother. Stop it. Please." She went into her bedroom and shut the door. When she came out, she looked at me and tossed her head. She had the key, but she wouldn't hand it to me. "I'll do it," she said. "I'm the one." She put on one of my father's overcoats and climbed the stairs. Our breaths clouded the air in the room. She tried the lock but couldn't turn it. "Let me. Let me," I said. I opened the lock and lifted the lid. The inside of the trunk was lined with blue paper the color of a robin's egg. Fitted across the top, like a second lid, was an empty shelf. I lifted it out and stared down. It was empty except for another shelf that fitted the space halfway down like a false bottom. I lifted that out and leaned over. At the very bottom was a skull in three pieces and a letter in a blue envelope.

"Satisfied now?" said my mother. She turned and left. I lifted out the biggest piece of the skull. Its top had been neatly sawed off, and tiny brass rivets driven around its rim. I reached down and found the top. Little holes had been drilled around its edge. If the holes were aligned with the rivets, the two pieces fitted together so well that they had to be pried apart. I reached down and came up with the jaw. It had finely wound brass springs on either side that hooked to eyelets screwed into the skull's temples. I fitted the pieces together and looked at what I'd made. A little skull it was, amber-colored, toothless, the original property, perhaps, of an old lady that had fallen into the hands of an anatomy class and then been passed on to my father. I reached for the letter. Blue ink on blue paper. It began with "Dear Max," my father's name, and ended with "Sadie," my mother's. It was a love letter. A letter my mother had written my father after they'd met and decided to marry. It had all happened very soberly. He'd left Ireland one summer to visit his sister in Cleveland. A relative had introduced them. They'd walked by the lake and agreed to marry, partners pledging their goodwill. He'd promised to send for her. She'd travel to London and be married in his brother's house. They both knew what would happen next: she'd return to America and wait. Fifty years later, he lay on the couch in the study with his eyes closed, while she sat in the kitchen staring into the storm, and I stood reading the only evidence I'd ever had that they'd once been in love. It was a wonderful letter she'd written, bright, sprightly, teasing, pining, and coquettish. Best of all, she'd written it as if she were speaking, with all the fits and starts, jumps and runs, pauses and pirouettes of a woman talking to a man she loved, missed, and knew she'd marry. She hadn't sent him a letter; she'd sent him her voice.

I took a cold deep breath. I looked up at the frost on the window. That's what I'd choose; that's what I'd keep. It's what I'd always had. Not the books and furniture and china, but the skull and the letter—the death's-head of my father and the voice of my mother. The melancholy of one, the sprung rhythms of the other. The very subject at hand and the very means to express it. Two days later, I packed my bags, and a week after that, I began my journey.

PATHOLOGISTS

*I*f you die in the university hospital, the nursing staff lets your family sit with you for what they call "a reasonable interval." Then they ask them to leave and they call the transport service. The transport service sends a man with a trick gurney to get you. The gurney's flat, covered with a sheet; it looks like all the others that carried you back and forth while you were alive. Except this one has a hidden shelf. Instead of laying you on top, the man from transport puts you underneath and drapes the whole thing with a sheet. Anyone who sees him coming thinks he's pushing an empty gurney, on his way to X-ray. Only he's not headed there. If your family's signed the proper forms, he's headed downstairs to medical pathology, to a little room with its own locked door. Unmarked, as I recall. The whole arrangement's like those fake meat-market vans Solzhenitsyn said the Soviets use to carry political prisoners out of Moscow on their way into the Gulag. Says the Intourist guide, "Political prisoners? No. Not here. None at all. And hardly any crime. As you can see." In the hospital, the same fiction prevails: out of sight, out of mind. Says the administrator, "Death? Of course we lose some. The fight goes on. But let me show you our magnetic resonance generator. It's just down here to the left." Meanwhile, the man from transport has closed the door behind him, put you on a tray, and is ready to transfer you to one of the lockers. I believe there are twelve of them, their stainless-steel doors forming a unit that fills one wall of the room. No one ties any tags to your toes. After all, you're still a patient in the hospital. Dead, maybe, but you're still wearing your ID bracelet.

Mr. Driver and Mr. Taggart from medical pathology have been expecting you. Just like long ago, when you were alive and the milkman used to deliver the milk. Remember? The milkman walked up the drive, in the snow, opened the door of the milk box, collected the empties, and put in two fresh bottles. An hour later, you woke up, opened the milk box from the inside, and discovered two glistening bottles, heavy and white, where two empty ones had been. A little bit of everyday magic. A loaf in the oven, a bottle in the box. Just open the door and start the day. Which is what Mr. Taggart and Mr. Driver plan to do with you. When they're done, they'll put you back, and someone from a funeral home will come to collect what's left.

Taggart was the one who told me about the trick gurney. He called autopsies "posts" (instead of postmortems), and bodies "patients." He spent two hours explaining things. A decent, friendly man. When he first came out of his office, he looked small and a little bent. He had blue eyes, but his left one kept going as if it might turn the corner. A muscle imbalance, surgically correctable I'm told, but socially disconcerting, since a stranger doesn't know which gaze to address. He was in his late twenties, but he looked as if he'd been wearing the same face since third grade. An innocent, serious face with hair combed and parted, the teacher's pet. In college he'd studied biology, then got a master's in pathology. He was in charge of the lab, the way a line producer is in charge of a movie: everything looked as if it was his, but it wasn't. Above him were the professors of pathology, men with medical degrees who worked in their own labs, assisted by pathology residents, evaluating diagnoses and conducting research based on tissue samples supplied by Taggart and the hospital residents he supervised.

Driver was Taggart's partner. He did the heavy work of opening and closing the bodies. He made a Y-cut to get into them. He began, on either side, at the outer edges of the collarbones. The cut converged at the base of the sternum and then went straight down the midline from there. He used a high-speed electric circular saw that whined like a dentist's drill to cut a triangular section out of the rib cage and expose the lungs and heart. After he pried off the breastplate, he took everything out, or, as Taggart said, he "eviscerated the patient." It all came out in one piece, like an engine block. "All in one piece?" I asked. "Sure," said Taggart, "we're pretty tightly packed." Also, Driver was very good at it. He came from a family of morticians who for four generations had been embalming the people who lived in the small, black, country towns around Asheville. He had a degree in mortuary arts and sciences, so he knew what not to cut to keep the funeral directors happy: he tied off the subclavians near the collarbones, and never went near the carotids in the neck or the femorals in the thighs. That way, when the lab had taken everything out, the embalmers still had all the plumbing they needed for the funeral.

Taggart told me all this while we were standing in the lab, leaning up against the autopsy table: the room, brightly lit, well ordered; the air smelling faintly of formaldehyde. I tried to keep on looking at him, but sometimes I'd follow the curve of his left eye and notice some details. For instance, there was a band saw that looked like the kind professional meat cutters use. There were quite a few kitchen knives laid out on corkboards, next to scalpels and scissors, and on the counter, above the sink, next to the radio, there was an Osterizer electric knife sharpener. At one point, Taggart reached into a cabinet and pulled out a heat-sealed plastic pouch, the kind that housewives with a passion for freezers use to preserve leftovers. Taggart's had an esophagus connected to part of a stomach, all of it awash in a bit of clear formaldehyde to keep it fresh. Taggart looked more like a technician than like a cannibal, more like a lab man than like a meat cutter, but I wanted to know if he ever got upset with the more carnivorous parts of his work. "Sometimes," he said. "When we have to do five or six a day. Then you're just cutting. The pressure gets to you. You don't have time to think." "Think?" I asked. "Think about what?" That's when he told me about the death of organ systems. Let me explain:

The day before I met Taggart, a friend of mine who was in her third year of medical school told me about the first time she'd seen Death come into a room and kill a man. The man had been her patient. The surgeons had opened him up to remove a tumor from his right lung. He was lying in the intensive care unit, recovering, hooked to a respirator. Lorna noticed he was trembling. She thought it was an aftereffect of general anesthesia, but wasn't sure. She found an anesthesiologist and brought him to look. By then the man was shaking. "No," said the anesthesiologist. "It's not the anesthesia. I believe this man is fighting for his life." First he'd been trembling, then shaking, and then, in spite of having a needle plunged into his heart and his chest reopened as he lay in bed, he died in ten minutes. "To see it happen! To see death roll over him!" said Lorna, her eyes wide from the sight of it.

Taggart took it a step farther. "We're all mammals," he said. "We're no different once we're opened up. A cow, a dog, or a pig looks about the same on the inside as we do." Taggart spent his days looking at the way death marked the organ systems of a group of mammalian vertebrates called humans. He said those who died from AIDS had organs that looked as if they'd been detonated, and those who'd smoked had lungs that were black and stiff like old rubber. Nothing was hidden; everything was visible. There were no abstractions, only subtleties. Death was a literal, visible fact. Even a pathologist's assistant like Taggart could follow it from the heart to the lungs to the kidneys, like a hunter following a beast through a forest. Five times a week, 250 times a year, he and Driver looked inside and saw something some of us believe in and all of us think about but never witness: they saw fate. If they found it in the bones, they measured it; if they found it in the glands, they weighed it. They cut it up and took samples: everything from the right side went into a small glass jar; everything from the left went into a big one. Choice examples went to histology to be made into slides for closer study. They did all this on behalf of the pathologists who sat in the research labs, waiting to pass judgment or confirm the outcome.

"Thirty percent of the time," said Taggart, "patients are misdiagnosed." Sometimes doctors were just wrong. Sometimes, instead of counting five fingers on a hand, they counted only three. The pathologists told them the truth. "We're the physicians' physicians. We're the bottom line, the quality control." For some reason, I thought of Roman priests who'd killed sheep to read their livers and predict the future. Pathologists read the past, but weren't they just as priestly? They looked inside, saw the marks, and told their meaning. They revealed secrets. They announced the wages of sin. I thought of how Death had come to Abraham the patriarch: one day, when he was very, very old, he saw a bright light and smelled a sweet odor. It was Death coming toward him in great glory and beauty. Death said to him, "Don't think this is the way I appear to every man, only to those who are righteous. To those who've sinned, I come in great corruption and horror." Abraham said, "Then show me." Death showed him two heads, one like a serpent, the other like a sword. All the men who were sitting near Abraham looked up and died from the sight, but Abraham lived. He lived because he was righteous. What about the pathologists? What did they see, and how did they bear it?

Taggart was only their assistant, and he was a man with a zoo-morphic vision. What about the people he worked for?

It was lunchtime when Taggart finished talking about organ systems and mammals and I had begun to think about fate and Roman priests. He said Dr. O'Brian wanted to meet me at 3:00 p.m. Dr. O'Brian was an assistant professor of pathology and laboratory medicine. "Fine," I thought. "He can find out if I can be trusted and I can find out if he speaks Latin." In the meantime, I was hungry. Halfway to the restaurant, I passed a bookstore with a skeleton in the window. The skeleton had a stethoscope around its neck. Instead of fountain pens, the display case was full of surgical instruments. Taggart's talk about subclavian veins and midlines and femoral arteries had made me a little uneasy. I thought I remembered where they were, but maybe I needed a review. I started looking for a standard anatomy text. I saw one with a skull on the cover and the title *Color Atlas of Anatomy*. "All right," I thought, "I'll just look in the index and then have lunch." I didn't notice the subtitle, *A photographic study of the human body*. I flipped it open, took one look, and stopped breathing. On the left, there was the head of an old man with his eyes closed and all his skin peeled off. There were lines connected to numbers, sticking into him from both sides, like acupuncture needles. The caption read, "Facial muscles. Anterior aspect. Left side: superficial layer; right side: deeper layer." I turned the page, thinking, "This is extraordinary. How could they do this? Look at all the detail. They can't keep this up." But they did. He was there on the next page, in profile, in color: "Lateral superficial aspect of the face. Peripheral distribution of the facial nerve." Not just his facial nerve, but his muscles, glands, ducts, veins. He had brown eyelashes and temporal arteries that converged like the Monongahela and the Allegheny. I kept turning the pages, and as each new plate came into view, my breath fluttered out of me.

When I was ten, I used to close the doors of my father's library behind me and take down his copy of Gray's *Anatomy*, the one he had bought in Dublin in the twenties when he was studying medicine at Trinity. His Gray's was on the same shelf as his *Collected Works of Sigmund Freud*. By the time I was twelve, I had started to read the Freud. I went back and forth, from one to the other, for years. First the visible, then the invisible; deep, then deeper; outside, then in; appearances, then meanings. The Gray's was as incomprehensible and thrilling as the Freud. Overlays of lines, crosshatches of meaning, books of abstract revelations, as dense as silk, but without weight or tactile presence: the Gray's illustrated with engravings, printed in only three pale colors; the Freud a set of abstractions and analyses clustered around a few truncated stories. The book I had in my hands now was different, as different as an engraving was from a woodcut, or a gaze from a glance. Everything was there before me in color, in detail, four hundred pages of exquisite plates, numbered and labeled. Photographs of people or parts of people, peeled layer by layer, their fat as yellow as chicken soup, their flesh as ruddy as beef, their limbs as finely articulated, veined, nerved, boned, and sinewed as—there was no analogy, only fact: what I saw before me were pictures of people revealed to a depth and with a clarity that was so unprecedented that I was as frightened as I was amazed. I took the book up to the counter. I wondered if the clerk would sell it to me. Would he ask me to prove my good intentions or my professional qualifications or my need to know? All he did was take my MasterCard. It cost $42. I now owned a book I could hardly bear to look at. I took it with me to the restaurant, asked for a table in the back, ordered a sandwich, and looked again. First for five minutes. Then I shut it and waited. Then I opened it and looked a bit longer. And then a bit longer, opening it and closing it until I could bear to look for fifteen minutes at a time, conducting an autopsy by turning the pages. By then it was time to meet Dr. O'Brian.

O'Brian was in his mid-thirties, dark-haired, bearded, and carefully dressed. He spoke rapidly and precisely, the voice pitched at an alto, the eyes quick, alert, and responsive. I thought, "If he were a priest, he'd have been too refined to have ever had a parish; this one would have gone straight into the curia." When I asked, he said he was from Boston, raised a Catholic. He'd studied philosophy and then gone into medicine. I would have asked why, but he had too many things he wanted to tell me. The first thing he wanted me to know was that he was a medical, not a surgical, pathologist. The surgical ones, he said, worked against time; the judgments they made were matters of life and death; the words they used were "malignant" or "benign," "active" or "in remission." The medical pathologists sat in their labs and considered the evidence after everything was quiet. They were studious and reflective, students of truth, not adjuncts of treatment. "We're the gold standard," O'Brian said, and I thought of assayists in a tower, locked away from the world, separating the gold from the dross. It was the research and analysis, he said, that had attracted him, the chance to spend nearly all his time quietly thinking about how and why and what. Pathologists, he said, were among the most intellectual of doctors. And, he said, some of the most visual. They insisted on *seeing* the evidence. Unlike surgeons, he said, whose life was a mad rush from crisis to crisis, operating almost blind, guided only by their sense of touch. I asked him then about the rate of misdiagnosis. Was it actually thirty percent? Yes, he said, but, even then, there were deaths that no one could explain, deaths that made him believe in the will to live. After Taggart's talk about humans as mammals, I couldn't believe my ears. "A will to live?" I asked. "Won't that disappear as your tests get better and better? Isn't that just a superstition that'll vanish as your analytic techniques improve?" No, he said, there was such a thing. The mind and body were linked. He knew it sounded religious, but . . . He would have gone on, but I interrupted him. I wanted to be sure. Was I talking to a cleric disguised as a doctor? Was he a Catholic who'd studied philosophy or a priest who read entrails? "I would never have brought this up," I said. "I would never have mentioned religion myself, but . . ." Now he interrupted me. "Not at all. I think you'll find pathologists to be more religious than other doctors; not as literalist, not as materialistic." I wondered if he was talking about himself. I thought, "If he can do it, so can I." I said, "I've long had the suspicion that the reason some people choose to become artists or writers or scientists, and the reason they make the art they make or think the thoughts they think or write the books they write, is their attitude toward death. That at a certain level of culture, the presence of death, real or imagined, shapes the work of creative people. It's death, not sex, that drives them on." I looked at him and said I was sorry I mentioned it. He said no, he didn't disagree. He wouldn't have used those words, but he wasn't bothered by the idea. "We're all tempted to hide behind the intellectual part of our work, the challenge of the investigation," he said, "but when you see a death that's tragic, it's better to acknowledge it. Some deaths are sad. If you ignore how you feel, the feelings will build up and get you."

There was a pause. I showed him the book I'd bought. "Very good," he said. "At least you can tell it was an old man." Then he asked me why I wanted to see an autopsy. I said I wanted to write about people who deal with death routinely. I wanted to find out how they did it, how they managed it. I knew, no matter how often they did it, there must have been a first time. I said I wanted to see an autopsy so I'd be marked by it. That way, I'd be able to recognize the marks others bore and they'd be able to recognize mine. O'Brian watched me as I spoke and I watched him. "Fine," he said, "but I just want to warn you. If someone who isn't a doctor comes on the scene of an auto accident and sees the victim all bloody and bent, the gestalt of the scene will do him in. If a doctor comes, though, he thinks immediately of tying off the major blood vessels and preventing shock and leaving the broken bones for later. His training lets him take one thing at a time. The gestalt doesn't overwhelm him. It's the same with us at a postmortem. We look at specific things: this organ, that organ; its size, shape, color, weight. We don't see the whole gestalt, the body laid out on the table. You might, and that might be too much." I said I knew that, but I couldn't give him any guarantees.

The phone rang then. O'Brian answered it with a voice pitched a whole octave lower. "Medical pathology," he announced, like a lawyer answering the call of a client. He listened for a moment, then said, "No. It's our policy not to begin any posts after 3:00 p.m. But if he's been dead for twenty-four hours, whatever degeneration might have occurred has already set in." He listened. "An endocrine problem," he said. And then, "Yes. If you tell the funeral home, we can schedule a post for 11:00 a.m. tomorrow. Fine. Thank you, Doctor." O'Brian hung up, turned, and smiled at me. "There. You'll have your post tomorrow." The lab had been asked to investigate the death of a seventy-four-year-old man who had died the day before in a nursing home. He'd been a manic-depressive with seventeen separate psychiatric admissions over the years to the university hospital. He'd been maintained on lithium. He'd died for no apparent reason. His doctor said it was depression, but that was like saying it was a broken heart. His physician wanted the lab to examine the brain and the pituitary.

Since O'Brian's specialty was neuropathology, he'd probably drop by to take a look sometime tomorrow, once Driver got the skull open.

I didn't want to miss the preliminaries, so I came an hour early the next day. Taggart said some first-year medical students would be coming to watch, once Driver had finished the heavy work. It was the heavy work I wanted to see. I went into the lab, but Driver hadn't taken the man out of the refrigerator yet. The radio was on to a rock station. There was a bearded man sitting hunched over the second autopsy table, finishing a post on a twenty-week-old fetus that had been spontaneously aborted the night before. The child was fully formed. It would have been a boy. He was lying on his back, on a corkboard, his chest and abdomen split open, the curve of his ribs and the flaps of his belly forming a thin-walled, empty shell. He had been eviscerated. All that remained in the cavity of his body were some shallow puddles of clear, pale red fluid. His face, his ribs, his hands and feet were beautifully detailed. The bearded man looked up. He was a third-year resident in pathology. "Who are you?" he wanted to know. I said I was a writer. "What are you writing?" he asked. "A book about people who deal with death." "Death??" he said. "We don't deal with death. Go upstairs and talk to the oncologists. They deal with death. Their patients die all the time. They talk about extending life expectancy by four weeks. But what's that like? What do the patients get out of it? The oncologists get a new batch of statistics. They get another grant. But what about the patients? Ask the oncologists. Down here, we get them when they're dead. We never knew them, never talked to them, never had them as patients. They're dead." As the spoke, he delicately unwound the child's small intestine, holding one end with a forceps, while gently pulling it between the blunt blades of another, stripping it of its outer mucous membrane by opening and closing the forceps so rapidly that its pincers behaved like the beak of a little bird, nibbling at its feathers. I looked at the child on the corkboard. I was going to ask the man if he'd ever had one of his own. I was going to ask him if his wife had ever lost one. But that wouldn't have been fair. I thought, "If you don't deal with death, what are you doing now? Isn't the kid dead? Aren't you taking him apart? What if I went upstairs and talked to the oncologists? 'Death?'

they'd say. 'We don't deal with death. We deal with a disease process. It's fatal now, but so was tuberculosis.' None of them would admit it. It would be like watching a shell game whose object wasn't to find the pea but the empty space." Then I thought about it again. This was just a variation on a theme. First there were Taggart's mammals, then O'Brian's body and mind, and now this resident's denial. Blame it all on someone else. The worms would probably tell me to ask God. I wondered what Driver would do.

Driver walked in, smoking an old pipe. The lab was posted no-smoking, but it was his to do what he wanted. He was a handsome man, brown-skinned, maybe fifty, but flat-bellied and well built. He said I could change in the staff locker room. All I wanted to do was watch, but I stripped anyway. The uniform was a short-sleeved surgical top, a pair of drawstring pants, a pair of surgical gloves, and a throwaway plastic apron that hung down like a bib to my ankles. Just as I came back in, Driver opened the refrigerator and I shivered. He pulled the man's tray halfway out and hooked it to the chains of an industrial hoist that ran on tracks along the ceiling. He looked at me and said, "We used to have to do this by hand." Then he pulled the tray all the way out, pushed it over to a heavy scale, and lowered it. The man was still covered with a fresh, clean sheet, white and crisply wrinkled. I asked, "Why do you weigh him?" Driver said it was just part of the procedure. "One thing for sure," he said. "They sure don't gain any weight." He laughed, with the pipe between his teeth. The man weighed 124 pounds. Driver swung him over to the autopsy table. I had to back up to get out of the way, but before I knew what I was doing, I was halfway across the room. Driver pulled the sheet off, and from where I stood I saw the man for the first time. He was an old man, thin but not emaciated, his back slightly arched. Gray hair covered his body; white hair framed his face; he had a high forehead, dark eyebrows, and a white mustache. "A good face," I thought. "An intelligent face. God, he looks so human!" I caught myself. "He looks human because he is! What do you think? Walt Disney made him for the tourists? He was alive two days ago. No one made him for exhibition." Still, he looked like a replica.

Driver picked up a yardstick to measure him. He wore a pair of surgical gloves on top of a pair of clear plastic throwaways. That way, if the man had died undiagnosed from TB, hepatitis, or AIDS, Driver was protected. Driver gave him a little pat on the side, like a man patting a horse before he saddles him. He tapped him the way a teacher does when he half taps, half touches a little kid to get his attention. That's all Driver did to let him know he was there. Then he measured him and wrote his height down on a form. The form had the man's name on it. I was looking at Alvin Kleinman. Driver checked him for scars and birthmarks, front and back. It was when he turned Al over and Al lay stiff on his side that I understood, for the first time, about Al being dead. Then, when Driver opened Al's eyes to check his pupils and Al's eyes stayed open, I understood again.

No doubt about it: Al was dead. He hadn't felt that little pat on the side. But if he was dead, why was I calling him Al? If his son had walked in and someone had asked him, "Who's that over there on the table?" he would have said, "That's my dad. That's Al." Al wasn't my father and he hadn't been my friend, but he looked like a man to me. Even if he was silent, he was resonant: even if he was still, I could hear him. Once, years ago in Washington, I had visited the Pentagon and asked to see the photographs made of the dead in Dachau by the U.S. Signal Corps. The intelligent part of me knew I was just looking at pictures, forty years after the fact. But some other part of me started reciting the Kaddish under my breath. Now it happened again. Even though I knew Al was dead, I started talking to him. Not out loud, of course. Part of me was shocked. "What are you doing??" it said. "Have you lost your mind??" I felt bad about it. But by the time Driver was ready to cut him open, I was saying things to Al. Things like, "I'm sorry." I can't remember all the words, but by the time Driver had cut Al's chest open, part of me was carrying on an intermittent, one-sided conversation with a dead man.

Driver tied off Al's subclavians with some string, sawed through the ribs, lifted out his breastplate, and leaned it against his shoulder. He tied off Al's small intestine in two places and cut it, as a doctor ties off an umbilical cord and then severs it. Then he reached in until he found the end of Al's large intestine. He looked at me and said, "Feels like this guy could have used an enema." The room started to smell like rotten garbage. That's when I understood about Driver's pipe. I asked him about such unpleasant things. "This place is pretty well ventilated," he said, "but if you want to smell something, you ought to go over to the city morgue. No fans, nothing. They had us over there for a month when I was in mortuary school. They gave us all the worst cases. Burn cases. Bad stuff. Stuff you wouldn't believe. To test us, to see if we could stand it. I was going out with this girl then. I kept asking her out but she kept telling me she was busy. Then her girlfriend called me up and said, 'You know, she really is thinking about you, but you've got a smell.' You couldn't get rid of it, no matter how much you washed. She said, 'You're going to have to choose either her or your work.'" Driver looked at me again and grinned with the pipe between his teeth. "You can see what I did." Then he turned back to Al. He made a few more cuts and lifted everything out, the heart, the lungs, the liver, the pancreas, the kidneys, everything out, all in one piece, into a tray.

Al was lying there as empty as that twenty-week-old fetus I'd seen when I first walked in. Except for the smell and the sound of the electrical saw going through his ribs, one at a time, it had been pretty peaceful. Driver made two cuts on either side of his head, behind his ears, and one cut along the hairline at the nape of his neck. Then he peeled Al's scalp up and over his head and draped it over his eyes. I moved to the foot of the table and bent down to try to see Al's face. I'd never seen anyone with his hair down over his eyes like that. I knew what was coming. I said, "Al? You in there? Al? You hear me? Thanks, okay? Thanks a lot." Because by then Driver had fitted a larger blade into his saw and was cutting the back of Al's skull open. When he was done, he pried the whole thing off in one piece. It made a sound I'd never heard before, half plant, half animal, as if, to peel a grapefruit, you had to pry off something as hard as an eggshell. Taggart came in just then, along with a third-year resident named Jo Ann. Jo Ann took one look at things and called O'Brian to tell him they were ready if he had a minute to come down.

Driver took out Al's brain, put it in a glass jar, and poured formaldehyde over it. It would be two weeks before it was firm enough to be sectioned. Al's skull was empty now. The base of it was divided into four hollow quadrants that looked like odd-sized cups arranged in a circle with their edges touching. At the center, in the space where the hollows touched, cradled in its own tiny cavity, was the pituitary. Driver used a fine, thin chisel to carefully chip away the cradle of bone where it nestled. Then he lifted it out and put it on the table next to Al's ear. It was about the size of a pinto bean, oval-shaped, and colored a ruddy pink. For the moment, Driver's work was done. He straightened Al a bit, turned on the water lines built into the table to wash away what little blood there was, and waited for O'Brian to appear. We all did.

O'Brian arrived in an eager rush. He saw me and smiled, then raised his hands to me, like a pope giving a benediction. "Congratulations," he said. I nodded back. O'Brian pulled on a pair of surgical gloves and picked up Al's pituitary. He still wore his street clothes. "What's this? What's this?" he said. "Water? This won't help tissue preservation." A drop or two must have splashed on the pituitary, not enough to damage it, but enough to break the rules. We all gathered around. O'Brian held Al's pituitary in his palm and turned it over with the blunt end of a small forceps. He looked like a gem merchant examining an emerald. He seemed very pleased. He leaned down toward it, turned it over again, smiled, looked up, and began to speak rapidly. "You can see, of course, the difference between the anterior and posterior portions: the anterior has the gray pulpy appearance of brain tissue; the posterior, the red color of heart tissue." I leaned closer and looked. I could see nothing, even as he pointed it out with the tip of his forceps. "Now, my guess," he said, as he turned Al's pituitary over and over like a precious stone, "is that we'll find a node in the right anterior portion." He picked up a scalpel and sliced the pituitary open on his palm. "What assurance!" I thought. "Street clothes, unaided sight, and a blade sharp enough to slice open his hand." "Well!" he said. "I'm surprised! It looks like the node's in the left posterior! Well, we'll see. May I have some formaldehyde, please?" Taggart handed him a jar, and O'Brian tipped in Al's pituitary, as gently as if he were returning a tropical fish to water. Then he stripped off his gloves, smiled at all of us, and left as quickly as he'd come. "What a performance!" I thought.

As soon as he was gone, Driver put everything he'd taken out of Al's chest back in. Then he fitted Al's breastplate back in, and closed the flaps of his chest. "What are you doing?" I asked. "It's for the medical students," Taggart said. Jo Ann was going to take them through the rest of the post, step by step. Soon they began to arrive, one or two at a time. They acted shy. They'd been exposed to cadavers in their anatomy classes, but this was the first time they'd been near the body of a man who'd just lost his life. They were all in their second year of medical school, all at least twenty-two years old, but they milled around, trying not to touch anything or talk, like a bunch of high school students. Once everyone had on gloves and aprons, Jo Ann called them over to the table. She began by asking them if anyone had ever seen an autopsy before. No one said a word. "Well, today," she said, "we're going to be conducting a postmortem on a seventy-four-year-old white male who died twenty-four hours ago in a nursing home." She told them Al's medical and psychiatric history, and then she opened the skin of his chest and rather gingerly lifted off his breastplate. "Now," she said, as she pointed to Al's right lung, "who can tell me the name of this organ?" No one said anything for a bit. Then a boy said, "That's the lung." Jo Ann said, "Very good, that *is* the lung." Then, pointing to the heart, she said, "And what's this?" I began to get impatient. "What do you mean, 'What's this?' " I said to myself. "Is this the eleventh grade? What are you doing?" Jo Ann didn't hear me. She just went on with it organ by organ, until she asked Taggart to lift everything out and carry it over to the table where I'd seen the resident work on the fetus. Then, with the help of the medical students, she and Taggart began to take Al apart. "Who wants to weigh the adrenals?" she asked. "Barbara, would you weigh them, please?" And so on, piece by piece, for the next two hours.

No matter where they looked, they couldn't find anything wrong. Al had been perfectly healthy. I stayed until they cut open his aorta and found it, as Jo Ann said, "clean as a whistle." By then, Driver had stuffed Al full of paper, sewn him up with some string, and put him back in the refrigerator. I left and got dressed. Then I went upstairs and tried to find the cafeteria. The hospital was so big and the cafeteria so far away and so crowded that I had plenty of time to think. I felt angry. O'Brian I could understand and appreciate. He'd cupped Al's pituitary in his hand like a gemstone. But Jo Ann had treated him like a chicken in a high school zoology class. No wonder, no awe, nothing but the most prosaic of teaching methods. Maybe that was all for the best: the kids had been scared; the best way to calm them may have been with the step-by-step question-and-answer method they'd known since they were fourteen. But there was more to it than that. The whole process of the autopsy had reduced Al to a shell stuffed with paper and two jars full of shreds. They had done that while hunting the cause of his death. But even the Indians, when they hunted, thanked their quarry after they killed it. They said, "We're sorry, but we needed to do this so we could live." No one in the lab had done that. No one but me, and I was just a civilian who talked to himself. No one had lit a candle or burned some tobacco or struck a bell or said a prayer. None of the professionals but O'Brian acknowledged that there had been something in Al besides his organs, or that they were dealing with anything but a mass of ripe flesh that had somehow gone wrong. Al had once had life in him. He might not have enjoyed being a manic-depressive, but some aggregate of energy had animated him from the moment of his birth until he died in that nursing home. Something that he had in him had left him, because if it hadn't he wouldn't have died. O'Brian wanted to call it his will to live. I would have called it his spirit. No one in the lab had acknowledged it. All they wanted to know was what had killed him, not what had allowed him to live. Of course, that was their job. But at least they could have admitted in some way, with some sort of ritual like saying grace before meals, that Al hadn't lasted seventy-four years just so they could pick him apart one Tuesday afternoon in the middle of November.

I calmed down. What I'd seen was just another variation. First Taggart, then O'Brian, then the resident, and now Jo Ann. No one could stare at death steadily. Some acknowledged it, some transposed it, and some denied it. Jo Ann had reduced it to a lesson plan. I still wondered about Driver. I walked back to the lab and found him in the office. It was the end of the day; he'd been on his feet for five hours; now he was leaning back. It was a time to talk. I asked him how he got started. His whole face, especially his eyes, smiled at me. "My great-grandfather brought me up in it," he said. First his great-grandfather, then his grandfather, then his uncle, and now him. He was nine when his great-grandfather and his grandfather took him along to pick up a body. His great-grandfather had a wagon and two horses. That's what he used.

Someone would send word and he'd harness his horses and go get the body. Driver paused while he thought about that. Then he told me a story:

One night, he said, his great-grandfather got word that a man had died. It was a bad night, pitch-black, thunder and lightning. The man had lived in a little settlement fifteen miles down the road. Driver's great-grandfather hitched his horses and set out. At last he found the house, put the man in the box in the back of the wagon, and headed home. It was raining hard. When he got home, he went to take the man out, but the box was empty. It must have been raining so hard that the body had just floated up and out. So he headed back the way he had come, but he didn't have to go very far. A man came riding up, all excited, and told him to come quick, there was a body lying in the middle of the road, in the center of his village, ten miles away. He said everyone was going crazy. When Mr. Driver's great-grandfather got here, he explained everything and then loaded the body back in the box. It was almost light when he got home. He brought the body inside, set it on the embalming table, and went into the kitchen to make himself a cup of coffee. When he came back, the man was sitting up, blinking, staring around. He must have been in a coma and the fall and the rain and the cold must have revived him. Mr. Driver's great-grandfather gave him a cup of coffee and got him some dry clothes. Then he sat him down on the seat next to him and drove him back home. When the man's wife looked out the door and saw him coming, she said to her son, "Son, you better go and get me a gallon of whisky, 'cause that's the only way I'm gonna stand this!"

Driver let out a laugh and rocked back and forth in his chair. He roared. He slapped both his knees and laughed some more. "Death and resurrection," I thought. "Not bad work if you can get it."

DETECTIVES

I walked into a large, low-ceilinged beige room: beige carpeting, beige walls, beige steel desks. There were only two people there: a typist wearing earphones, and Sergeant Kelt, who gravely rose from his chair and solemnly shook my hand. Kelt was a tall, thin man, bespectacled, middle-aged, with the face and bearing of a farmer painted by Grant Wood. "Glad to have you with us, Mike," he said. He looked at me from a distance, without a smile or a frown. What he saw was a man with a fresh haircut, dressed in a gray suit, trying to impersonate a rabbi. "Now what exactly is it you want?" "Sergeant," I said, "I'd like to ride with the detectives under your supervision. I understand that's a privilege. I don't want to get in anyone's way; I don't want to get anyone in trouble. If you want me to change names, I'll change names. That's not important. What's important is the meaning of what the men who work here do, how they do it, and why they do it. There are a whole lot of things I don't know. But one thing I do is that I'm here with your permission: if I don't walk right or talk right, I know I'll be gone. I'm an ignorant man. I'd be grateful for your help." Kelt cleared his throat ever so slightly. "Well, Mike," he said, "we'll do what we can. Changing names is a good start. Now what exactly do you want to know?" I looked around the empty room. "To begin with, Sergeant, I'd like to know how you run this place." "That's one thing I don't do. The lieutenant does that. There are two of us sergeants; all we do is keep things in order. There are fourteen detectives in the section: six teams work the day shift, eight to four-thirty; ten men do follow-up; two men are on call—if anything happens, they go to the scene. From four to midnight, two other men take over. They go home at twelve, but they're on call until sunrise. Homicide responds to all suspicious dead bodies, suicides, murders, floaters, burn victims; we go to plane crashes along with the FAA; we investigate crib deaths; we follow up all aggravated assaults and batteries; we keep tabs on all violent sex crimes. Vehicular homicide responds to road kills; everything else in the city is ours. Which reminds me, Mike. If you're going to change names, you ought to change the city, too." "That's fine with me, Sergeant, but this is my first time in Florida. Do you have any suggestions?" Kelt looked at me with a little smile. "Didn't you say you were a writer, Mike?" "That's true, Sergeant, that's true. How does Tampa sound to you?" Kelt smiled again. "Tampa sounds just fine, Mike." There was a portable, eight-channel Motorola on his desk that had been making noise as we talked. A dispatcher's voice had been quietly calling a series of numbers, followed by a pulse tone, followed by something that sounded like "8460." "Hold it," said Kelt. He listened and then stood up. "That was a suicide." He smiled. "Looks like you're going to get your first chance to take a ride. Want to come?" "Of course, thank you." Kelt picked up his radio, buttoned his sports coat, and we took the elevator down to the garage. Kelt looked around; he'd forgotten where he'd parked. "Here it is," he said. It was a four-door emerald-green Buick Electra. "Is this yours or the department's?" "The department's," he said. "It used to be the chief's, but he got himself a new one." Power brakes, power door locks, power windows and seats, plus factory air-conditioning. Kelt reached for the car mike, recited a series of numbers that identified him, his departure, and his destination. The dispatcher echoed his last four digits, and we pulled into traffic. No lights, no sirens, just a Buick on its way to a suicide.

We crossed a causeway onto a six-lane expressway lined with twenty-year-old motels, two-story apartments, and shopping centers. Kelt waited in line for an arrow, made a left that turned into a U, and pulled off in front of a big new sporting-goods store. The front parking lot was empty. There was a handwritten "Closed" sign taped across the front doors; we turned down the side and saw the action: four patrol cars, a county medical rescue truck, a news van, two Chevy Malibus that belonged to homicide, a hearse, and a rusted-out Firebird that belonged to the assistant medical examiner. A quadrant of yellow plastic tape marked T.P.D. DO NOT CROSS fluttered in the breeze. Outside the tape, a patrolman stood watching the news crew scamper up and down the perimeter looking for a camera opening. Inside the tape area, all I could see was a dumpster and a crowd of men. Kelt said, "Mike, you stay with me." Then he hung his ID from his breast pocket, stopped the car, picked up his radio, and walked straight for the tape like a preacher headed up the aisle. The patrolman turned his head. Kelt nodded, said, "Get 'em back; that's not right," looked at me, said "Stay close," and we stepped over into the crime scene.

What had happened was that the son of the store owner had taken a brand-new .357 Magnum out of the display case, loaded three rounds of fresh ammunition, and walked out the back door of the store with it. The kid had been in and out of drug rehabilitation centers for years. This time, when he got out, his father had given him a job in the family business. The boy didn't think he was making much progress. So he climbed up on the dumpster, balanced himself on the edge, put the gun to his temple, and shot himself. When his father came out a half hour later to empty his wastebasket, he found his son in the trash. The man and his daughter and his wife were inside now. Outside, there must have been a dozen patrol officers, emergency medical people, detectives, and criminal-evidence technicians standing around watching while the assistant medical examiner, a dapper little Pakistani, put on a pair of surgical gloves to examine the body. While Kelt talked quietly to an old uniformed patrol sergeant, I circled the crowd and looked on. The kid was lying on his back on the ground; his face was pale gray; the front of his shirt looked as if he'd spilled a pot of spaghetti and meat sauce down it. There were brown paper bags over both his hands. The Pakistani was very gingerly unbuttoning the kid's shirt when someone leaned over and said, "You the writer?" I turned. It was the patrol sergeant Kelt had been talking to. The man was between fifty and sixty years old, short, stubby, strong, and bald—a New York Irish cop come south for the sun.

The patrol sergeant had many things to confide. "You know about .357s?" he asked. "No," I said. "Cops are queer for guns; you don't watch 'em, they'll pick 'em up and spin the cylinder. That can make life complicated, especially for a suicide: you try explaining how a live round's still in the chamber after there's one in the head. Now this kid shot himself in the right temple, but you see his shirt?" The Pakistani had borrowed a towel from one of the medical people and was wiping off the kid's chest. "Yeah," I said. "Blowback," he said. "The .357's a supersonic round; it makes a vacuum behind it, so the tissue gets pulled out the entry wound." "What about the paper bags?" I asked. "Powder residue, barium, antimony, and lead. The lab'll swab the kid's hands and then do a neutron activation test. If he really killed himself, the samples'll convert to isotopes." "You been at this a while?" I asked. "Thirty-five years," he said. "I got a son who's an Eastern pilot and my daughter's a speech therapist." He opened his wallet to show me his grandchildren, when I saw Kelt walk through the back door of the store. "Sergeant," I said, "I'd love to see your pictures, but I'm supposed to stay close. Would you excuse me?" I followed Kelt through the door into a storeroom stacked with boxes of uniforms and equipment. In one corner were two racquet-stringing machines; in the other was a hot transfer press for decals. In between stood two homicide detectives, silently playing grab-ass. One was white; one was black. The white man looked like a basketball player gone to seed; the black looked as if he could still run a few plays. They were talking to each other in stage whispers. "Where'd you get that goddamn tie, Melon?" hissed the black man. "You look like a goddamn pussy." "Hey, show some respect, show some respect," Melon whispered back; then he reached around and flipped the black man's coattails above his waist. I followed Kelt down a corridor into the store's office.

The boy's father was sitting in a stenographer's chair, his arms at his side, his legs apart, tears running down his face. His daughter knelt between his legs, knees on the floor, arms around his belly, head nestled between his thighs, nuzzling him, rocking back and forth. Next to her sat her mother, holding her head in her hands, her hands over her eyes. The two women were weeping in a way I'd never heard before. I'd heard dogs groan and whimper when they were dying. I'd heard cattle bellow and cry when they were hurt. But I'd never heard two women weep so deeply or so helplessly. The sound they made drained the blood from my hands and feet.

Melon, the ex-basketball player, followed us in, buttoning his coat over his paunch and clearing his throat. His voice came out like honey from a jar. "Mr. Wasserman," he said, "I know how you feel, sir; it's a terrible shock, terrible, but I need to ask you a few questions about Jimmy." Mr. Wasserman didn't look as if he'd heard a thing. "Mr. Wasserman, sir, Mr. Wasserman," said Melon again. Mr. Wasserman looked as if he'd fallen from a great height. I edged out the door, down the hall, back to the dumpster. The assistant medical examiner was popping off his gloves, the evidence technicians were packing their Rolleiflexes, and the undertakers were asking the medical crew if they could transport the kid to the morgue. Kelt came out, followed by Melon, who looked a little embarrassed. "Mike, this is Detective Paul Melon. If he says it's okay, you can ride with him this afternoon. All right, Melon?" "Absolutely, Sergeant, just so long as he spells my name right. It's got just one 'l,' son, rhymes with felon." He gave me a grin that must have worked wonders on cheerleaders. "One 'l,' " I said. He started walking toward his car. "Now, why don't you come on over here and let me set down and get my notes in order and then we'll take care of some business." Melon got in his Malibu, turned on the ignition, and started up the air-conditioning. He looked in the mirror, checked his tie, ran his tongue over his teeth, brushed back his hair, and settled down with his notebook. "We're going to visit the widow. The kid was a dirtbag. He left a wife and an eight-week-old baby. The father says they weren't married but he bought a house for them. The kid was doing a lot of drugs, coke and 'Ludes, now and then some Percodans. A real winner. He probably did everyone a favor. You all set?" I wanted to say no, but it might have ended our relationship. The blood had come back to my hands and feet, but I wasn't looking forward to the sound of another woman weeping. "You sure you want me around for this?" I asked. "You got anything better to do?" he said.

When we reached the house, he looked in the mirror, picked up his radio, and we shuffled up the drive; behind us, the Malibu dieseled in place, ignition off, rattling around like a can full of nails. "Piece of shit," he said as he rang the bell. The girl who opened the door was so pretty that Melon forgot his lines. Black hair, blue eyes, clear white skin, lips like a valentine, holding a baby in her arms. Melon showed his ID, mangled my name, and said that something had happened to Jimmy. "Is he hurt, is he hurt?" said the girl. Melon kept his mouth shut until she'd closed the front door and sat down. Then he told her that Jimmy had shot himself. She winced, then shivered, sobbed, and wept. Her girlfriend came running in from the kitchen and held her. The baby began to cry; the girlfriend joined in; I sat on the couch next to Melon and wanted to leave. The room was empty: bare stucco walls, orange shag carpeting, one chair and one couch— an ugly little room full of nothing but two girls and an orphan crying. Once things quieted down, Melon found out more about Jimmy's drug habits. The girl said he'd beat her when she was pregnant and threatened to hit her with a chair after the baby was born. Definitely a dirtbag. Melon gave her his card. "I want you to call me, anytime. If there's anything you need, I want to hear from you." The girl sniffled and said, "Thank you so much, Officer." As we walked down the drive, Melon handed me his radio. "Hold this for a minute, son, I got to fix something." Then he reached down his pants and adjusted his privates. "There, now," he said. "That's much better. You talk about a hard-on. That was a sweetheart. All alone in the world. She's gonna need some help." "Are you thinking of giving it to her?" I asked as we drove away. "Now, son, whatever gave you that idea? I'm a married man, a deacon in the church. I was only talking about a damsel in distress." "You got a lance for your horse?" I said. "Never you mind," he said. "You just pay atten- tion; we have work to do." He pulled a color mug shot from his visor: a young black man looking at the camera as if it was a wall. "This boy," he said as he handed it to me, "robbed and murdered an old lady in my neighborhood and we are going looking for him." "Your neighborhood?" I asked. "Place where I started as a patrolman, boy. My neighborhood, my people."

A half hour later, we were in a war zone. Convenience stores run by cashiers locked behind two inches of safety glass; corner bars called the Tropicana and the Date Palm, places so poor their names were written in spangles that blew in the wind; men sitting on broken dinette chairs lined up in the shade, looking at nothing but the curb as Melon drove by. "Just trying to make a living," he said. "See that fat man, that old boy wearing the captain's hat? He's been sitting in that chair for ten years. I reached in his pocket one time and got stuck with two needles, put me in the hospital with goddamn hepatitis. Wait now. What do we have here?" What we had was a group of six men in their early twenties, standing around some gas pumps, drinking Colt 45s.

Melon slowed down, fumbled around on the floor for his gun, and put it on the seat between his legs. "Gimme that picture, son," he said. I handed it to him, as he stopped ten feet from the men, who looked at him and then pretended he was invisible. Melon was looking for trouble and I didn't want to be around for it. The problem was that sitting next to him was the safest place to be. He rolled down his window. He didn't say anything; he kept looking back and forth from the men to the mug shot. They kept pretending he wasn't there. I was getting scared, but Melon was enjoying himself. "Hey," he said to no one in particular. "Don't I know you? I do; yes I do. I know you." He waited for one of them to look. Two of them did. Melon grinned. "Yeah, I know you. Definitely. Now, what are you doing here, drinking like that, no paper bag, no nothing. That could get you in trouble with the police." He said "poé-lease." That did it: four of them laughed. Melon handed me the mug shot and put his hand between his legs. I didn't know where his testicles were, but mine had gotten out of harm's way. "Now that I have your attention," he said, "I want you gone in three minutes. Read my lips. Watch carefully: three minutes. Catch you later." He rolled up his window and we drove off. "You like looking?" I asked. "Love it, son, love it. Looking and asking, looking and asking. I got a ticket to ride." We spent another hour seeing the sights. Then Melon said, "It's getting too hot for this, let's go to the morgue. You ever been to the morgue? We'll go visit Jimmy." "Jimmy?" I said. "You sure you're a writer? How come you don't remember names. That's the little lady's ex-husband."

Jimmy was there when we arrived. "You ever been in one of these things?" Melon said. "Yeah," I said, thinking about Driver sliding Al out of the refrigerator in medical pathology. I didn't know if Melon was playing chicken with me or just trying to be helpful. My testicles had returned to their usual place, and I didn't hear any women weeping, but I wasn't interested in the next part of the tour. Melon held the door open, and a cold smell came out, as distinct as a cigar store, except it was animal, not vegetable, halfway between stale and rancid, like three-week-old hamburger gone gray. Jimmy was lying on his back on a gurney just inside the door, surrounded by what looked like choice company—a few derelicts, some burn victims. Melon gestured:

"After you." "Melon, you're all heart, but I've been through it." He closed the door. "Come on, then, I got to talk to my girl-friends."

I followed him down the hall to the lab. He clapped his hands; two women looked up and smiled. "What'd you find in the kid?" he said. "Nothing for you," said one. "Especially for you," said the other. Neither of them was very young or very pretty, but it didn't matter to Melon. "Why are you so mean to me?" he said. "You know I love you." "Melon, we're working." "Girls, gimme a break. What did the kid have in him?" "A little of this, a little of that, some coke, some heroin. We're working on it." "You want to hear a joke?" he said. They both sighed. "No, I mean it; this is a good one; you never heard this one before." "Okay, okay, Melon. Tell it and leave." "You ready?" he asked. "Go." "You ever hear the one about Roy Rogers and Trigger?" he said. They didn't say a word. "No? Okay. Roy's out riding one day and he gets ambushed. They pull him down and they beat the shit out of him. Then they tie him to a tree and they beat him some more. When he wakes up, they're gone, but he's still tied to the tree. He calls Trigger. "Trigger," he says. He can barely talk. "Trigger, I'm hurt bad. Go get help. Bring a posse. You understand, boy? A posse. A big posse." Trigger nods and paws the ground and gallops away. Roy passes out. When he wakes up, he sees Trigger coming for him with a big, beautiful blonde, naked, riding on his back. "Goddamn it!" he says. "I said a big *posse*, you stupid ass!" Melon clapped his hands and let out a hoot. "*Posse*, get it? A big *posse*!" The two women didn't even smile. Melon couldn't have been happier. The three of them looked as if they'd done this before. "Melon, you have a dirty mind," said one. "Why don't you transfer to vice?" "I can't, darling. The sergeant says I might corrupt 'em." He looked at his watch. "Gotta go. Let me know about the kid. Love you both."

"Sex and death," I thought. "It's as good an antidote as any." It was four o'clock when we reached the section. I checked in with Kelt. "How'd it go, Mike?" "Just fine, Sergeant. Very exciting. Melon's got a great sense of humor." "Glad to hear it, Mike." He looked at the clock. "This is the end of the shift, Mike. If you like, you can call it a day. If you want to ride tonight, I can introduce you to George Schultz." "George Schultz?" I said. "Sounds like the

Secretary of State." "People often get them confused." He smiled. "I'm sure you and George will get along fine." He looked over my shoulder. "George?" he called. Schultz had been sitting at his desk in the very last row at the very back of the room, farthest from Kelt, leaning back, hands behind his head, chewing a tooth-pick, while a cigarette burned in his ashtray. He'd been watching me. When Kelt called his name, Schultz tipped forward, picked up the cigarette, and came walking up, toothpick still in his mouth. "George," said Kelt, "this is Mike—Lacey?" He looked at me. "Is that right?" "Why not," I said. "Mike's a writer, but he's okay. The office says he can ride with you if you say so. All right?" Schultz took the toothpick out of his mouth and smiled. "Why not," he said. "You eaten?" Schultz's hair had gone gray, but he was on the light side of fifty. A big chin and a hawk nose gave him the profile of a Renaissance duke. He smiled again. "Writer, huh? You eat shrimp?"

We ended up in a seafood place on the edge of a bad neighbor-hood. The owner gave the police sixty percent off so they'd come and keep away the robbers. "He couldn't get insurance," said Schultz. We settled into a booth. The menu featured shrimp baskets. "So what do you want to know?" he said. "The usual stuff," I said. "How'd you get started. What you do. What it's like." Schultz seemed so relaxed I forgot he'd been watching me. "Nothing to it," he said. "Born in Ohio, enlisted in the Marines, got sent to Florida for the missile crisis. Fell in love with a local girl and got married. Went to work for Sears, but they kept me in automotive, never would move me to appliances. You can sell all the tires you want, but the money's not there. I held on until I was twenty-seven, then I told 'em to shove it. I said to my wife, 'I've been doing the right thing for years. Now I'm gonna do something for myself.' Went to the Police Academy, then into patrol, just like everyone else. Patrol's hard on you. Hard on you, hard on your family. First, you're stuck in the same neighborhood, day after day. You drive the same streets; eat in the same place, you feel trapped. The sergeants run your life; everything you do is supervised. One month they have you work days; one month, evenings; one month, nights. You can't plan ahead. They move you around like a chess game. Then, when something happens, you're the first one there. You get a signal 61, a fight, or an 88, an assault, or a 23, a holdup, and you go, and while you go, you think about it, and the thinking is worse than when you get there. Then it's just you and whatever's happened. You're the one standing there when the shit hits. Just you. You learn two things: first, you learn to stop thinking about it. Whatever you saw, when you're gone, you're gone. Whatever happened, it didn't happen to you. Whoever's on the floor, it's not you; it's not your wife; it's someone else, *something* else. It's dead, you're alive. So, the first thing you learn is how to separate. Unless, of course, it's a kid. If it's a kid, it's hard. The first case I ever had in homicide was a two-year-old boy who drowned in a cesspool. That's one I remember." The shrimp baskets arrived. "You want lemon with yours?" he asked. "I'll pass." Schultz took a bite. "What's the second thing?" I asked. "Right," he said. "The second thing you learn is to move up." "What's up?" I said. "Traffic homicide, burglary, vice." "What happened to you?" "Burglary." "What's that like?" "It doesn't go anywhere. You don't accomplish anything. You spend all day chasing TVs and CBs." "And traffic homicide?" "That's a real mess. You go out and pick up the pieces. You walk around what's left of a family spread all over the road. Did Melon tell you his first death on patrol?" "No." "First time it happened to him, it was a head-on, mother, father, three kids; he had to reach in the guy's pocket to get his wallet. That can get to you after a while: innocent people. It wasn't for me. I did five years in burglary, then they gave me a choice: vice or homicide. Things were changing; vice was getting more and more of a budget. Not just whores and gambling, but dope. You remember the War on Drugs? I said, 'No, thanks.'" "How come?" "Because in vice you can't trust anyone. In vice, the name of the game is 'The Price Is Right.' Plus you can get yourself killed. In homicide, it's just you and your partner and the action's over. No one's getting up off the floor. You go in, make your notes, write your narrative, make your case. Most of the time, no one's breathing down your neck. You go to a scene or you're given a case and you've got ten days to clear it, and ten more if you need it. How you do it is up to you. You're not stuck in one place. Every day's different." "But isn't it just more of the same?" I asked. "One death after another? Doesn't that get to you?" Schultz pushed away his shrimp and lit a cigarette. "All right. But it's not the death that does it. If you make it through patrol, that doesn't bother you. Patrol's your combat experience. You get through that, you're fine. It's the I-don't-give-a-shit factor. You burn out." "How?" "Different ways for different men. You don't just burn out and that's it. It's a cycle. My first one took me three years. It takes most guys five. Five years and you're in your prime." "How's it work?" Schultz looked at me. "No one's innocent, not the drunk on the floor, not the drunk standing up, who shot him. Everyone knows everyone else. If you're black, your friends kill you most of the time. If you're white, most of the time it's your family. Or a stranger, a white stranger. Most of the time, whoever gets killed is no angel. The one standing up could just as easily be the one on the floor. I've seen guys killed over a 38-cent piece of chicken." He smoked for a bit and thought. "I've seen guys killed over a 25-cent game of pool. That was a good one." He grinned. The smile brought his chin up and made him look like Bob Hope. "Listen to this: this guy walks into a poolhall and walks up to a table. There're two guys finishing up a game. He puts his quarter down on the table and waits his turn. The two guys finish up; they put their quarters on top of his and they start another game. The first guy gets upset. 'Hey! What are you doing!' he says. 'It's my turn. The rules are: you put your quarter down and you shoot.' The two guys go on playing. 'Hey now!' he says. 'Hold it! My turn.' One of the guys looks up. 'What'd you say?' he says. The first guy repeats himself: 'I said, the rules are, you put down your quarter and you shoot.' The second guy says, 'Okay.' He puts another quarter down on the table, then he takes out his gun and he shoots him." Schultz looked at me. "You see that every weekend, you get tired of it. You stop thinking about people's motives. You don't ask why. You determine if there was a crime and if there was evidence of a crime. You make your notes, collect the evidence, and go on to the next one. Which is as much a waste of time as the one before. You want coffee? No? Then come on, I got something to show you."

We walked back to his Malibu. He finished his cigarette and stuck a toothpick in his mouth. I noticed a baseball cap on the ledge of his rear window. Blue visor, blue lettering: "Our Day Begins When Yours Ends." "You wear that to crime scenes?" I asked. He laughed, very relaxed, the laugh of Bing Crosby. We climbed in. He switched on his police radio, then turned on the car radio, soft rock underneath the dispatcher's voice. "You ever seen communications?" he asked. A series of rapid Morse tones sounded. "What's that?" I said. "That's the station ID; it's an FCC requirement. They used to give it verbally, but it interfered with the dispatcher, so they switched to Morse. I was trained in communications. We've got a nice setup. I'll show you." We drove back to headquarters and took an elevator to the top floor. The door to communications had a numerical key-pad lock. Schultz fingered the combination and pulled; we walked into a glass-walled corridor. A sergeant on the other side nodded to Schultz and buzzed us through a steel door into a main room that looked like a half-scale version of the telemetry center at Cape Kennedy. "Nice, huh?" he said. I nodded. "Come on in here, I'll show you something else." I followed him into a smaller, separate room where three women in uniform sat at consoles. "This is the computer link to Washington, National Crime Information Center, plus regional centers, plus secure lines for domestic intelligence." I was going to ask him what domestic intelligence was, when he gave me his Bob Hope smile and said, "Let me see your license." "What?" I said. He kept smiling. He had his hand out. "Let me see your license." He sounded like Bing Crosby, but he was serious. He turned to one of the women. "Pat," he said, "can you run this guy?" I'd forgotten he'd been watching me. The man was a cop—cigarette, toothpick, and all. I started to sweat. "Sure," I said. I handed the license to him and he handed it to Pat. I quietly reviewed my criminal past: a disorderly-conduct charge during an anti-war demonstration; two years on the staff of an underground newspaper that was financed by voluntary contributions from marijuana wholesalers. Schultz hummed and twirled his toothpick. I smiled and sweated while Pat typed in my social security number. I could be gone sooner than I'd imagined: the underground where I worked had given gainful employment to three separate intelligence units—local, state, and federal. By the time Nixon was forced to resign and the Freedom of Information Act was law, the editor discovered there was a file on him suitable for a full-length posthumous biography. I'd never known what there was on me, but I was about to find out. The printer whined; the paper rolled. Pat tore off the sheet and handed it to Schultz. Schultz took the toothpick out of his mouth, scanned the page, and handed it to me with a smile. File numbers, followed by search codes, followed by null signs. I'd escaped the Ten Most Wanted. "Keep it," he said. "A souvenir." I folded it and stuffed it in my jacket. My inside breast pocket felt as if someone had dumped a glass of water in it. "You do this for all your new friends?" I asked as we stood by the elevator waiting to go down. He gave me another smile. "Forget it," he said. "Come down to the section, I've got something to show you." "Let me guess," I said. "An interrogation room?" "Relax. You asked me; I asked you; now everyone's even. I want you to see a file." We walked into the section and Schultz led me into an adjointing room lined with file cabinets. He jerked one open. "You're gonna like this," he said. He handed me a brown alligator file marked, "Creal, John Edward." "What is it?" I asked. "One of mine. A triple murder, a mother and two kids. He was their next-door neighbor. We had him charged in twenty-four hours." "Where is he now?" "On death row. Sit down. I've got to finish up. You read, then we'll get coffee."

The first thing I saw were the pictures, $5'' \times 5''$ color prints from well-exposed $2\frac{1}{4}''$ negatives. A blond little girl, maybe four years old, in a Muppet bathrobe, sprawled on her side, lying in the middle of a thickly carpeted hallway. Her belly had been torn open by a slug, like a jackrabbit hit by a .30-30. Then her sister, ten years old maybe, a very pretty little girl. Her hands had been tied behind her back; she'd been made to kneel at the foot of a big, four-poster double bed. She wore a yellow top, purple slacks, red-white-and-blue tennis shoes. Her hair was in twin ponytails held by heart-shaped, purple barrettes. There was a single gold earring in her right ear. She'd been shot between the eyes, at such close range that there was soot around the hole. And then their mother, on her back, near a nightstand, on the floor, at the head of the bed where her daughter knelt. The woman looked as if she'd been hit by a car and then dragged a few blocks. There wasn't much left to her face. "What is this shit??" I said. "What the fuck happened to the woman??" Schultz looked up. He'd lit another cigarette. "He beat her. See those pieces of metal on the floor? That was the butt of the gun. He used a Ruger Black Hawk, belonged to his dad." "What the fuck happened?" I said. "Read on," he said. "I'll read, but this is a real piece of shit. What happened?" "Did you get to his picture yet?" I looked: his was next. A big, frowning, gray-haired man with a black mustache, arms at his sides, dressed in a splattered T-shirt, standing in the corner of the section's interrogation room. Short, blunt fingers; a tub of a belly. Thirty-seven years old, said the file. "How big was this guy?" "Maybe six-two, three hundred pounds. His folks called him Little Eddie." "Oh, shit," I said. "What happened?" "He lived next door with his folks. Worked as a welder. He was out on parole for armed robbery. When he was nineteen, he'd molested a little girl." "Who were these people?" Schultz inhaled and smiled. "Just your ordinary, white, upper-middle-class family. Innocent. The mother was active in the PTA. The father was an engineer. He was out of town when it happened. The company sent him back on the corporate jet. The little girl, the nine-year-old, was getting ready for her birthday." "And??" "He walked in through the back door. The mother and the youngest girl were out front. He tied up the nine-year-old and started fooling around with her. The mother and the other little girl came in and discovered him. He panicked. Who knows, maybe he was just going to rob the place. Business and pleasure. Probably knocked out the mother, then got the little girl with a grab shot on the run. Then shot the oldest girl. Then beat the mother to death." "How'd you get him?" "He didn't look right. Here's this guy, looking like he did, in this nice neighborhood, driving a ratty old pickup, working as a welder. His parents lived next door to the family. The first thing his father said when I talked to him was his gun was missing. Then Little Eddie told me he was out on parole. Then his father told me he believed his son was the last person to see the woman and her kids alive. We checked his record, and I asked him if he'd take a polygraph. He said he would. He took it and he failed it, utterly failed it, right off the scale. Then it got strange. The polygraph operator went back in and told him the results. He wouldn't look up. Then we sent in a woman, a detective, to talk to him. He kept twiddling his thumbs and getting redder and redder in the face. I thought he was going to stand up and throw the table against the wall. We got the woman out of there. Then we had a detective who's a Baptist walk him around the station. Check out page 22." The narrative quoted the detective: "I told John Creal that he needed to confess any problems to the Lord since he told me he was a Baptist and had been baptized when he was nineteen. He then said, 'I think it's too late to confess to the Lord.'" "Okay," I said. "You tried technology; you tried a woman; you tried a Baptist. Then what?" "Then we brought him back in and I sat down with him. We shot the shit. Talked about cars, talked about welding. Then I said I wanted to run through what happened. I took it one step at a time. When I got to shooting the nine-year-old, he looked up and said, 'John Edward Creal would never do anything like that.' He sounded like he was talking about someone else; like there was him and me and John Edward Creal in the room. I said, 'Eddie, did you do that?' He said it again. 'John Edward Creal would never do that.' I said I didn't know about John Edward, but I was charging him with three counts of murder. I advised him of his rights, and we took his picture. He was in jail twelve hours after we found the bodies." "A good cop, definitely a good cop," I thought. "The man can check my records any time." "Congratulations," I said. He shrugged. "It was lucky; it was one of those that makes you feel good. The nine-year-old was two years younger than my daughter. The father insisted on sitting in court. We had a plainclothesman sit behind him every day. He didn't know it. We didn't want him standing up and blowing Creal away. You all set?" I handed him the file. He locked the cabinet and we headed out the door.

"Where do you want to go?" he said. I would have preferred another planet. "It doesn't matter," I said. "How about the Hilton?" "Great." A suicide in the morning; Melon, and the widow, and the morgue in the afternoon; all that weeping, then Schultz and a triple murder in the evening. A change of place, plus a change of species, would have been great. The Hilton did its best. A fine, quiet dining room, decent crystal, fresh flowers. The waiter brought us our coffee. Schultz stood his Motorola next to the sugar bowl and lit a cigarette. "You okay?" he said. "You upset?" "Upset??" I said. "Eddie was a real piece of shit. I'm glad you got him, but goddamn! A mother and two kids. We're not talking about a 25-cent game of pool. He was a fucking animal." Schultz raised his cup and looked at me over the rim.

"You got it wrong. Little Eddie was human. We're all capable. We're all murderers." He took a sip. "You mind if I ask you something?" he said. "Go ahead." "You're Jewish, right?" "Yeah. And you're German. So?" "So, I got a question for you." "Okay." He gave me a sly look. "All right. Who are the intellectual elite of the human race?" "The what?" I said. "The intellectual elite of the human race," he repeated. I wasn't ready for that. "I don't know. Tell me." He looked at me again. He cocked his head. "Come on. You know." "No. Tell me. I don't know." He grinned. "You guys. The Jews." I didn't like where we were going. "Okay. Fine. We're the intellectual elite. Now what?" He cradled his cup in his hands. He looked straight at me. Bob Hope with powder-blue eyes. "If you grant me that, then answer me something else." I nodded. What was this, the riddles of the Sphinx? "All right," I said. "If you guys are at the top, who's at the bottom?" I sighed. "I don't know. Tell me." "The blacks," he said. "The what?" I said. "Are you kidding? The earliest human fossils were found in Africa." "Human?" he said. He leaned forward. "We're worse than animals. We're born killers. If it wasn't for outside intervention, we'd be gone by now." " 'Outside intervention?' " I said. "What the hell are you talking about?" "What I'm talking about is landings; what I'm talking about is Chariots of the Gods extraterrestrials. Without them, we would have vanished, killed ourselves off. We're all murderers." That did it. "Not me," I said. "Not me." Schultz leaned back and looked at me. He looked at me the way a psychiatrist in a lunatic asylum might look at an inmate who's just declared he isn't crazy. Schultz didn't know what to say. I was his guest; I had a clean record; I was a Jewish genius. He tried to be polite. He gave me a little smile, the way I'd smiled at my son when he was young and said something so stupid it was cute. "Okay," he said gently, "not you. Everyone else, but not you." "Thanks," I said, "I appreciate that. It's getting late. I'm going to bed. Can you give me a lift?"

Schultz drove me to my car and I drove back to my motel. I walked in just after midnight. I double-locked the door. I'd left the television on, and a detective show set in Hawaii was playing. Someone was trying to scare a little girl. Blond hair, white blouse, blue shorts, white sandals, ten or eleven years old, very cute. She ran from them. Down the street, up her drive, through her front door, up the steps, into her room. She locked the door and leaned on it. Then she looked up and began to scream. Someone had tied a noose around her doll's neck and hung it from the ceiling. I jumped at the TV and turned it off.

The next morning I walked into the homicide section at 7:30, singing a McDonald's commercial to myself, the one about "You deserve a break today / So get up and get away." The room was nearly full, detectives at their desks talking to each other or talking into tape recorders. A few inspected me, a few ignored me, one or two nodded, by now they knew. I said hello to Kelt, found an empty desk, wondered if it was okay, and sat down. The room sounded like a little red schoolhouse: everyone was talking, telling stories or dictating incident reports. What they were saying to each other had lines like "Shot him dead as a smelt, blew his goddamn chittlings all over the bathroom." What they were dictating had the drone of professional prose. The man next to me spoke in a monotone: "Upon arrival at the scene, this writer was advised by Mrs. S-H-E-L-L-S that the above-listed victim had been having some difficulty avoiding an old boyfriend who had apparently just been released from Raiford State Prison. Mrs. SHELLS stated that L-Y-N-N would say loudly, 'Please don't hit me no more.' Every time Mrs. SHELLS heard the hitting sound, LYNN would repeat this. There were also some scuffling sounds at the time LYNN was yelling. When the noise stopped, after some time, Mrs. SHELLS stated, she could hear A-C-E crying. ACE was saying, 'LYNN, please wake up. LYNN, please wake up.' At this time, this writer was advised by radio relay that the suspect had recently been released from Raiford State Prison after serving ten years for aggravated assault and rape." All around me, men were dictating, rewinding, listening, then beginning again, muttering like students rehearsing their answers before an oral exam.

At twenty to eight, Kelt stood up with a sheaf of fresh incident reports in his hand and distributed them, face down on each desk, like a teacher handing out homework. Every detective got one: an aggravated assault, a battery, an attempted rape, whatever it was—unless he was actively investigating a case; that was his work for the day. When Kelt finished, he stood at the front of the room, arms at his sides, silently whistling, waiting for everyone's attention. The stories stopped, the litanies ended; he began with a report of the night's happenings: Patrol reported a woman had jumped from the High Bridge at 3:00 a.m., an apparent suicide. "Course, I'm sure you-all know by now that it wasn't just one." Men shuffled their papers. "No, Sergeant," said someone. "It says it was a single, twenty-seven-year-old white female." Kelt smiled ever so slightly. "Sorry, Schrader, we now know there were two. First the woman, then her psychiatrist." Someone snickered. Kelt cracked a little smile. He cleared his throat and looked serious. "Now then," he continued. There had been a shooting outside a bar called the Pair-a-dice. Three of the suspects had dragged their intended victim into the street and unsuccessfully tried to run him over with their car. Someone yawned very loudly. Kelt cleared his throat again and began a review of everyone's cases. He went from left to right, desk by desk, row by row, the teacher making sure everyone understood his or her assignment. There were, of course, some differences between the homicide section and my high school Latin class. Such as the man in front of me, who had his feet up on his desk and a small chrome automatic in a holster strapped to his right ankle. The moment Kelt finished, the room broke up into sighs, groans, and the final minutes of late dictations. Melon came over, chewing gum, dressed in a yellow sports coat, gray slacks, and loafers. "You going to the club today?" I asked. "Tomorrow," he said. "This morning, I got to go out and find a boy who beat the shit out of his buddy. His buddy says it was a drug deal. The boy's girlfriend says he works construction at a nuclear plant. You want to come?" It was eight o'clock in the morning, but I wasn't awake. "I'm gonna pass and do some homework. You have any cases I can look at?" "You're gonna have to ask the sergeant, but I got some pictures, my private file, keep 'em in my desk, reminds me of all the good times I've had. You interested?" "Why, sure." "Well, then, sit down and make yourself at home." Melon went back to his desk, pulled open the bottom drawer, and started stacking packs of 5″ × 5″ color glossies on his blotter. After the twentieth one, I said, "That's fine, that's fine," but he just grinned and said, "I'm just getting started." When he was finished, the top of his desk was covered with them. "Knock yourself out," he said and left. The typist had put on her earphones; Kelt had gone off to a meeting; I was all alone with Melon's greatest hits.

Most of them were suicides, with a few bizarre murders thrown in. The first one I noticed was of a distinguished-looking old white man, dressed in blue linen pajamas, bent over his toilet, three .32 slugs buried just beneath the skin of his forehead. It had taken him three tries before he realized his ammunition was as old as he was. He'd finally managed it with a shot behind the ear. Then I saw an old white woman who'd been murdered in bed. Whoever had done it had dragged her body into the living room, spread her out on the floor, and buried her from the waist up, underneath a pile of feathers. The pictures on Melon's desk looked like outtakes from a film by Antonin Artaud and William Burroughs. There were two young white men, separate cases; each had killed himself in bed—one held a teddy bear, the other a dildo. There were three ancient black women, each of them found stuffed in their hall closet. There were the middle-aged white women who'd shot themselves in their garages; both had left notes to their daughters; both had spread out newspapers so as not to make a mess. The dead became punch lines in a series of absurd dirty jokes. Kelt came back from his meeting and saw me looking at the pictures. "Going through Melon's oddball file, are you?" he said. He put on his glasses and looked over my shoulder. "Is this something Melon does," I asked, "or does everyone have a collection?" "I don't know if you'd call it a collection, Mike, but everyone has his favorites. You never know what you're going to find. You go out, day after day, it gets to be kind of funny after a while." I'd gotten to one I couldn't understand. It was an outdoor shot of a concrete retaining wall. At the center of the frame, about shoulder height on the wall, was what looked like the aftereffects of a large watermelon. "What's this?" Kelt leaned down to get a better look. "Oh, that one. That was a strange one." After the woman and the feathers, I wondered what I was in for. "What happened?" "Boy rode up on his motorcycle and met his girlfriend at the bus stop. He said, 'Watch this.' Then he drove straight into the wall. Must have been going fifty miles an hour. He might have been trying to do some trick or other to show off and it went wrong, who knows. Anyhow, he went into the wall head-first. He was wearing a helmet, but all the bones in his head were broken. His face looked like some kind of rubber Halloween mask. They took him to the morgue. Melon says he was standing around talking to the medical examiner when one of the attendants came running up looking like he'd seen a ghost. He couldn't talk. He pulled Melon into the cooler and pointed. It was the goddamnedest thing: the boy was lying on his back and there was this thin line of smoke trailing up out of his nostrils. Turned out the boy had been smoking a cigarette just before he went into the wall. The impact crushed his trachea, but moving him around had opened it and let the smoke out his lungs. Melon said it was the strangest damn thing he'd ever seen."

Kelt gave a little chuckle and went back to his desk. The secretary was still typing. I decided to open one more packet. It was of a salesman who'd checked into a Ramada Inn and then swallowed five bottles of aspirin. His room looked a lot like mine: gray carpeting, burgundy drapes, white-tiled vanity. After the aspirins, he'd gone to work on himself with a razor. The cuts in his neck and wrist were so wide and deep he looked as if he'd been attacked by a stranger. They'd found him on the floor between the beds, next to the phone. The beds in his room could have been in mine; the phone looked as if it was. I had to sleep there at least one more night. The little girl on TV hadn't been funny. The salesman wasn't that amusing. I put all the pictures away and walked into the room with the file cabinets.

When Schultz took me in there and showed me Little Eddie's file, I'd noticed bulletin boards on the walls. Pinned to them were mug shots, artists' sketches, alerts, advisories, and bulletins from all over Florida and all over the U.S. In the center of them all was a color mug shot of an extraordinarily handsome but very bored-looking man with sun-bleached blond hair. The police in Palm Beach had found him driving the car, dressed in the clothes, and carrying the wallet of a man he'd killed in bed after they'd had sex. Once he was in custody, he'd admitted killing twelve other people in four states, all with a buck knife—all homosexuals, whores, or transvestites. The Palm Beach police offered his palm-, finger-, and footprints, as well as his photograph and a short description of his predatory habits, to any police force who had a homosexual homicide without a suspect. What puzzled me as I admired his picture was that Little Eddie had looked the part but the blond didn't. Eddie could have played the gorilla in *Murders of the Rue Morgue*; the blond looked good enough to have his own TV series. According to the Palm Beach police, after he'd killed his sex partner, he'd taken a shower in the man's bathroom, left his knife in the tub, changed clothes, and gone out for a drive before dinner. His habits reminded me of a female spider. What I wondered was why his palm-, finger-, and footprints looked so human.

I went back to the main room and asked Kelt if the section had any reference books. "The lieutenant's got himself a whole library in his office. You're welcome to look." Where the lieutenant was, or even who he was, I never did find out, but he was obviously a man who liked to read. I scanned the shelves and started pulling titles: homicide textbooks written by retired investigators; bound back issues of the FBI's *Law Enforcement Bulletin*; loose-leaf notebooks full of articles on epidemic violence compiled by the Center for Disease Control. I stacked everything on a table and settled down to it. I was looking for something other than bad jokes and atrocities. If I'd had my choice, I would have preferred meanings; what I found, instead, were facts. To begin with, I ran into a variation on something Schultz had said: the leading cause of death for young black men between the ages of fifteen and twenty-four was murder. For young white men ages twenty to twenty-four, it was a bit different, not homicide but suicide. Jimmy, the kid on the dumpster, was only acting naturally. Statistics for suicide confirmed the intuition of poets: April was the worst month. Year after year, homicides peaked near Christmas, even though their frequency steadily increased from week-end to weekend throughout the summer and early fall. According to eighty years of homicide statistics from Iceland—a place so quiet that every victim and every murderer could be thoroughly studied—33 percent of all murderers were lunatics; 60 percent were drunks and drug users. Little Eddie talking about John Edward Creal fit right in.

The *Bulletins* from the FBI analyzed victims and murderers as if they were rowers facing each other, chained to the same oar: for every push, there was a pull; for every mark there was a maker; for every kind of corpse, a certain killer. According to the Feds, victims weren't puzzles but primary clues; every body was a negative that could be processed to reveal a suspect. Wounds and blows to the face revealed the killer knew the victim; wounds and blows from behind revealed a stranger. Bitemarks and their locations displayed the suspect's sexual nature: if the victim was a man and he was bitten on the chest, arms, and abdomen, the suspect was a heterosexual male; if the victim was bitten on the upper back, or on the back of the shoulder and arms, or the buttocks and genitals, then the suspect was a homosexual. Bloodstains had their own language: drops shaped like bowling pins revealed a push, a shove, the swaying motion of a bloody hand or instrument, a struggle or a blow; stains shaped like sunbursts revealed wounds that were already bleeding when the victim was struck or fell; where they appeared indicated the direction of the blow. If the victim was a woman, if the kill was quick and sexual, and if the weapon was something from the scene itself, then the murderer was a young man, inexperienced, mentally disorganized, a recluse who lived nearby. If the kill was slow and sexual and no weapon was found, then the murderer was a man in his prime, methodical, self-aware, sadistic, a lone wolf who lived at a distance.

The homicide texts, written by veteran investigators, combined obscure facts with common sense, helpful hints with standard procedures. Three hours of reading them taught me more than ten years of crime novels on airplanes. If a victim was killed by a handgun, and if grains of gunpowder were found under the skin, then the suspect had been no more than two feet away; if blood droplets were found sprayed in a fine mist on the wall, then the suspect had killed from a distance, using a high-velocity weapon. If a stain was moistened with Benzedrine and then with peroxide and turned blue, it could be blood; unfortunately, it could also be apples, apricots, beans, potatoes, or turnips. Every hour, in the first few hours of death, a body lost 1 degree F. of heat. The fresh corpse of a well-nourished, fully clothed man didn't reach room temperature until twenty or thirty hours after he'd died. To determine how many hours had elapsed since death, an investigator subtracted the rectal temperature of the body from 98.6 F. and then divided it by 1.5.

By the end of the afternoon, I'd learned everything except how a spider could look like a TV star. I bought a cup of coffee and walked into the section, just after the shift changed. Schultz was bent over his desk, thumbing through a file, toothpick in his mouth, cigarette in his ashtray. If I had a chance that evening, I decided to ask him about insects who looked human. Maybe he'd tell me a story about spaceships. "You want to eat?" he said. "Why not?" He grinned, and we ended up at the same place as the night before. Schultz's task for the evening was to drive fifty miles into the countryside and make sure that a set of witnesses who'd been subpoenaed to testify the next day showed up. "What's the case?" I asked. "Old one of mine," he said. We'd been driving in the dark for thirty minutes down a road that didn't rise, fall, or curve. The dispatcher recited her numbers; the Morse tones sounded; Cat Stevens played on the radio. Schultz chewed his toothpick. "So?" I asked. "The guy's a scumbag," he said. "Twenty-eight years old, long stringy hair, looks like Charles Manson, got a starburst tattoo between his eyes. Christmas Eve last year, he beat up a seventeen-year-old boy and then shot him to death. He said the kid had stolen some Quaaludes from him in a drug deal. He took the boy in the woods and killed him and then dumped him in the river. This was Christmas Eve. Christmas Day, he got drunk and started boasting. He told a hitchhiker; he told his girlfriends; he told everyone. If murderers just kept their mouths shut, they wouldn't get in so much trouble. The day after Christmas, the boy floated up in the Bay. We arrested the guy fifteen hours later. Now I gotta make sure the people he talked to testify. The boy hadn't done anything. He didn't know enough to steal. He didn't deserve to die."

We pulled off the road, bounced over a culvert, skitted up a dirt track to an unlit trailer. Schultz turned on his overhead and checked his names and addresses. "You stay put," he said. Then he walked up, beat on the door, and woke everyone up. I watched him do it three more times to three more witnesses. The last one came out and stood in his carport, dressed in his underwear, drinking a beer. I heard him whine, then I saw Schultz start tapping him on the chest as if he was a touch-tone phone. "Whatever happened to Bing Crosby?" I thought. Schultz came back, slammed the door, and we drove away. "Asshole," he said. "He was scared to testify. I told him if he didn't, he better be more scared of me." Schultz rolled down his window and didn't say anything for a while. It probably wasn't the right time to ask him about blond-haired spiders, but there was something I wanted to know. "Detective," I said, "you mind if I ask you something?" He lit a cigarette. "It's a dumb question, a basic dumb question, but that's what I get paid for." "Glad to hear you admit it." He looked at me and grinned. Old Bing was back. "All right," I said, "let me try this out on you: here you are, a pretty bright guy, doing what you've been doing for how long?" "Eighteen years," he said. "Seven more and I get retirement." "Okay," I said, "you've been in police work for eighteen years; five years patrol and burglary, then thirteen years homicide, right?" "Right." "And homicide's top of the line; it's something a lot of guys shoot for. Correct me if I'm wrong, but you guys consider yourselves the best, don't you?" "Yeah," he said. "All right then, I want to ask you something. What I want to know is how come you deal with shit all the time, triple murders and guys with tattoos between their eyes? In patrol, when you started out, they said, 'You do good, and one day you might make detective.' Then one day you did and it was a big deal: your own car, no uniform, no one breathing down your neck. But what you're dealing with is garbage. So I have a question: How come? Why do you do it?"

Schultz listened, but he didn't answer right away. He rolled up his window, then rolled it down. He threw out his cigarette. "You ever hear of the Ten Commandments?" he said. "That one about 'Thou shalt not kill.' You ought to know about that: you people invented it. That's one reason. Killing people isn't all that hard. You kill one and don't get caught, it can get to be a habit. What I do is make sure it doesn't. I've got the power to stop that. The power's very important. I've got the power to stop anyone and ask anyone a question. I can do that, and if I don't like what I hear, I have the power to arrest them. That's something I can do, but I have to be very careful, because freedom's very important. You take away someone's freedom, you take away just about everything." "But what about the bodies?" I said. "I spent the morning looking at Melon's pictures. They weren't that funny." "That depends," he said. He smiled. "People do some strange things. As far as I'm concerned, a body's about the same as a burnt-out Studebaker. A body's part of the scene. I'm not interested in the body by itself. If there's no body, there's no crime. The body leads to the suspect. The suspect's what I'm interested in. Whoever's dead is dead. I'm interested in the son-of-a-bitch who did it." Schultz lit another cigarette. We were on the same road as before, dark, flat, and straight, back to the city. "Okay," I said, "I understand. But I have one more question." Schultz looked annoyed. "Yeah?" he said. "You sure you're not Jewish?" He laughed and we drove back to the station. I leaned over and shook his hand. "Goodbye," I said. "I'm leaving tomorrow morning." "You'll be back," he said. "You like this stuff." I shook my head. "I don't know," I said. "It's pretty nasty." He grinned. I waved. When I got back to the motel, the tube was off and the room didn't look like the one in Melon's picture. A man could do worse than enforce the Ten Commandments.

A SLAUGHTER-
HOUSE

*F*or two weeks after I got home, I kept asking myself how creatures like Little Eddie and the blond who killed his sex partners managed to do what they did and still remain human. The closest I came to an understanding was a three-hundred-year-old quote from Hobbes about life being "solitary, poor, nasty, brutish, and short." That described what I'd seen, but still left the question hanging. I decided I'd have to leave it there unless I was willing to go back to Florida.

In the meantime, I had an appointment in Omaha with a man named Lee McTier, the operations director of a packinghouse. I'd discovered McTier after days of blundering telephone calls to one packing company after another, every conversation eventually reduced to a monologue, where I groped for words while the man on the other end waited until I'd shut up long enough for him to say no. By the time I called McTier, I'd learned to say "beef kill" instead of "slaughterhouse" and "kill floor" instead of "pit." All that, plus the assurance I wasn't a vegetarian or an animal-rights activist, must have helped. "Sure, what the hell," said McTier. "We've got nothing to hide. We've got USDA inspectors up the ass; we've got a company that comes in every day and scrubs the place down with germicides: the floor's so goddamn clean you can eat off it. You want to know what we do, I'll tell you. You want to see, it's no problem. You ought to know, 'cause if we didn't do what we do you wouldn't eat. Come up and we'll talk." I'd been to Omaha once before, to interview the surviving relatives of a lunatic recluse who'd spent the last fifteen years of his life taking sixty thousand pictures of New York City. When I'd been there then, I'd ordered steak and eggs once for breakfast and been served a sizzling three-quarter-pound filet crowned with a pat of melted butter as if it were a stack of wheatcakes. If I was going to find out how and why men routinely killed other large mammals for food, I'd find out in Omaha. McTier said Mondays and Tuesdays were the plant's busiest days. His offices were on the eighth floor of the Livestock Exchange Building in the middle of the stockyards. "You meet me at eight o'clock Monday morning and I'll buy you a cup of coffee," he said.

I flew into town Sunday morning, found a room in a Best Western, and asked the clerk for directions to the stockyards. He looked at me the way a kindhearted New Yorker might look at a Chinaman who'd asked the way to Central Park. When I saw the place from the expressway, I pulled off onto the shoulder of the exit ramp, stopped the car, and looked. From sixty feet in the air, half a mile away, the yards looked like a gigantic honeycomb laid flat on the ground, its grid of corrals forming a huge quadrant, perhaps a mile long and half a mile wide, divided into smaller quadrants by narrow roads closed off by cattle gates, all overlaid by an elevated network of wooden crosswalks connected by stairs to the roads and corrals below. At the outer edge of this plane of rectangles, rose the Livestock Exchange Building, only twelve stories high, but—because it was the only vertical in a shabby landscape of low wooden horizontals—it looked like a massive tower, sharply outlined, made of bricks the color of dried blood ornamented with limestone.

I drove down the exit ramp and turned onto a bridge that ran along the outer edge of the yards, straight to the Exchange. Its doors were of glass and polished bronze, set beneath limestone arches that rose two stories high, carved, ornamented, and columned as if framing the portals of an eleventh-century cathedral. Outdoor loudspeakers, fixed to the façade high above the entrance, broadcast easy-listening music just loud enough to form a cone of melody twenty feet around the doors. The calls and cries of unseen beasts occasionally broke through the music, their squeals and grunts sounding like the cries of gigantic infants lolling in some distant nursery. The air smelled of cowshit, pigshit, and hay.

I walked through an orchestral arrangement of "Rocky Mountain High" into the lobby. The only light came from the screen of a video game that glowed in a corner. The floor was of black marble, worn, pitted, and gouged, inlaid with ceramic tiles that framed large squares of yellow stone the color of buttermilk. To the right, next to a column, was a replica of a covered chuckwagon bearing the motto: 1884–1984 OMAHA STOCKYARDS. To the left was a coffeeshop that sold canes used as cattle prods, and coin banks shaped like black Angus bulls. To the right, taped to another column, was a color poster of an attractive young family standing, laughing, next to a big plate of lean beef, cooked carrots, and sliced kiwi fruit. "BEEF GETS YOU GOING / Beef Gives You Strength" was the slogan. Underneath was a Xeroxed memo that described how the poster, used "in conjunction with radio and TV spots as a point of purchase theme in 22,000 supermarkets in 12 states," had produced "a 16% increase in beef tonnage (1492 lbs. per store) in an 11 city test." Along a wall was a row of elevators with semicircles of numbers above each door. One of them would carry me to McTier's office the next morning. I stood listening to the video game play like a hurdy-gurdy, then I walked out into the light.

At five o'clock the next morning, I woke up twisted in the sheets from a bad dream. In the dream, I'd arrived at the stockyards late for my appointment. I rushed in and took the elevator to McTier's office. I hurried down the corridor, looking for his number. The hallway was wide, faced with cream-colored marble, lined with dark wooden doors inset with panels of frosted glass. I noticed the doors were ajar. As I walked, some opened behind me and men in bloody smocks came out and looked at me. "Are you the sucker looking for McTier?" they called. "You're late. You're late, sucker." Then, in front of me down the hall, another door opened and a man dragged out a huge bag full of dead dogs. The bag was made of white plastic that had been stuffed so full and stretched so thin that it had become almost transparent, like an amniotic sac. So many dogs had been stuffed into it that I could see not just the outline of their muzzles and haunches but the color of their hair. I made out a black-and-white German shepherd, a black Labrador, and a rust-colored English spaniel. The man dragged the bag after him as if it were a huge sack of cold cooked macaroni. I watched him and thought, "Goddamn it! Why are they killing dogs? They're supposed to be killing cattle. Why do they have to kill dogs?" Then I woke up. I turned on the light and untangled myself. "You went back to the lab where you'd worked where they'd killed the dogs," I thought. "Now you're in a place where they do it on a bigger scale. This time it's worse, but this time you can see through it. Don't look away. Look at the memory. Look at this world. See it for what it is. This is the lowest point of the journey. Begin here, then rise."

McTier's reception room looked like a law firm's. A secretary led me down a gray-carpeted hallway, past a glass-walled room of men wearing shirts and ties sitting in front of video terminals, talking into telephone headsets. "Lee'll be off the phone in a minute. Can I get you some coffee?" She led me into a blue-draped conference room, set out a cup and saucer, a cream pitcher shaped like a cow, and a carafe of fresh coffee, then left me. A half hour later, a blond man with a broken nose stuck his head in the door. "Mike?" he said. "Mr. McTier?" He shook my hand. "Call me 'O.K.' Come on in." I followed him into his office, teak-paneled, gold-carpeted, a leather couch and chairs on one side, a conference table on the other, his desk in between. It was 8:30 in the morning, but he was dressed for golf. He was somewhere between fifty and sixty years old, lean and tanned, a man who would have looked as good dressed in Levi's, riding a horse, as in a golf cardigan. He smiled—white, perfect teeth. "What can I do you for?" "Well, Mr. McTier . . ." "Call me O.K., Mike." "All right. O.K.," I said and explained things. "No problem," he said. "You can go where you want, see what you want, just don't name the company. Deal?" "Deal," I said. He leaned forward and we shook again. "In this business, a man's hand is good enough; a man breaks his word and he's finished. Now, what can I tell you?" "To start with, I'm curious about that room of guys wearing ties and headsets back there." "That's sales. They're talking to restaurant chains and supermarkets. We deal in 'fat cattle,' known as USDA Choice. We kill one-and-a-half-year-old steers and young heifers who haven't had more than one calf, most often none; they're in the same shape as a nineteen-year-old girl who hasn't been knocked up." He grinned at me. "We don't kill cows. Other companies kill cows; they sell to the big hamburger chains." I looked surprised. "You didn't know that? As soon as old Daisy stops giving milk, she turns into a cheeseburger. Yes, sir. Now, what was I saying?" "You were saying something about young heifers." He nodded. "We kill one-and-a-half-year-old steers and heifers and sell them to places like Kroger and Winn Dixie. That's who those guys were talking to back there." "What kind of money's involved?" He laughed. "A lot for a little," he said. "An animal comes in at eleven hundred pounds. At birth, he weighed a hundred; most everything else is three to six months on the feed lot. You go down to Amarillo, take a plane and look down, you see five to ten million animals in a fifty-mile radius getting fattened up. A single lot'll have a quarter million head. For USDA Choice, we pay $700 a head, about sixty to sixty-one cents a pound. Dressed out, gutted, no head, no legs, no organs, that animal weighs seven hundred to eight hundred pounds. If we're lucky, we make eighty-five cents a head after we pay the help and the government." "That's all?" I said. "That's nothing." He smiled and nodded. "It's a living. The only way to make it in this business is volume and export. The only trouble is, we have tremendous over-capacity. Occidental Petroleum bought Iowa Beef Packing years ago; now Iowa Beef runs two lines, sixteen hours a day; each line kills 380 an hour. We're talking six thousand kills a day. Compared with them, we're very modest. Modest is one line, two shifts, six-teen hours a day, 110 an hour." I must have looked surprised again. "Don't get excited," he said. "The numbers are deceiving. Iowa Beef can run six thousand; we can run 1,760, but it doesn't matter because no one in the U.S. is eating red meat anymore. In ten years, there's been a 14 percent increase in population and only a 7 percent increase in beef consumption." I remember the smiling family with the kiwi fruit in the lobby. "So what do you do?" I asked. "What you do," he said, "is export. You sell the livers to the French and Germans, the tripe to the Italians, and to the Japanese . . ." McTier leaned forward and smiled as if he'd been waiting for this. "You know what we sell the Japanese?" "No, O.K. I don't." "We sell them assholes. They eat assholes. Rectums. We boil 'em, box 'em, and ship 'em. I got twenty-five guys in the plant, that's all they do. And you know what else?" McTier propped his elbows on his desk and rubbed his hands together. "This Japanese buyer comes to me. He says he's very satisfied with our rectums, very good quality, very consistent. But—he's interested in some-thing else, in addition." "Which is?" I asked. "Uteruses," said McTier. "Uteruses?" I asked back. "Yeah, uteruses. I say, 'How very interesting, Mr. Tagawa. How do you prepare them?' 'We barbecue them,' he says. 'That's strange,' I say. 'In this country, we eat them raw.' " McTier let out a laugh and slapped his desk.

"That's great, isn't it, pussies and assholes, but I tell you, without them, we'd be up shit's creek. Everything we can sell, we sell. You ever heard of calf fries?" he asked. "No, I haven't," I said. I wasn't sure I wanted to. "They're very popular in Texas, considered delicacies. They serve 'em as an appetizer, deep-fried, with cocktail sauce. Up North, no one'll eat 'em but the blacks." "What are they?" I asked. I could feel it coming. "Balls," he said. "Testicles." He looked at my face and laughed. "What's the matter? You said you weren't a vegetarian." "That's true. I guess there's no accounting for taste. You mind if I change the subject?" He laughed again. "I want to ask you about the people who work for you. Who are they?" McTier folded his hands on his desk. "Everyone in this office who has any responsibility started on the kill floor. I started there. I took my two sons there when they were five. During high school, that's where they worked, every summer. They used to bring home the eyeballs and prop 'em up on the shelf of the refrigerator to scare their mom. You know what they are now?" he asked. I was about to say brain surgeons but I caught myself. "No, what?" I asked. "Electrical engineers," he said. "The kill floor's the place to start. The work never hurt anyone, but no one wants to do it anymore. We still have a few whites, and we have some blacks, but the blacks aren't worth shit: they think Monday's part of the weekend. Now we have Mexicans and Vietnamese. It's a buyer's market. I have 125 men in that plant, and there're ten applicants for every opening. Pay used to be $12 an hour, unskilled, on the line; now it's $6, and skilled is $8.25. The Mexicans are good with knives; they *like* knives; the Vietnamese do anything you tell 'em, good steady workers. Alcohol used to be a problem, now it's dope. My guess is 80 percent are high on something, but things take care of themselves: you can't get too high or you'll cut off something that belongs to you."

McTier leaned back and looked over my head. "I've got a conference call in five minutes. You can listen to me talk prices, or I can get Dwight in here, and he'll take you over to the plant. What's your pleasure?" I would have preferred if he'd used another word, but I chose the plant. "One more question, though," I said. "Save it. When you're done, Dwight'll bring you back and we can talk more." "Fine," I said, "but I wanted to ask you about the music." "What music?" he said. "The music outside the front door." "That? That's for people who come in from the yard. It's a signal they're back in civilization. I used to run a plant in Minnesota; I used to play classical music for the animals before they went up the chute. They'd be all spooked; no one could explain it. Some people said they could smell the blood of the kill; some people said it was because they had no depth perception, to them dark shadows looked like deep holes. They'd be skittish, but the music calmed them down." I wondered if McTier had ever heard of Orpheus. I wondered if he'd ever heard of Auschwitz. I was thinking about asking him, when Dwight walked in and shook my hand. "Hey, all right," he said. He looked down at my trail boots. "Looks like you're going camping. Let's head out." McTier nodded and we left the office.

Dwight was another blond, thick, and beefy, somewhere in his twenties, wearing Western boots and a down vest. In Georgia, he would have qualified as a good old boy; in Omaha, he was probably known to his friends as a shitkicker. I figured we were headed for his pickup, but instead we climbed into his LTD. "What do you do, Dwight?" I asked. "I'm a buyer." He spoke in a flat voice. "I buy maybe forty thousand head a year." We drove out over the bridge. "Look at that yard," he said. "How many you guess are out there?" I looked out the window. "I don't know, Dwight. How many?" "Maybe three thousand, and this is the busiest day of the week. The yard's dying. I hear in Chicago, on a Monday, there used to be forty-five thousand. Now Chicago's gone and Omaha's not long, and you know why?" I nodded, no. "Guys like me. We go out and talk to the farmer, cut out the commission agent; the farmer sells directly to the company. We truck 'em in, fifty head at a time, right to the plant." "What do you buy, Dwight?" "Good-looking Holsteins, black Angus, Baldies, Chardonettes. If they got a nice fat ass and a good size brisket, they're mine." "Dwight, I'm sorry, but all this is new to me. What's a brisket?" He grinned. "Breast meat, from the neck down, between the forelegs, that's brisket." He turned left, swerved to avoid a cattle truck lumbering up the middle of the road; we drove downhill, under a railway bridge, into a long cul-de-sac.

I didn't know what I'd expected, maybe a tall chimney belching black smoke, maybe a gate with a wrought-iron motto arched above it, maybe the sounds of a string quartet or a light opera carried by the wind. What I saw was a low, block-long, narrow building made of cinder blocks that had once been painted white, cars parked along it, pens at one end. Dwight began looking for a place to park. "Dwight, do you mind if I look at the animals first?" "No problem." He pulled up alongside the corrals and I climbed out. There were thirty steers, wedged in a tight circle, up against the fence, standing nose to nose, their breathing loud, moist, and rhythmic, their tails turned to the world, their heads to each other, broad, powerful creatures, their smell rising like heat from a building after sundown. Thirty-five hundred years ago, Egyptians believed cows were incarnations of Isis; three thousand years ago, the priests of Solomon's Temple used the ashes of a red heifer to purify themselves after contact with the dead. Long ago, Cretans danced with bulls; the Minotaur ruled the Labyrinth; and bull effigies stood everywhere in the Aryan city of Mohenjo-Daro. In India even now, Lord Krishna, God of Gods, is said to pass eternity happily tending a herd of sacred cows that graze on his home planet at the center of the universe. In Omaha, though, cows were bought by guys like Dwight and left to stand in the mud. The air smelled like hickory smoke, part shit and sawdust, part hay and blood. Dwight drove around to the other side of the building, still hunting for a parking space. The wind tasted like beef jerky. This was going to be a hard one, I thought, the lowest kind of death, the most common, the most ordinary, the death we give to creatures under our control. This was the base from which all other dyings ascended. Dwight walked by and I followed him up the steps of the building.

There was no reception room, just more steps up to a landing, then dark, narrow corridors to the left and right, and straight ahead a broader one, brightly lit, painted white, that led through a steel door fitted with safety glass into the plant itself. The door slammed open, and a big Mexican with long black hair braided into pigtails decorated with red ribbons, wearing a white hard hat, bloody white boots, and a bloody white smock, flounced in out of a cloud of steam, looked straight at Dwight and me, gave us a coy little wave, and pivoted left out of sight. "Faggot," said Dwight. "Come on in the office and get yourself something to wear." I followed him down the corridor to the right into a room where a sad-faced, middle-aged white man in overalls sat alone at a steel folding table, spooning pinto beans into his mouth from a thermos. He looked up. "Hey, Bradley, gettin' any?" called Dwight. Bradley looked down at his pinto beans and went back to his meal. "Find yourself a coat and a hard hat and meet me outside." The only hard hat I could find perched on my head like an egg; all the coats on the rack were too short. According to the posted regulations, Dwight should have issued me a pair of ear protectors, but since he didn't need them, he decided neither did I. He opened the steel door, and I followed him into the plant.

I took a step and skidded. Steam clouded my glasses. The air was filled with the clatter of chains and hoists; men shouted; animals bellowed; klaxons blew; animate and inanimate, human and inhuman, everything sounded at once, thumping, clanking, grinding, and whining. To the left, I could see carcasses swaying, suspended from chains. Dwight walked in a bent-shouldered crouch; I followed, wiping my glasses, looking up and down, as afraid of slipping as of colliding with something hanging from above. Everywhere, there was steam, hot water, and a bright film of blood. Pockets of air smelled of fresh blood, singed hair, sawed bone, and shit. Off to one side, twenty-five men, standing shoulder to shoulder, dressed in splattered white coats, each holding a small circular electrical saw, were shaving off the animals' hides, each man making a single set of gestures that were added to by the man beside him, until the hides slipped down around the carcasses like heavy, wet blankets. To their right, a single man rode up and down on the platform of a small open elevator, holding a huge electrically driven chain saw that cut straight down the animals' spines, slicing them in half. Lines of men in soiled tunics stood in front of lines of heads stuck on moving armatures or stood beside conveyor belts splayed with organs, each holding a chrome-plated hook or a steel sharpening shank in one hand, and a knife in the other, either a broad-bladed, curved skinner, or a straight, sharp, pointed boner, all of them making their cuts and slices, then rapidly sharpening their blades and repeating the gestures, their faces slack, their eyes dull and steady. Any minute, I thought, they'll try their knives on each other. Dwight put his mouth to my ear and shouted, "You want to see the kill?" I nodded. He gestured and I followed, ducking and slipping between a line of swaying carcasses, up a short flight of stairs to a concrete platform where a man stood looking down at an empty concrete chute three feet below him. "This is it," shouted Dwight. "He's the knocker. Stay out of the way. I'll be back." He turned and left; the knocker nodded; I backed up against a side wall and watched. Suddenly a man shouted, "Come on, you son-of-a-bitch, move it, move it!" The knocker lunged to the left, grabbed an overhead lever, and opened the door to the chute as three steers, single file, thundered in, nose to asshole, bellowing, kicking, and rearing. As the first one slammed into the far end of the chute and the last one rose up onto the haunches of the one in the middle, the knocker released the lever, and the door through which the three had been driven closed behind them like a guillotine.

Until twenty years ago, knockers had been called knockers because they swung hammers; heavyweight boxers came out of the packinghouses of Chicago with right hands that could kill. Now the industry had switched to air guns. As the animals kicked and raged, the knocker turned and pulled the gun toward him, the weapon shaped like a caulking gun without a tip, suspended from an overhead pulley, counterweighted, connected to a long yellow air hose. One hand around the weapon's cylinder, one hand around its lever, the knocker leaned down, bent at the waist above the animals' heads. He killed first the last one in line, the one nearest him, so that the two in front, who couldn't turn around, couldn't back up. The gun had a hard rubber ring around its muzzle. He pushed the ring down onto the middle of the animal's forehead and squeezed the lever. A charge of air drove a three-inch-long, solid-steel rod into the animal's brain. The gun pumped, thumped, and recoiled, the animal dropped and shuddered; the rod retracted, and the knocker leaned down toward the middle one as the one behind it collapsed. He knocked the second one as he did the first, but the third, who'd been the leader, was farthest from him and harder to reach. This one he knocked in the back, not the front, of the skull, but one blow wasn't enough. The animal reared back in pain and rage, and the knocker hit him again, this time on his crown. By now the other two had fallen on their knees, panting and trembling, their heads back, their tongues lolling, the broad muscles of their backs in spasm. Finally the last one collapsed and the knocker turned and mashed a red lift button with his thumb.

Outside, the herder began yelling again at the next three, "Come on, come on, move it, goddamn it, move it."

The whole left side of the chute, a thirty-foot section of stainless steel, groaned and rose up on chains, and the three animals, still twitching, but more dead than alive, slid sideways three feet down a concrete slope into a pit whose floor and walls were thick with a mash of blood, urine, and mud. There in the pit danced another man called the shackler who hooked a heavy steel chain with a wheel at one end around the left rear leg of each animal. With one hand he held the shackle; with the other, he pushed a button and pulled down a chain with a hook at one end that descended from the ceiling, thirty feet above his head. The knocker on the platform was already in the middle of his next kill; the animals in the pit were still kicking and twitching: the shackler slipped the hook of each chain onto the wheel of each shackle and then pressed a lift button. As the knocker finished off the next three and slid them down the slope toward the shackler, the others rose, one at a time, twirling slowly, nose down to the ceiling, where the wheels of their shackles dropped into the moving links of an overhead trolley track. Thirty seconds before, they'd stood on their feet; now they hung thirty feet in the air, head down, one leg up, stretched eighteen feet from hoof to nose. The one in the middle trembled like a plucked string; the one to the left shivered as if it had a chill; the one to the right swayed back and forth like a pendulum. The shackler looked up, afraid that that third one might slip out of its chain and fall on him. The overhead trolley clanked, jerked, and slammed them, one at a time, into a bloody wall, as the track turned ninety degrees and carried them twelve feet to the first stop on the disassembly line.

Three men in body-length yellow rubber aprons slimed and runneled with blood stood on a raised honeycombed steel platform, waiting for the animals. Each of the men had a narrow, sharp, pointed knife in his hand. As the animals passed in front of them, their heads level with the men's waists, the men reached forward tentatively, knife in hand, afraid the animals still had enough life in them to arch and kick them in the chest or face. As the animals drew in front of them, each man darted forward and made a slit that ran upward from the softest part of the animal's throat to the beginning of the animal's breastbone. Then, at arm's length, head back, each man reached in and flicked open the animal's jugular. At that very instant, before the man could withdraw his hand, dark blood, black to the light, gushed out of the animal, not in a steady stream like water from a broken hose, but in separate single bursts, as if a big bucket had been filled, then emptied, filled, then emptied, filled, then emptied. The blood looked black as engine oil as it burst out, but as it fell on the men and poured through the holes of the platform where they stood, and spread on the floor beneath them, and ran down a storm drain into a cooling tank in the basement, light bounced off it, and for the first time I saw its true color. It was crimson red, brighter than a candy apple, shinier than the finish on a fast car, much more alluring than the reddest lipstick. I stared at it and stared at it as more animals collapsed under the knocker and more animals slid toward the shackler and more animals rose toward the ceiling like nightmare hippos in a Disney film. I kept looking at the blood, amazed at its color, amazed at its beauty. "Hey!" shouted Dwight. "You seen enough?" I jerked around and looked at him so dazed he yelled at me again. I nodded and followed him out.

"Something the matter?" McTier said when I walked back into his office. I sat down on the couch against the wall. "You all right?" I didn't want to tell him; I didn't know how. "What happened?" "Dwight showed me the kill, O.K. I was"—I didn't know the words—"deeply moved." "Are you upset?" "I don't know if I can say this right, but I want to ask you something." "Shoot," he said. "O.K., when you started out, when you were young, did the kill bother you? Did it ever bother your sons?" McTier stood up, walked around his desk, sat on the edge of it. "I didn't think any more of it than if I went out to the garden and pulled up a carrot. We raised those animals. They were bred, born, and grown to be slaughtered. They were born to die to feed us. Like a crop, like corn or cabbage or wheat. We harvest them." "What about the kill, the steel bolt in the brain? The ones I saw didn't like it. Would you?" McTier stood up and looked down at me. "Who the hell knows? What difference does it make? When you're dead, you're dead. When the rod goes in your brain"—he snapped his fingers—"that's it, lights out, adios, you're gone. You don't feel anything.

Even if you do, for a second, how the hell do I know; I've never asked; no steer's ever told me." He sat down on the edge of the desk again. "You don't look so good. Why don't you take it easy, go back to your motel, take the afternoon off; we can talk tomorrow. You're coming back, aren't you?" I stood up. "You bet. I didn't come all the way up to Omaha just to go home. I'll see you tomorrow." We shook hands and I left. I don't remember what they were playing when I walked out the front door. I don't remember much of the drive back to the motel. I didn't notice much of anything, good, bad, or otherwise, until I got back to my room and started to take off my clothes. I noticed my shirt smelled as if it'd hung in a smokehouse. I looked down at my pants: the cuffs were spotted with blood and spackled with little flecks of fat. I looked at my boots: the cleats were clotted with pieces of fat. The boots I couldn't throw away: I'd have to clean them. The clothes I put in the garbage. Then I took a shower. I washed once, climbed out, and dried off. I sniffed my skin. I climbed back in and washed again. Then I turned off the lights, lay down and let the covers settle on me. I woke up three hours later and turned on the TV.

It was the last twenty minutes of *A Night to Remember*, about the sinking of the *Titanic*. As I watched, the deck upended. Beautiful women in evening gowns, pretty little girls in party dresses, handsome men in dinner jackets, they all skidded screaming down the deck, tumbling over the side, sucked down in a whirlpool as the ship slipped out of sight into the night sea. I watched, and as I watched I realized something: the manner in which a creature meets its death could either degrade its nature or confirm it. Just as the passengers were transformed into terrified creatures, sliding and skittering down a slope, no different than the crockery and furniture that crashed past them, so the animals at the plant were transformed from creatures, once sacred, equivalent to forces of nature, into helpless beasts, driven up a chute, trapped in a narrow defile, and then punched in the skull to meet a production quota by a man they couldn't see. The steers hadn't died; they'd been exterminated, and because they'd been exterminated, they'd been transformed at the moment of their deaths into beasts. The kill had trapped them, reduced them, and made them helpless. Men in tuxedos tumbling down the deck, and steers driven into blind alleys, they were all the same—living creatures, made helpless, their natures denied. The idea was obvious, but the facts weren't. McTier had talked about carrots, but I'd seen cattle; I'd seen them, heard them, and smelled them. I had one more day to understand how men who killed animals could do what they did.

I called McTier the next morning and asked if I could go straight to the plant. "I figured you might want to do that. Ask for Bradley; he's the foreman; he's worked for packinghouses for forty years; he'll take care of you. Call me later if you want. Otherwise, good luck." Bradley I remembered: he was the sad-eyed man sitting eating pinto beans. When I arrived at the plant, I found him in the same room, sitting at the same steel table, keying figures into an adding machine. I told him McTier had sent me and he straightened up. "Weren't you the fella with Dwight?" he asked. "That's me. Dwight ran me through here, but I can't say I understand things." Bradley stood up and gave me a tired smile. He could have been Dwight thirty years later, gray, nearly bald, his body soft, spread-out inside a pair of bib overalls. "Come on, then," he said. "Let's get you fixed up." He led me to a supply room and unlocked the door. "Gotta keep things in here; they'll steal anything, scrub pads, sharpening rods, you name it. What's your shoe size?" He handed me a new pair of rubber boots, a clean, full-length white coat, a hard hat that fitted, and a pair of earplugs on a lanyard. Then he took me out to the plant and led me from place to place like a worn-out, kindly tour guide. The earplugs deadened the noise. The confusion of steam, carcasses, and men was patiently explained, step by step. All that remained was the kill. Bradley led me up to it and pointed at the knocker. "That's Zeke," he said. "He's a good boy, has a good hand; he's got some personal problems, but I told him if he can lay off the booze he's looking at eight and a quarter an hour, steady as she goes." Bradley sounded like an old coach talking about a rookie. He gave me a sad little smile and left. Zeke nodded and mouthed a hello. I leaned up against the wall. "This is the place where it happens," I thought. "Not in the plant. Here they die. Zeke's the killer." Bradley had been kinder to me than Dwight. I was better protected than before. I pushed in my earplugs. I'd stay and watch as long as I could. This was the meanest death. If I could bear it, then, wherever I went afterward, I'd know the difference between something evil and something good.

Outside, the herder yelled, and suddenly the steers charged through the door, heads down, ears back; the herder shouting; Zeke shouting, an electric prod in one hand, the door lever in the other. The door slammed down; the animals banged, bellowed, and kicked; Zeke reached for his gun and bent at the waist; the animals twisted and jerked away; the gun went *wump-phump* and recoiled, *wump-phump* and recoiled; Zeke swore; the animals dropped. Zeke shouted down to the shackler, the shackler looked up and stepped forward; the side of the chute rose and the animals slid down. Outside, the herder yelled again, as the shackler looped the first animal and sent it straight up in the air, head down, tongue down, like the stem of a divining rod pointed into the earth; the animals rising to the ceiling then, one at a time, slamming into the wall while the gun thumped and the next three fell to their knees, just as the first ones reached the bloodletters, who danced forward and back like fencers. The blood arced out and splashed down; Zeke shouted to the shackler and the shackler shouted to Zeke; the side of the chute rose as the chains descended from the ceiling. The herder yelled and the air filled with the rattle of chains and the whine of the bonecutters' saws as the time-driven, death-driven ballet of the men and beasts passed in front of me. I looked across at the bloodletters again, mesmerized by the color of the blood as it splashed over them. "Redder than a kiss" I thought, "it's so fucking red . . ." I would have stared at it longer, but I heard Zeke shout in alarm. I looked and saw him jerk back and his hard hat fly off as one of the steers rose almost straight up on its hind legs, rearing out of the chute, bellowing, outraged, trying to escape, climbing onto the back of the animal in front of it. "You *goddamn* son-of-a-bitch," Zeke shouted, as his hard hat bounced, clattering past me, and he lunged at the animal and killed it with his air gun. The animal fell backward onto the one behind it. I reached down and picked up the hard hat. Zeke reached for it with one hand while he punched the chute button with the other. The inside of the hat was wet and cold with sweat. I handed it to him and he grinned. The herder started shouting again; the animals galloped up the ramp; Zeke spun to open the door, then he looked back at me, pulled down the air gun on its pulley, and shoved it at me. "Go on," he yelled. The animals slammed against the side of the chute. "Go ahead," he shouted. I didn't hesitate; I didn't give it a thought. Maybe it had been the hard hat as it skittered across the floor, me picking it up and feeling the sweat. Maybe it had been the beauty of the blood or the time/motion dance of the kill. Maybe it had been the ear-plugs and the new rubber boots or Bradley's explanations and Zeke's grin. Whatever had done it, I grabbed the gun, leaned down, and pressed it against the skull of the steer closest to me. The animal tossed its head to shake it loose. Its skull was as broad as my forearm, brown, muddy, and hard as stone. I leaned down, and as my weight balanced against the strength of the steer's neck, I squeezed the lever. The gun bounced up and back. The steer dropped away as if the ground had opened under it. "Nothing to it," I thought. "As easy as hitting pop flies to the outfield." Zeke grinned and nodded. "Go for it," he whooped. I leaned over to knock the second one. "Sweet-fucking-Jesus," I thought, and straightened up and shoved the gun back at him. "It's all yours," I shouted. Then I turned and found the door and went out into the air. "What the fuck did you just do?? 'Pop flies to the out-field'?? You just killed a steer." I took a breath and leaned up against the wall of the building. I started laughing, but the laugh turned into a tremble. "I'll have to tell McTier," I thought. I felt as if I had the chills. "All he has to do is charge admission to guys like me. Five days in the office at a desk, getting shafted, then going home and getting ignored, and McTier could charge me $30 for thirty minutes every Saturday morning. I could put on boots and a hard hat and hit a few. Instead of telling my boss to fuck himself and my wife to eat shit, I could go to the plant and knock 'em in the head. McTier could meet his expenses, I could get my rocks off, and nobody but some animals would get hurt. McTier could make up his shortfall; people like me could blow off steam, and someone would have roast beef for dinner. I smiled, then I stopped: I remembered the conversation I'd had in the Hilton with Schultz, the homicide detective. "We're all murderers," he'd said. And I'd said, "Not me." "Not me," I'd said, and he'd looked at me as if I was crazy. He was right. I'd just done it. They were animals, but if killing them wasn't murder, what was?

Unless, of course, it was genocide: dead Jews, dead dogs, dead steers. I'd always assumed I'd be a victim, not a participant. Schultz said I'd be back. He'd smiled. "You like that stuff," he said. I'd always thought killing was something other people did. I was wrong; Schultz was right. I needed to tell him. I'd have to leave town and head south. I stood there until I stopped shaking. Then I turned in my gear and caught a plane.

A MURDER

*W*hat I thought I'd do was go home, repack, and drive down to Florida. I thought it'd be easy: a change of clothes and I'd be gone. Instead, I climbed in my car one morning to buy some fruit and never made it to the supermarket. I drove right by it, found the interstate, and headed north. An hour later, I turned east, then south, then west, driving past the limit, tailgating semis, playing tag with pickups; whoever got in front of me was in trouble; whoever crowded me was asking for a fight. I was half-way to Alabama when I realized that I was trying to get myself killed along with someone else. I turned around and headed home. I was in trouble. The next morning, I called Robert Lifton.

Lifton had been one of the first American psychiatrists to enter Hiroshima after the surrender. While the rest of the army medical team compiled statistics for long-term leukemia studies, Lifton began to ask the survivors what it meant to them to be alive. Out of their answers came *Death in Life*, a book that gave a name to the rage and sorrow of survivor guilt. After that came book after book about life on the dark side of the twentieth century, studies of brainwashing, studies of battle fatigue and post-traumatic stress. I'd read and admired every one of Lifton's books because he'd had the courage to try to understand the human aftermath of the organized violence modern nations called war. Lifton was a writer, a doctor, and a historian. If anyone could understand what was happening to me now, it was him. He and I had met only once, perhaps a week before I had seen the autopsy performed on Al. I'd made an appointment with Lifton, then spent an hour describing my hopes and fears to him. At the end of it, I'd asked if I could call him in case I needed someone to talk to. He'd listened sympathetically to all I'd said, but then, in a kindly way, he'd expressed his doubts. "I've never done what you intend to do," he'd said. "As far as I know, it's unprecedented. I've always been at a distance from such things." He spoke with the clear voice of a singer. "The events I've studied have always been after the fact; the people I've interviewed have always spoken in retrospect. I've never walked into the middle of things as you want to do. I don't know anyone like you who has." He paused and thought a moment. "All right," he'd said, "let's say we'll talk—just so long as it remains mutually beneficial. There are things you can tell me that I don't know. And, as you say, you might need someone to talk to." He'd paused again. "Perhaps you know I'm finishing up a book on the Nazi doctors, the ones who aided in the extermination. That's something you might find interesting. I'm almost done with it. Perhaps we could share some of that." I was surprised. I'd been prepared for a polite dismissal. "Thank you," I'd said. "It's more than I'd ever hoped. I'd be honored. The camp doctors were at the heart of darkness."

All that had been said months before the slaughterhouse. When I called and Lifton answered, I told him what had happened in Omaha. Then I told him about my drive on the interstate. There was a long silence, then he replied. "From how you describe it," he said, "I think you understand it already: killing the animals is a way to express your rage while you obliterate it. You express the beast in yourself, transfer it to something outside yourself, and then destroy it. Of course, the rage remains because all you're destroying is a symbol, not the cause." "What blew me away," I said, "was when I realized I was carrying that around. I always thought it came from the outside. You know the clichés: 'Don't let your kids play in the mud or they'll get dirty. Don't let them watch TV or they'll become violent.' I always thought wanting to kill something was a disease you caught, not something you carried in your gut." "We all carry it," he said, "not just you. Rage and guilt; guilt and rage. First you have to acknowledge it, then you have to understand its origins. Good luck. Call me when you want to talk. We'll take it one step at a time."

The next afternoon I called the homicide section and asked for Schultz. It was four o'clock and he was at his desk. "Yeah?" he said. "You were right," I said. "I'm coming back." "Where you been?" "In Omaha, at a beef kill." "Business or pleasure?" he asked. I told him what happened. "I tried it. It was pretty easy, nothing to it. The only trouble was, I remembered what you said." "About what?" "About everyone being a murderer." "That's true, but so what?" "So what is: you remember the conversation we had in the Hilton about Little Eddie? You said everyone was capable of it, and I said, 'Not me.'" "Yeah?" he said. "Well—up in Omaha I realized you were right." He didn't answer. "Schultz? You there?" "Yeah, I'm here, but I don't know if you qualify. I don't think I told you, but the woman was four months pregnant when he killed her. Her husband didn't even know. We found out at the autopsy. We never told him. Killing a bunch of cows isn't the same thing. When'd you say you'd be down?" "In a couple of days. Are you still working nights?" He groaned. "This week and next. Tell you what, though—what you say reminds me of a guy we had two years ago. Worked in a chicken plant. Used to stand in a room all day, cutting their heads off as they came by. He was real nice. I'll pull his file. You ought to look at it. You better check in with Kelt, though."

I walked into the homicide section two days later, paid my respects to Kelt, and sat down at Schultz's desk. The file was under his ashtray. There were two packets of pictures clipped to the inside of the folder. I opened the first one, expecting the worst, but instead of a corpse, I looked into the face of a dreamer, the eyes dark and heavy-lidded, framed by long black hair, the eyes of a man in reverie, the face of an ecstatic. After that came pictures of his body, stripped to the waist, the light so even, the camera so intent that the images were erotic: three-fourths-length views of a St. Sebastian, flat-bellied, long-limbed, and sinuous, torqued to the left, then torqued to the right, a tattoo that said "Jan" over his left nipple, a crescent-shaped scar on his right shoulder. What he'd done was in the next packet. What he'd done was tie up a young woman, stuff her panties in her mouth, and then punch a dozen holes in her, knife wounds that looked like pucker marks, all across her breasts and belly. The knife he'd used was his knife from the chicken plant.

I read the file. Half of it was an interview with his girlfriend; half of it was his confession. He was twenty-three years old. One Saturday morning, he'd got up, chewed a couple of grains of cocaine, swallowed some Thorazine, and then gone down to the corner to buy a bottle of R.C. On the way home, he'd stopped at a house to buy an ounce of marijuana. The dealer wasn't home, but his wife was. She was babysitting two little kids. He took her into the bedroom, locked the door, and tied her hands and feet behind her. First he raped her, then he sodomized her, then he stuffed her panties in her mouth and stuck his chicken knife up her. Then he started filling her with holes. When he finished, he locked the bedroom door behind him and left the two kids in the house with the corpse. "It was okay. I don't remember much," he said. His girlfriend described her life with him. He liked to tie her up, she said. She'd let him, but when he suggested she let his dog do it to her, she'd said no. He liked her to shove things up his rectum and bite him until he bled. He liked pain. "He liked pain better than anything," she said. I closed the file and looked back at his pictures. Two arms, two legs, a head, two eyes, a nose, and a mouth, perfectly human.

I closed the file, left the section, and walked out to the street. Ten blocks away, a huge Maxwell House roasting plant filled the air with the smell of coffee. It was the tallest building in the neighborhood. I turned and walked toward it. Schultz was right again: I didn't qualify. The kid with the chicken knife was like the blond I'd seen on the bulletin board: they looked human, but they weren't. I walked in a cadence: "looked-but-weren't, looked-but-weren't, you're left, you're left, you're right." I looked up: I was half a block from the coffee plant. High on its side I could see a big neon sign, blinking on and off, barely visible in the daylight, a giant coffee cup and some drops, blink, blink, blink, good to the last drop. I turned and walked back to the station.

The shift was ending when I came back. I stood outside the door and said my hellos, Melon pulled a punch at me; I sat down at Schultz's desk and waited. A half hour later, he came padding in, toothpick in his mouth, coat over his shoulder, as free and easy as Gene Kelly dancing down the set of *Singing in the Rain*. He noticed the file had been moved. "How'd you like the boy?" he asked. "It makes me wonder," I said. "I'll bet it does. You want to eat?" "Sure. Why not?" This time we went to an all-you-can-eat buffet packed with people who took the offer seriously. Widows, retired couples, single women with children—they sat in clusters around banquet tables, methodically eating their way through piles of underdone roast beef, overcooked vegetables, and thick crusted fried fish. Every once in a while, a gang of kids would jump up and make a dash for the dessert table and the soft-drink machines, only to be called back by their mothers, who knew the price difference between carbohydrates and proteins. Old women sat in front of plates piled with boiled shrimp, eating and pausing, eating and pausing, filling their bellies as if they were dropping nickels in a change purse. "Save room for the banana pudding," said Schultz. "You eat and I'll watch." I said, "I'm still thinking about that chicken killer. Anyway, the roast beef looks a little red." Schultz shrugged and came back with a plate of fried chicken, mashed potatoes, and string beans that had gone gray at the tips. When he was halfway through, I asked him.

"Detective," I said, "did you interrogate that kid?" He nodded. "What was he like?" Schultz swallowed and wiped his fingers. "Very matter of fact, no big deal, didn't seem upset, just told us what he'd done." I leaned forward. "Okay, then, what I'm wondering is: there you are, listening to the kid, looking at him; you know what he's done. Did you ever wonder whether someone like that may not be human?" Schultz blinked. "I mean, the kid looks like a human being, he talks like a human being, but what he's done isn't human. It's not animal, but it's not human. What I mean is—I'm sorry I have to use this word—but do you ever think about the existence of evil, I don't mean the Devil or anything like that, but something that exists the same way lightning and thunder exist, something tangible, something present in the world, a quality and quantity, not an idea but an actual thing?" Schultz looked at me as if he was watching a circus act, maybe an acrobat. Then he smiled. "I see you've been doing some thinking. You sure you don't want dessert?" I shook my head. He stood up and laid his hand on his belly. "I'm going to get some coffee; be right back."

When he came back, he put down his cup, checked the volume on his radio, and then looked at me. "You ever hear of the Roswell incident?" he said. "No." "It's supposed to have happened just after the Second War. When I was a kid, I had an uncle in Dayton; he worked at Wright-Patterson Air Force Base. He said they had a big black hangar with no windows. No one ever went in it, except once or twice, and those were people like Curtis LeMay. He said they had parts of a spaceship in there, a spaceship and what was left of the crew, in a cooler. He said everyone knew about it; it was a big rumor. He said the ship went down in New Mexico, in the desert between Alamogordo and Roswell, a little while after they tested the Bomb." I looked around at the old ladies and the kids and shivered.

"Okay," I said, "I'm listening." Schultz cocked his head and looked at me. "You ever hear of Flight 401?" "Oh, Schultz, tell me." He took a sip of coffee. "Four-oh-one was an Eastern flight to Miami, an L-1011. It got hit by lightning and went belly down in the Everglades. No one died but a cabin steward. Just the cabin steward. The FAA investigated it, then released the wreckage to Eastern. Eastern salvaged it and used the parts for replacements in other airplanes." "All right," I said. He took another sip. "One evening, on an Eastern flight to Miami, some stewardesses were standing in the galley, talking about this and that. All of them knew the steward who'd died. They began to reminisce. All of a sudden one of them smelled something. So did the others. It was the strangest thing. They all smelled the cologne the guy used to wear. Very spooky. Then, on another flight, same type of aircraft, same destination, the plane flies into a thunderstorm on its approach. It's a bad storm; the plane's bucking around a little; the crew's worried. One of the officers on the flight deck, I can't remember which one, maybe the third officer, he looks up and there's the steward standing there. He looks up and sees him; the steward says something like, 'It's okay, don't worry'; the guy turns to tell the co-pilot. When he turns back, the steward's gone. This time the crew reports it. After that, the reports keep coming, always the crews, never the passengers, they see this guy. The management gets worried: if word leaks out, they got a Flying Dutchman, no one's gonna go Eastern. They investigate; they check the crews, the aircraft, the times of day, all that, and what they discover is that every goddamn time the steward appeared, it was on a plane repaired with parts from the L-1011 that crashed and killed him." I would have shivered again, but Schultz didn't give me a chance. "Let's get out of here," he said.

As soon as we were in the car, I said, "All right. I get the point: 'There're more things in heaven and hell than are dreamt of in your philosophy.' Fine. So I have one for you: the first thing you ever said to me was about Chariots of the Gods. Now it's spaceships and ghosts. If that's what you believe, that's what you believe. But the question is: Have you ever walked in on one? I mean: you go to all these crime scenes; sometimes the guy's been there for a while; sometimes it's a fresh kill. Have you ever walked in and felt that the man's soul is still there, bobbing up against the ceiling like a helium balloon?" Schultz lit a cigarette, looked at me, then looked back at traffic. "To tell you the truth: it's never happened. I ask 'em, though, but they don't talk. I walked into one place, the guy was way down at the bottom of a stairwell. I couldn't figure out how he got there. So I asked him: I went down and I leaned over and I said to him, I said, 'How did you *ever* end up *here*?' I asked him, but he didn't say a word." Schultz grinned; I laughed. "I'm not kidding," he said. "They don't talk."

"So much for Schultz telling me something I don't know," I thought. I laughed, but I was disappointed: the Ten Commandments were as far as I was going to get. There was something else, though. We drove for a while; the radio was so quiet Schultz switched back and forth through the frequencies and fiddled with the volume just to be sure it wasn't broken. "Looks like it's going to be a quiet night," I said. "It happens," he said. "Since there's nothing else to do, I've got another one for you." "What a surprise," he said. "You interested?" "Why not?" "I promise I won't say a word about evil." "Fine," he said. "This is a practical question." "Go ahead." "I want to be sort of delicate about this." "I'm listening," he said. "All right then: sometimes something happens, people get a little carried away; people make mistakes, and a suspect doesn't make it to the station." "You mean still breathing?" "Right. So, to begin with, how does it happen?" Schultz didn't pause. "It happens very easily. In this town, in a hostage situation, if you call in a special weapons squad, you call in the killers. In other towns, you call in a SWAT team, it's just to intimidate the son-of-a-bitch so you can talk him out of it. Here it's to kill him. That makes for problems. Because every police homicide, whether it's a weapons team take-down or a cop who shoots a junkie in the back, whoever, whatever, it doesn't matter: we get called and we have to have the complete report, witnesses, evidence, everything, typed up and on the chief's desk the next morning. *That* is a pain in the ass." "Have you ever been called on one?" "Yeah, sure, a couple of times. Once was a hostage situation. The asshole came out with the woman in front of him. He tripped, a space opened up, and they blew him away. Once was a guy who'd made the mistake of robbing a bank where a cop moonlighted as security. He shot the cop. Half the people in the Department chased him, and when they caught him, they beat the shit out of him. He died on the way to the hospital. Policemen get very upset if you kill one of them. And then, once"—he started laughing—"you're gonna love this: this patrol officer is called to a burglary. The owner comes home and realizes there's someone inside, taking his house apart. The officer pulls up just as the kid runs out the back door. The patrolman yells, 'Stop! Stop!'; the kid heads for the back fence. The officer draws his gun and fires a warning shot into the kid's back. When we get there, I ask the officer what happened. 'He had a knife. It was him or me. I had to shoot him.' The kid's lying where he fell, with a hole in his back. 'He had a knife?' I say. 'Where's the knife?' 'He dropped it,' he says. We spend the next two hours looking for the knife. We walk up and down the back yard. It's a big back yard; lots of trees and bushes. It gets dark. We can't find the knife. We tape off the scene. The next morning, we'll come back and look again. So—the next morning, we come back and we find sixteen knives." Schultz started laughing again. "Penknives, hunting knives; we even found a goddamn letter opener. His buddies had done it, only they hadn't told each other. The Department conducted an inquiry, then they fired him—for being stupid." "Terrific," I said.

Schultz spent the rest of the evening telling me about the time he'd worked undercover for a federal sting operation. I spent the time nodding and laughing, listening for the dispatcher to call a homicide. The only call that came across, though, was a Be-on-the-Lookout for a biker named Two Time Tony, sought by police in South Carolina, for a drug-related homicide. Schultz stopped his story to listen. "Oh, yeah," he said, "I saw the bulletin in the section: six foot three, 250 pounds, blond, military crew cut, Fu Manchu mustache. They want him for cutting the head and hands off a guy with an electric hedge trimmer. Wonder how he did it?" We discussed that for a while. Then Schultz looked at his watch and we drove back to the station. "I feel pretty strange, waiting for a homicide, but I'd like to see you work." He grinned. "In this town, you don't have to worry. Stick around; you'll get your chance." He gave me a salute that turned into a wave. "See you tomorrow."

I had such a good night's sleep, I woke up at dawn. I hadn't come to Florida to watch television and fiddle with the thermostat, so I dressed and drove to the station, thinking I'd ask Melon if I could ride with him during the day. It was 7:30 when I walked into the usual clutter of idle talk and dictation. I sat down at Schultz's desk, nestled my head in my arm, and waited for Kelt to call the class to order. "Hey, Mike." I looked up. It was the black detective I'd seen playing grab-ass with Melon the first day of my first visit, in the back room of the sporting-goods store. I stood up. "Detective Worth," I said, "I'm sorry we haven't met before." He waved my words away. "Don't pay it no nevermind," he said. "I got something for you." He pulled a cassette out of his shirt pocket. "You up for a Redd Foxx tape?" he asked. "Sure," I said. It was a little early for a raunchy nightclub act, but I thought it might lead to something else. "You got yourself a machine?" I shook my head. He handed me his. "You know how it works? This is volume; here's the speaker. You load it, close it, hit the button, and you're ready to boogie." He grinned, turned his back, and walked away. I stood the machine up on the desk, put my head down next to the speaker, and pressed the Play button. I was expecting a laugh track interrupted by some dirty jokes. Instead, I heard a woman screaming for her life.

"Peoples!!! Peoples!!! Please help!!! Peoples!!!" She was screaming an inch from my ear. In the background I heard a peculiar clicking noise, a dull, hollow, plastic sound I couldn't identify. Then I heard a man's voice, clear, calm, and white, and I realized he was a police dispatcher and the clicks were the sound the keys of his console made as he typed the call into his terminal. The woman kept screaming. "Send help!! Send help!! There's a man in my house with a shotgun. Please! *Please!* Send help!" "Ma'am, do you know his name? Ma'am, stop crying and tell me his name." She wept and panted. "Turner," she said, "William Turner." "A black male?" he asked. "Yes," she said as if she were being squeezed in a vise. I heard another voice then, a woman's voice, just as white but not as calm as the man's: "Officer, you've got a pay phone." The dispatcher acknowledged. The line stayed open; more keys clicked. The woman panted and wept. The operator and the dispatcher spoke back and forth, their words professional, their voices hopeless, dumbstruck, and resigned. "Can you give me a location?" asked the dispatcher. "One moment," said the operator. I heard some more clicks, then the woman began screaming, "*William! No, William!*" She still held the phone. I heard him then. A deep, slow voice. "Yes-you-did," he said. They fell into a rhythm, like two loggers sawing through a tree. Then the woman's voice became very shrill, high, and keening, and the tape ran on without a sound. I raised my head and clicked off the machine. I felt as if someone had pounded a wooden spike through the side of my head.

I looked up at Worth. He'd been watching me. He winked. I walked over to him with the machine in my hand. I wanted to throw it at him. "What the fuck was that?" I said. He shrugged. "The sound's not so great, but you can get into it. We used it at the trial." I took a deep breath. I wanted to be sure my voice was steady. The words came out very softly. "What happened?" I said. "He stabbed her to death in the phone booth," he said. "That's what was going on?" I asked. "That back and forth? Him stabbing her and her saying 'No'?" Worth nodded. "Twenty-six times for her," he said. "His wife got forty. See, the three of them were living in the same house. He said they were lesbians. He accused the girl of alienating his wife's affections. So first he got his shotgun and blew some holes in the house. Then he got worked up and stabbed his wife to death. Then he took off after the girl. Here's the pictures." He handed them to me. I didn't want to touch them. "This your case?" "All mine. Take a look. They won't bite." "Chicken, chicken—say no and he'll take it the wrong way," I thought. I handed him his machine and took the pictures back to Schultz's desk. First came the wife, a fat woman, dead in her housecoat, her right breast nearly sliced off. Then came William Turner himself, three hundred pounds, covered with blood, looking frightened and ashamed. Then the woman in the phone booth. When I looked at her, I realized Worth had said "red fox," no proper name. She'd been light-skinned and pretty; now she was colored by her own blood. The nipple of her right breast showed stiff through her wet nightgown. She lay on her back, on the grass, her knees so flexed and drawn up that her vagina showed pink between her light brown pubic hair. Her hands were clawed, like the paws of a digging animal; her upper arms stretched straight out, her forearms straight up: she'd surrendered. I handed the pictures back to Worth, nodded to Melon, who'd started to say something, and walked out the door of the section. Television and the thermostat looked like good ways to spend the day.

It was 4:30 when I walked back into the section. Schultz was at his desk, sucking on a toothpick. "Damn!" he said. "We thought Worth had got rid of you." "Note quite, Detective. I didn't want to miss your act." "You might get your chance. Tonight's a full moon." He stood up. "Come on, it's Friday. They got a fish-and-chips special." We drove to the same buffet as the night before. Time hadn't improved it. I took a hint from the old ladies and settled down with a plate of boiled shrimp. Schultz ate his way through the perch and french fries, then finished off with a piece of choco- late cream pie. "You sure you don't want dessert?" he asked. "If tonight's like last night, we'll have plenty of time for a snack," I said. "You never know." He scraped his plate, licked his fork, and we left.

We'd been driving aimlessly for ten minutes, talking about the moon, when the radio sounded a warning tone, followed by Schultz's call number, followed by a signal 60, a suicide. Schultz acknowledged; the dispatcher said, "Stand by." When she came back, she changed the call to a murder. Schultz kept driving, chewing a toothpick, smoking his cigarette. "Shit," he said. Then did a U-turn. "I guarantee you, it's gonna be a murder-suicide, two bodies, a wham-bam-thank-you-ma'am. We'll be there an hour and then get coffee." I wondered how he knew that.

The call was on the other side of the city; we took the express- way, but it was Friday night and we hit a traffic jam. We sat it out for twenty minutes. "Shit!" said Schultz. "I don't have to take this crap." He groped under his seat and pulled out a blue spotlight tangled up in its cord. He plugged it into the cigarette lighter and handed it to me. "Just point it out the front window and keep it like that, straight ahead, don't move it." I pointed it and he crossed over the five lanes we were in, then over the five others that were headed at high speed in the opposite direction. The sun was just setting. I kept pointing the spotlight in people's faces, whistling along with the radio, hoping we wouldn't get broadsided by some guy late for his date. We rocked along the shoulder on the other side of the road, pulled off onto an exit, shot through some underpasses, and drove back up an entry ramp, two miles past the traffic jam, headed in the right direction again. Schultz had taken all the curves at fifty, arms braced along the top of his thighs, hands hooked under the wheel, chewing his toothpick, smoking his cigarette.

We found the apartment just before dark. It had already been tramped through by a Fire Department rescue crew and an emergency medical squad. It was now occupied by three patrolmen, a patrol sergeant, and a police evidence technician. The dead woman had been discovered by her mother and her own two teenage daughters, stretched out on her back on her bed, her dress slit open and peeled back like a potato skin. They were the ones who'd called every emergency service and rescue squad in the book, hoping one of them knew how to raise the dead. The firemen and the medics had come and gone; the patrolmen had taped off the scene; now it was Schultz's turn. Schultz ducked under the tape, said hello to everyone, and stuck his head in the bedroom. The place was a three-room, one-bath, ground-floor apartment. Schultz glanced at the dead woman, then turned and asked the patrol sergeant if he could borrow his flashlight. "Be careful with it, Schultz; if you break it, it's gonna cost me a lotta money." The light was a long black new one, with a high-intensity beam and a lens that could be focused. Schultz turned back into the bedroom, switched on every light, then leaned down between the woman's legs and shone the beam into her pubis. The light was so bright it turned her hair white. He straightened up and shone the beam into the stab wound in her chest. Then he went into the living room and asked the dispatcher to contact the lab at the Florida Department of Law Enforcement. He was going to need some special hardware and the evidence technicians that went with it. This was not going to be a one-hour visit. This was a dead, very attractive white woman of good family and more than comfortable circumstances who'd been raped, strangled with her own socks, cut, chewed on, and then stabbed to death in her own apartment, with no signs of forced entry and with no obvious loose ends: whoever had killed her had even washed and wiped the kitchen knife he'd used. We were going to be there a long time.

There were seven of us now, standing around the living room. Since there was nothing to do but wait for the people from the state crime lab, one of the patrolmen turned on the TV. The dead woman had cable. The cops sat down on her sectional and tuned in HBO. Schultz walked outside. There was a crowd of women out there, standing on the other side of the parking lot, their arms folded, watching the door. He was fifteen feet from them when they started telling him things: "When she came back from work, she always walked her dog," one said. "There's a strange man who lives in a trailer in the woods next door," said another. "The apartment manager has tattoos and beats his wife," said a third. Ten minutes later the van from the state crime lab nosed down the parking lot and pulled up next to the patrol cars near the front door. Schultz asked the women to excuse him and turned back to the apartment. The van's front doors opened and two tall, skinny white guys jumped out. It was the summer before *Ghost-busters*, so their jumpsuits, gum-popping, laid-back looks were a little ahead of their time. As it was, they could have been the Smothers Brothers hosting *Saturday Night Live.*

I'd spent night after night riding with Schultz, listening to his stories, reading his reports, looking at his pictures. I'd read stories about evil lunatics and heard the tape of a woman dying in a phone booth. This was my first murder, though, where the victim and the suspect weren't interchangeable ciphers. The victim had been a well-bred woman, and the suspect had disappeared without a trace. I could hardly wait to see Schultz start work: Sherlock Holmes played by Fred Astaire I imagined. What I imagined, though, never happened. Instead of pulling out his magnifying glass, Schultz told the guys from the lab what he wanted. Then he sat down to wait. HBO's feature presentation was *Brainstorm*, starring the late Natalie Wood and Christopher Walken. "Terrific," I thought. "There's a dead woman in one room, and a movie about mind reading and transmigration of souls in the other." As the credits rolled, one of the patrolmen said to the sergeant, "Hey, Drury." "Yeah?" said the sergeant. "Why did Natalie Wood go over the side?" The sergeant just looked. "Okay, smartass, why?" " 'Cause she wanted to wash up ashore." Everyone groaned and I went in the bedroom to introduce myself. The Smothers Brothers looked up, nodded, then finished unpacking their cameras. "Okay," said Dick to Tom, "let's take it from the top." I put my hands in my pockets and leaned back in the corner.

"What we have here is a dead forty-year-old white woman," Dick spoke. Tom wrote. I watched; as they talked, I thought. She lay on her back, diagonally across the bed, her left foot flexed, drawn up under her right calf, her right leg stretched straight down, toes extended, like a dancer *en pointe*. Her fingertips had turned purple, the blood pooled under her skin, just as the textbooks described. Dick held her right hand and bent her arm at the elbow: stiff but still flexible. That plus her fingertips, plus her temperature, would help them establish the time of her death. All that plus the fact that she hadn't come to work that morning. Her boss had called her mother; her mother had collected her granddaughters, and together they'd driven to the apartment. Her mother had found her with her terrier lying next to her, barking at her, trying to wake her up. The old lady had drawn a sheet over her and covered the hole in her chest with a washcloth. "My little bluebell," she'd said. Dick continued the preliminary exam: a pair of woman's white socks had been knotted and then wound but not tied around her neck. There was a knife wound in the middle of her throat, just above the breastbone. Tom probed it with his pen: not deep enough to have penetrated the windpipe. There was a stab wound over her left breast. Tom laid a metal ruler beside it: three inches wide. He probed it: deep in her chest, a mortal wound. The knife was lying next to her, a twelve-inch kitchen knife. When the murderer had finished, he'd rinsed it off and wiped it down with some Kleenex. Now it lay next to her in a nest of shredded tissue.

Dick stepped back and looked at her. "Definitely a ten," he said. Tom shook his head. "Not my type." She was red-haired, pale-skinned, well-shaped, her blue eyes open but filmed, staring up at the ceiling. On her dresser were pictures of her two daughters, girls not as pretty as their mother. Until recently, she had been married to a vice-president in charge of international sales. He'd landed in Amsterdam that afternoon. He was headed back tonight. "Complete with an alibi," Tom said. Dick looked around at the room: it hadn't been ransacked. "Okay," he said, "let's blow some 'roids.'" "'Roids'!" I thought. "The last time I heard that was from a photographer who made a fortune taking pictures of chocolate cakes for Pillsbury. He'd shoot some Polaroids, check his light levels, then switch to Vericolor." Tom and Dick were about to do the same thing. I turned the corner into the living room.

While I'd been gone, Christopher Walken and his boss had developed a device that not only could videotape people's memories, thoughts, feelings, and sensations, but could replay them for anyone else. The director of their research institute had just told Walken's boss that her invention was about to be used for military purposes. I came in just in time to see her throw a tantrum, have a heart attack, and stumble back to her lab. As I watched, she struggled to connect her brain to the tape machine while she died. She was going to record her last moments in full-format, one-inch color, complete with taste, touch, sound, and feeling. I turned back to the bedroom.

Tom was leaning down, brushing the woman's pubic hairs with a fine comb. Every few strokes, he'd shake the hair into a small white envelope. The lab would determine which were hers, which were her rapist's, and what his race was. Dick came in carrying some metal tent poles. "What are you doing?" I said. He looked as if he'd been waiting for that. "Camping out," he said. Tom left and came back with a sheet of clear vinyl, folded up, draped over his arm. "Now what?" I asked. "You just wait and see," said Dick. They laid a long pole down one side of her and a long pole down the other; they laid a short crosspiece by her head and another at her feet. When they clicked them together, the poles formed a frame around her. Next they screwed eight-inch rods into the frame's four corners, and the frame became a box. Then they draped the box with the clear vinyl and suddenly everything changed: the box they had made turned into a crystal sarcophagus, and the dead woman turned into a saint, laid out in a reliquary, uncorrupted and incorruptible. Her attendants raised the flaps at either end of the casket and hung two packets, one at her head, one at her feet. "What are those?" I asked. "Super Glue," said Dick. "Super Glue?" "Just watch," he said. Then he and Tom reached under the vinyl and ripped open the packets. The tent clouded with fumes. "First we fume her, then we scan her, then we dust her. We're looking for latent prints and bite marks. We've got six minutes." He looked at his watch. "Come on, let's check out the tube."

By now, Christopher Walken had been fired and was plotting to penetrate the lab's computer to discover how the institute had perverted his invention to evil ends. We watched for a while, then went back to the bedroom. Tom lifted off the vinyl and snapped apart the framework; Dick pulled a stubby little neon light out of his bag and plugged it in, just as Tom turned off all the lights in the room. I stood in the dark and waited. The tube snapped on and glowed purple, ultraviolet. All I could see was Dick's hand moving the light up and down her body, his face a few inches above it, hovering like a pilot, scanning the terrain. Below him, the earth glowed pearl-white, her skin luminous in the darkness. I thought of all the times I'd danced in rooms papered with Day-Glo posters, lit by the same sort of glow. "Ah-hah!" Dick said. "Vhat half ve here?" He'd spotted something around the nipple of her right breast. He hovered above it, moving the light to the right, then to the left. "*Velly* interesting." Tom craned his neck. It was a perfect set of bite marks, upper and lower, around the areola of her breast. In room light, they'd been invisible; under ultraviolet, they showed deep and clear, more than enough for the crime lab's orodontist to make a plaster cast.

Tom turned on all the room lights and Dick looked at the bites. "They're post-mortem," he said. "How can you tell?" I asked. "No blood in 'em. He must've taken one for the road. If we're lucky, he left some saliva. We might get his blood type from it." Tom pulled a roll of pressure-sensitive labels from his bag, peeled one off, and pasted it horizontally beneath the lower set of marks; he peeled off another and pasted it vertically beside them. The labels were marked in millimeters and centimeters; they'd establish scale in the photographs Tom was about to make. He shot two rolls, twenty-four exposures, bracketed, from every angle, then he put his camera away and pulled out two jars of carbon black and two camel's-hair brushes from his bag. Dick took one set, Tom kept the other, and, one on one side, one on the other, they dusted her from her toes to her neck, avoiding only her pubis and the quadrant they'd marked off on her right breast. As they powdered her, I thought of how it would have tickled her, the soft brushes, the strokes, the two men on either side, working their way up like makeup artists preparing a model. As they moved up her legs to her waist, and her pubis showed white, untouched by the powder;

as they moved up her waist to her shoulders, and her breast showed pale, circled by the carbon black, she changed again, from a saint to a carnival dancer, made up for a Mardi Gras she'd never celebrate.

Tom turned out all the lights again, and this time Dick scanned her with the same sort of intense white light Schultz had used when he first examined her. Dick kept his head low again, moving the light at an oblique angle across her skin, looking for ridges formed by the carbon black where it had stuck to the Super Glue, ridges that would have revealed the latent fingerprints of her murderer. If he'd seen any, he would have pressed them with a pad, then photographed the transfer, but this time he found nothing. Tom hit the lights again and took out a wide roll of transparent tape from his bag. They were going to turn her over, but before they did, they wanted to tape down her breast to protect the bite marks. Dick folded a washcloth over the stab wound in her chest, and Tom laid long strips of tape across her rib cage, covering both breasts. As he did, she changed one last time, from a dancer to a Barbarella, dressed in transparent sex armor, her breastplate glinting in the light. They turned her over. Her backside was as discolored as her fingertips. They looked, found nothing, pulled her over on her back again, and went in the hallway to check for telltale blood splatters. Tom found one the size of a pinhead. He ran back to the bedroom to get his camera, but I'd grown bored and turned into the living room to watch the tube.

It was a big mistake. Much had happened to Christopher Walken since I'd seen him last. For one thing, he'd penetrated the institute's computer and discovered a set of nightmare tapes, tapes of full-blown, flat-out crazed terror, straight from the brains of psychotics. Military Intelligence wanted to use them on difficult prisoners: no more electric shocks to the genitals, just sit the fellow down, put him in harness, and give him five minutes of the worst fear imaginable. Vicarious horror in the Ministry of Truth. Walken had nearly died monitoring the tapes' first few minutes. He'd barely managed to pull off his headset in time. He'd made copies, though, and now he had them, all spooled up on the machine in his study, ready to use as evidence against the director of the institute.

I walked into the living room about the same time Walken's

thirteen-year-old son walked into his dad's study. The boy saw
Walken's machine and the thought crossed his face: "I wonder
what Dad's up to now?" His father had warned him never to touch
anything. If the living room had been a movie theater, everyone
in the audience would have been sending the kid some message:
"Kid! Stay away! Don't do it, kid!" The boy paid no attention. He
sat down, put on the earphones, and flipped the machine to Play.
The tapes began with a blinding flash. I'd seen the movie before.
I'd been in that audience sending the kid the warning. I knew
what was going to happen.

I turned the corner into the bedroom. Tom and Dick were in the
hallway taking pictures of minute blood spots; Schultz and all the
cops were glued to the tube; I didn't want to see the kid get his
brain blown out his ear. I didn't want to see him scream and
convulse. The tapes turned him into a catatonic. I was in no mood
to sit and watch a child be deformed by terror. I shouldn't have
gone in the bedroom, though. There wasn't anywhere else to hide,
but the bedroom with the door closed wasn't a good choice. Tom
and Dick had filled the room with their banter, their hardware,
and their work. Their jokes had kept the woman away. She was
still on the bed when I walked in, but this time I was alone. Maybe
it had been the "red fox" tapes I'd heard that morning, the woman
screaming, the man punching his knife into her, the back and
forth, the nightmare rhythm of that killing. Maybe it was that, or
maybe it was the evil lunatic who'd killed the woman with his
chicken knife. It could have been that. Or it could have been all
the pictures and all the stories and all the reports I'd read, heard,
and seen. All of it. Now I was alone in the room with the woman,
and she was coal-black, with her breasts taped down, staring up
at the ceiling. I got scared. Very, very scared. Not because she
looked ugly. But because, with the kid going crazy in the living
room, and all the tapes and photographs flashing through my
mind, I suddenly, without meaning to or wanting to, experienced
the dead woman's terror. Her panic, her helplessness, her pain, her
torture, and her death. The story goes that Tiresias the prophet
had seen two sacred snakes coupling, and because he'd seen this,
he'd been turned from a man into a woman. God knows what I'd
done to deserve it. Maybe I'd spent too long in Omaha. Maybe I
should never have said anything to Al, the man in medical path-

ology. Who knows, but just then, in that bedroom, it was me and Tiresias. It didn't take long, and it didn't last long. I pulled out of that bedroom the way Christopher Walken had pulled off his headset after his first dose of the nightmare tapes: a little longer in there, all alone with the woman, and I would have lost more than my balls. I stumbled past Dick and Tom, tripped over the patrol sergeant's feet, and sat down, numb, on the couch.

By the time I woke up, Walken had managed to tap into the tapes his boss had made of her own death. Her soul rose from her body like a balloon, but it kept on going and going, past all her memories, through an asteroid belt of all the objects and trappings of her life, higher and higher, farther and farther, through bull's-eyes, mandalas, and star clusters, past beating pulses of light and energy, until at last she saw a distant, gigantic glow, and streaming toward it, in endless threads of light, she saw streams of souls, their tiny wings beating like the wings of shining butterflies, wending their way toward an immense, luminous center. I stood up, walked over to Schultz, and said, "Hey, George? Come on outside, I've got something to tell you." We walked out into the parking lot. All the women had gone. Schultz looked at me and smiled. "What's up?" "That movie," I said. "That's what you're doing. You're doing the same thing. Walken's in there, flying along with a dead woman, listening in, checking it out. You're doing the same thing. You don't have the equipment, but if you could, you'd raise that woman, bring her back to life, and ask her who did it. You'd stand her up and ask her to name the son-of-a-bitch who killed her. Don't you see the parallel? The coincidence? It's incredible that movie was on tonight." Schultz looked at me the way he did that night in the Hilton. "You okay?" he asked. "I'm fine," I said, "I'm great. It's okay. You guys are trying to raise the dead. It's terrific. I understand." "Well"—he smiled—"I'm glad someone does." We went back in, and an hour later it was all over. Tom and Dick closed up their bags; an ambulance came and took the woman to the morgue. Schultz checked his notes. The patrol sergeant went over the place for loose ends. Schultz locked the door and we drove away.

We'd been there five hours. It was two o'clock in the morning. We drove back to the station; Schultz parked parallel to the curb, the car pointed toward the Maxwell House plant. The air smelled of coffee. Straight ahead of us, ten stories in the air, the neon coffee cup I'd seen in the daylight glowed red, blinked on, blinked off. We sat and stared at it and didn't talk. The cup blinked on, then a red drop lit up under its rim. The drop blinked out and another one lit up underneath it. Then it blinked out and another lit up. Finally, the whole sign, cup and all, blinked out, and disappeared; then it paused and lit up again. I sat staring at the drops. I could see them in the night. They were shaped like tears and they were as red as blood. *Lacrimae rerum*, the "tears of things," Virgil had said. Schultz turned to me. He looked tired. "Well, lemme ask you something; you think those cattle in Omaha died any worse than that woman?" "I don't know," I said. "The cattle couldn't talk. The woman's dead. She probably died worse." We sat and watched the drops a little while longer. Then I pulled myself up, shook his hand, and said good night.

I drove back to my motel and slept without dreams. When I woke up, I packed the car and headed north. Before I hit the interstate, I stopped for coffee and bought a paper. It reported the death of the woman the night before. It said she'd been killed on Good Friday. "Good Friday?" I thought. "Killed on Good Friday?" Forty miles north of the city, I found a classical music station on the radio. The announcer said, "In honor of the death and resurrection of Jesus Christ, I'd like to devote this program to excerpts from two monumental works of religious conviction: Bach's *Easter Oratorio*, and Handel's *Messiah*. We'll begin with the Handel, the aria 'I Know That My Redeemer Liveth.'" The orchestra played, the soprano sang, and as she sang, I started thinking, "If she was killed on Good Friday, then Easter Sunday's tomorrow." I beat time on the steering wheel. "Goddamn! Maybe she'll make it. Maybe she'll be okay. Stranger things have happened. The timing couldn't be better."

I speeded up. "If Easter's tomorrow, then tonight's the first night of Passover. Sweet Jesus!" I passed three cars and a semi. I started singing along with the chorus. "You talk about homicide!" I thought. "First, the Egyptians killed us, then Moses killed one of them, then the Angel of Death killed more of them, then their whole army drowned in the sea. What a holiday! Freedom and retribution; murder and revenge."

I made it home long after sunset that night, but I didn't care: I read through the Seder anyway. At the end of it, I came to my favorite hymn, a hymn about a baby goat. "An only kid," it said, "an only kid." I read it through: "My father bought . . . an only kid / Then came the cat and ate the kid / Then came the dog and bit the cat . . . Then came the stick and beat the dog . . ." On it went: a fire burned the stick, then water quenched the fire. Then an ox came and drank the water. Then a butcher came and killed the ox. Then the Angel of Death came and killed the butcher. And then, at last, "came the Holy One, blessed be He, and destroyed the Angel of Death that slew the butcher that killed the ox that drank the water that quenched the fire that burned the stick that beat the dog that bit the cat that ate the kid."

A week later, I began to call rabbis to ask to meet a *shochet*.

SHOCHETS

Shochets are slaughterers, ritual slaughterers, Orthodox Jews who kill animals according to an ancient code that divides the world of flesh into things clean and unclean. The killing they do is religiously sanctioned, conducted according to an intricate set of laws that link men with God by sanctifying the most elemental acts. What they do is a sacrament, like the taking of bread and wine, a religious service commanded by God, that permits others to obey Him. From what I had read, a kosher kill is quicker and less painful than the one I'd seen in Omaha, done with a knife, not an air gun, done by hand, not with a machine. Its ritual protects the slaughterer from the moral consequences of what he does; its method spares the victim a painful death.

All this I wanted to believe, but not just because of what I'd learned when I was young. My Bar Mitzvah was far behind me, and all the books I'd since read about the secrets of Jewish mysticism and the ecstatic practices of Hasidism were just books. I was like the Jew in a story I'd once heard about the Holocaust: in one of the extermination camps, a pious rabbi and a Jew who was a Jew in name only became friends. One day, the time came for everyone to die: the guards herded a huge crowd of them out into the snow, marched them to a clearing, and told them to dig a pit. When the pit was dug, the guards said to them: "Listen to us: if you can jump across, we'll let you live; if you can't, we'll kill you." One by one, the men tried, and one by one they fell in and were shot. Finally it came time for the rabbi to try. Behind him, in line, stood the Jew. "It's impossible, I'll never make it," said the Jew. "Hold on to me," said the rabbi. "Close your eyes and we'll jump together." So together they jumped, and when the Jew opened his eyes, he and the rabbi were on the other side. "My God! How did we do it?" said the Jew. "It was simple," said the rabbi. "You held on to me, and I held on to my ancestors." Perhaps I'd lived too sweet and easy a life, but the death I'd caused in Omaha and the killings I'd seen in Florida had opened a pit in front of me. Perhaps I was more religious than the Jew in the story, but if I was to get across, I was going to need the help of a man who was devout.

Unfortunately, none of the rabbis I spoke with believed me. I told them I was a Jew, maybe not an Orthodox one, but I belonged to a congregation and observed the Commandments. None of that mattered. I told them where I was born, who my parents were, who my relatives were, where I'd studied. It made no difference: at best, I was a stranger; at worst, a troublemaker, maybe even— God forbid—a Jew who hated other Jews, a traitor, an apostate. They even had a name for such a person: an *apikoros* they called him. That sort of trouble they didn't need. So, Mr. Lesy, they said, good luck, but call someone else. Finally I did something sensible: two miles from my house was an Orthodox congregation. I went there, asked to see the rabbi, and explained. Until then, everything had happened on the telephone. This time the rabbi looked at me. Maybe he saw I was desperate, or maybe he saw I was just a harmless man in need of some help. He did what he could: he knew no *shochets* himself, but there was a rabbi in New Jersey, he said, a man famous for his learning, an authority on the codes of *kashruth*, a scholar of the Law. This rabbi, this sage, supervised a kosher slaughterhouse. "Call him, use my name if it'll help." I called the rabbi and it did. He spoke like a man never contradicted. "If you want to come, I'll see you," he said. "But, as far as spending much time at the plant, that is impossible, impossible; the men cannot be distracted. They have enough to do; it is very serious; they have no time to talk to anyone. But if you come, I'll see you. I'll meet you at the plant. I'll show you that there is no pain. You'll see it; you'll be satisfied, and then you'll say goodbye." "Rabbi," I said, "it's very far for me to come for a short visit." "How long do you need to know that something is good?" he asked. "What is good is good. The longer you're here, it won't change. What are you asking me?" "I'm asking for more than a quick tour." "That's out of the question. If you want to come, all right, fine, we have nothing to hide. Otherwise, *sei gesund.*" "Whatever time you can spare, I'd be grateful." "Fine," he said, "I'll see you in a week, on Monday. When you know your flight, call my secretary. Sunday, before you come, call me at home: it's possible I may be out of the country. Otherwise, the plant is close to Newark Airport. You can take a cab."

The idea of stepping out of an airplane and into a slaughter-house made me smile. "Something's better than nothing," I thought. "No matter what, I'll be able to visit Warren." Warren was Warren Susman, a professor of American history at Rutgers. Long ago, when I'd earned my doctorate, he'd been my teacher. Over the years we'd become friends, but Warren always remained the one who knew, and I the one who asked. What Warren knew were books. Great books, obscure books, remarkable books, trivial books. Warren was like the renegades at the end of Bradbury's *Fahrenheit 451*, the runaways who memorized and recited whole classics, except Warren was all of them combined, capable of cit-ing anything and everything, not just author and publisher, but content, and not just content, but context, spinning it all out in an intellectual lacework that filled the air with references, quotations, allusions, footnotes, and asides. In front of a class, he sounded like a finely tuned small orchestra; alone in a room, he raced along like a string quartet. Four years before, he'd had a massive heart attack and barely survived. When he woke up, he discovered that whatever had gone wrong had somehow freed him of the angina pain that had tormented him. His near-death left him elated. During his convalescence, he watched television and read Sontag's *Illness as Metaphor*. He displayed a copy of it on his nightstand, so he could watch the faces of his visitors when they noticed it. Now he was out, teaching and talking again, walking around in a body that might suddenly fail him, enjoying the risk. His father had been a cardiac invalid, confined to the house, cooking and clean-ing, while Warren's mother ran the family business. Warren had inherited his father's heart, but he refused to stay home and wait.

When I called to tell him I was coming to Newark to see a slaughterhouse, he laughed. "The perfect place." He chuckled. "But what on earth for?" I told him, and immediately he began to name books. "Philippe Ariès, of course, and McNeill's *Plagues and Peoples*, and certainly you ought to have a look at Hillman's *The Dream and the Underworld*." "Wait, Warren, wait," I said. "It's gone beyond that." I began to tell him what I'd seen. I told him of the medical pathology lab and the homicide section. I told him about the evidence technicians with their Super Glue, the black detective with his tape recording, and all the others with their collections of color glossies. I described my coincidences with the television, the overlaps between *A Night to Remember* and the cattle, and *Brainstorm* and the dead woman. I was about to tell him what I'd done in Omaha, when I stopped myself. "My God, Warren," I said, "I'm sorry. Maybe I shouldn't be talking about this. Does it bother you? Shit! I'm sorry." "No, no, no, no, no," he trilled back. "It's *fascinating*. I don't know if that's a good sign about me"—he laughed—"but it's *very* intriguing; it's so Kafkaesque. When did you say you'd be in Newark?" "This Monday," I said. "Excellent," he said. "I'll be in Minneapolis over the weekend. I'm on a panel at the Historical Convention. I'll be back Monday. You see your rabbi, and we'll get together Tuesday." He paused. "Just don't get too close to all that, Michael." "Oh, Warren," I said, "I can't avoid it. If I stay away, nothing'll touch me, and if that happens, I can't write. I've got to get dirty." "Just be careful," he said. "Stay well," I said. "Take care," he replied and hung up.

That was Thursday. On Friday, I went to a bookstore and saw Warren's face staring out of the pages of a literary supplement. His publisher had just issued a collection of his essays, twenty years of pieces that had appeared in obscure foreign publications, scattered about in film quarterlies and scholarly journals, now drawn together in a collection that the reviewer called a monument of scholarship. I looked at Warren's picture. His beard had grown white, his face thinner, his forehead higher, his eyes more intent, his gaze more centered. He looked like a wise old man, a truth teller and a skeptic. "How wonderful," I thought. "Maybe he can tell me what all this means."

Saturday evening, a woman called to tell me that Warren had died in the middle of his speech. The funeral would be Monday, she said. "Will you be attending?" she asked. "I don't know," I said. "Damn!" I thought. "It's as if he wrote the script." Surrounded by colleagues, accompanied by friends, riding on a wave of good reviews, he'd stood before an audience eager to hear him. His words had come without effort, his comments articulate and erudite, his observations precise and witty. Then he'd taken a breath, collapsed, and died. Died in mid-sentence, in mid-thought. For an intellectual, not a bad way to go. Not like some terminal case, hooked up to a respirator, robbed of the power of speech. Not like his father, puttering around the house. I walked outside and looked at the night. "Ah, Warren," I thought, "you always were a good teacher: I call you to talk about death; you offer books; I counter with experience. For once I thought I had you. Then you went out and died." "Goddamn it," I said out loud, "I don't want to go to your goddamn funeral. I don't want to and I don't need to. You won't be there anyway. You already made your point: 'Don't wait; die while you're still alive.' Great. I get it: you had no choice. But school's out now." Then I got frightened. "You talk about coincidences," I thought. "The stuff on the tube was bad enough, but this—what is this? You go out looking and it'll find you. You mess with this and it'll crawl right up your leg. You should never have called him. You asshole. Remember what you said? 'I'm interested in death.' What did you think you were talking about? Some kind of idea? 'Don't get too close,' he said. But you said you had to. As if you were an artist. How romantic. You get any closer and it'll take you along. You only think you know what you're doing."

Sunday morning, I woke up sure I wouldn't go. "I'll send a telegram," I thought. "The work will be my tribute. I don't want to lose my chance. I'll go see the rabbi." That evening, I called the rabbi at home. His wife answered. I introduced myself. "I'm calling to confirm my appointment." "Something's come up," she said. "Is the rabbi out of the country?" I asked. "No," she said, "it's something personal." "Excuse me," I said, "but 'something personal'—what personal?" "His sister," she said. "She's very sick. She's in a coma. It doesn't look good. He's with her in the hospital. It happened this morning. It's impossible for him to see you." "I'm sorry," I said, "but is there some way for me to see the plant without him?" "No, no," she said, "it's impossible. I'm sorry. Call tomorrow." I said goodbye. "You've got the touch," I thought. "You've done it now." I walked outside. "Okay, dumbo," I said. "You get the message? You want it spelled out in flaming letters, twelve feet high? Consider: a week ago you make plane reservations to go see a slaughterhouse. Then you call Warren. You talk about death. He says he'll be back Monday. He's right, except he's in a box. You get scared; you back away. 'Work's the best tribute,' you say. Then you call the rabbi: his sister's dying. You can't see him, but you still have the plane reservations. You thought you made reservations to see a beef kill. But you're wrong: the tickets were for your teacher's funeral. It's Abraham and Isaac in reverse: a man instead of an animal. School's not out. You still have some lessons to learn. You started asking questions and now you don't have a choice. You're going to a funeral. Pay attention, you might learn something."

Monday morning I flew into Newark, took a train, then took a cab to the funeral home. There were a hundred people there when I arrived, and more coming. In the crowd of strangers, I recognized two men, both academics, colleagues of Warren. "He'd nearly died at the convention in Montreal," one said. "When?" I asked. "A couple months ago, but that was nothing: he was in the hospital just a few days before we left for Minneapolis. His doctor told him he was taking a chance, but that's what his life was: he'd been holding on for years, waiting for the odds to change for a quadruple bypass." Overhead, from speakers in the ceiling, music began to play, and the crowd began to move into the main parlor. I looked around: maybe 250 people, ambling into a large, low-ceilinged room, gray walls, off-white trim, pale blue carpet. Everyone found chairs, and there we sat for fifteen minutes, listening to the music, waiting. The sound that came through the speakers grew so faint and garbled that it was difficult to know what we were hearing. I turned to the man on my right. "Shostakovich?" I asked. He shook his head. "Beethoven's *Eroica*. Warren's favorite." I turned to the man on my left. "Shostakovich?" I asked. "No," he whispered. "Sousa. Warren loved it." I looked around for the coffin. There was a big flat table in the front of the room, but there was nothing on it. I turned to the man on my left. "Where's the body?" I asked. "He was cremated," he said. "What does that mean?" I thought. "Are they going to bring him in on a platter, in an urn, surrounded by lilies, when the music stops? What's going on?" Then I noticed a big, beautiful pitcher on a stand next to the old man who looked as if he was going to lead the service. "That's it. Warren's in there," I thought.

The old man stood up, poured himself a drink from the pitcher, and welcomed us. He paid his respects to Warren, then introduced the first of four other speakers. Each of them tried to recall Warren in such a way that the rest of us could see him and hear him one last time. One read a poem, one spoke of Warren as a friend, another of him as a teacher, another as a colleague. The air stayed empty; the room stayed quiet. No one carried in his ashes or called his soul back to life. The old man rose and thanked us; music came from the speakers again; everyone stood up and began to move out the door. "Shit!" I thought. "Nothing happened. He's disappeared." I stared at the back of the suit jacket in front of me. Above us, the speakers went dead. We inched along. When the music began again, it was different. Maybe someone had changed the tape or changed the channel, but a new melody filled the room, loud enough to be heard clean and clear. It began as a simple organ solo, the tune of "My Country 'Tis of Thee." I smiled. "The perfect recessional for an American historian," I thought. But then it changed. It didn't stop after the first verse, or the second, or the third. The solo became an organ voluntary. I bent my head and listened. Each new refrain spun filigrees of sound around the old tune, each variation more exuberant and playful than the one before. The crowd came to a stop. I closed my eyes. Warren's mind took shape in the air above my head. It hovered just below the ceiling, then skipped across the room, as profligate but graceful, as inventive but true, as gay but serious as the music itself. The crowd crept forward again. Above them, the organ played and Warren danced. No one looked up. He'd been a brilliant man, entranced with the intricacies of this world. I'd loved him for that. I had tears in my eyes. As I reached the door, the music ended and Warren disappeared.

That evening, I called the rabbi's house. His wife answered. "His sister has died," she announced. "He has gone into mourning. In ten days, he can see you. We'll call you then. Goodbye." I knew I'd tripped a wire. "You're two for two," I thought. While the rabbi mourned, I waited in New York, counting the days. One morning, the phone rang: it was the editor of a literary magazine. Could I meet him for lunch? Of course, I said, but I was surprised. He and I had never met. We knew about each other. We'd exchanged letters about my work. He'd expressed an interest in perhaps publishing excerpts of it, but I'd never expected him to call. As I understood it, he was a man my age who'd made his reputation when he was the young executive editor at another magazine that published exposés about the Mafia, the CIA, and the assassination of Jack Kennedy. The fact that we'd lived through the same historical period was enough to guarantee us, if not a publishing relationship, then at least a decent lunch. At the proper time, I gave his name to the maître d' and was escorted to a table where a remarkably young-looking man rose to greet me. "Mike?" he said, extending his hand. "Alan?" I replied, wondering what I was doing there, dressed in a suit, with a smile on my face, halfway between a funeral and a slaughterhouse. We sat down and looked at each other. I wondered what he saw. I felt like the Sorcerer's Apprentice, dressed in robes that were too big for him, wearing a hat that made him look like a dunce, terrified he'd just unleashed a spell he couldn't control. The maître d' hadn't stopped me; Alan hadn't drawn back in horror. Whatever was happening to me wasn't visible. I looked across the table at him and was amazed. For a man close to forty, he didn't have a mark on him. Not a blemish, not a tear; his face was as perfect as a Dorian Gray; his manner as unaffected and fresh as Holden Caulfield's. I felt old and a little dirty.

We began by discussing flavored vodkas, then ordered a bottle of Chablis. He chose the venison; I decided on the salmon. "Well, Mike," he said, his voice casual but his gaze intent, "what have you learned so far?" He leaned back and looked at me like a buyer appraising a painting. I took a breath and lit a cigarette. A woman at the next table leaned over and said the smoke was endangering her health. I begged her pardon, and put out the cigarette. The editor was still sitting there, faintly smiling, waiting for an answer. I had no idea what he wanted to hear. None of what I'd seen was fit conversation for a decent restaurant. If my smoke offended the lady next door, only God knew what my words would do to anyone in range. I looked over Alan's head, down the length of the restaurant, full of chatter and bustle, to the front door. When I looked back, he was still waiting. I didn't want to offend him. He was paying the tab; the salads hadn't even arrived. If I told him the details, I might find myself sitting alone. He thought I was an author, a potential contributor—I felt like Calamity Jane. I looked at him. " 'What have I learned?' " I said. "That's a good question, Alan." I decided to keep it general. "You know, I've been riding around with homicide detectives in Florida for the past couple weeks. The place they're at's not like Miami or L.A.; it's a nice town, not too big, not too small. Most of the time, they deal with sort of petty stuff, rage and folly, that sort of thing. But every once in a while, every couple weeks, they deal with evil. Human evil. So, I guess, to begin with, to answer you, I'd say that's what I've learned: evil exists. Evil exists in the world; it's quantifiable and qualifiable; it's present, not historical, not remote. You don't have to read about it in the Holocaust, or take a plane to see it in Cambodia; it's tangible, like a rock, or a stone, or a piece of wood; it's . . ." As the waiter arranged a plate of hearts of palm in front of him, Alan said, "But isn't that all relative?" I closed my eyes and saw the Smothers Brothers combing the dead woman's pubic hair. "Relative?" I thought. "Evil? What did Alan think I was talking about? Breaking a publishing contract? Not meeting a deadline? He was talking about an idea, and I was talking about a fact." I opened my eyes and saw him watching the woman at the next table. He grinned at me. "So," he said, "what else have you learned?" "What I've learned," I thought, "is to tell the difference between someone who's been around and someone who hasn't." I felt like a veteran talking to a rookie, except the rookie might be paying for more than my tab. "What else?" I said. "Hard to say, Alan. Nothing much. The usual stuff. You know: life lives off death. That kind of thing. Nothing special. I'm working on it." "Well, good," he said. "Glad to hear it. Keep at it. We're anxious to have first look at it." Then he changed the subject to his Saab. The entree came and we switched to repair rates for BMWs. Over coffee, we talked about handball.

Three days later, the rabbi's wife called: I could come if I wanted. "To the plant?" I asked. "No," she said, "to the yeshiva." "Excuse me," I said, "but what yeshiva?" "The rabbi's academy. He wants to meet you there." She told me the time and named the place.

To get there, I had to take a bus. It lurched through the traffic on the interstate, past Newark Airport, a foot at a time. After an hour, the driver let me off. On the map, the town was marked in capital letters, but all I could see was a drugstore, some gas stations, and six lanes of traffic. I crossed the road and began looking for the yeshiva. Every building I passed looked abandoned, without a tree or an upturned face. I kept walking until I came to what looked like a public high school. "Hebrew Academy" said the sign. Inside, the halls were noisy with children. I asked directions and found the office. When I gave my name to the secretary, a little sparrow of a man, hunched over an adding machine at a desk behind her, turned his neck to inspect me. While I waited, a Russian Jew walked in, waving a federal income-tax form. "This," he said in English, "this is what?" Then he switched to Yiddish and the little man at the adding machine rose to help, clucking like a mother hen. The secretary turned to me and said, "The rabbi will see you now." As I stood up, I saw him at the end of a short hallway, standing by the open door of his office. We shook hands. He was a handsome old man with a full white beard, a black skullcap on his head, dressed in a black suit so finely tailored, its lines so distinct, its color so deep, that, as he stood framed in the light, he looked like a Hebrew letter, freshly printed by a scribe. His eyes sparkled behind his spectacles. "Come in, come in," he said. He sounded happy to see me, as if I were some travel agent, come to confirm his vacation plans. As soon as he reached his desk and sat down, he grew serious. "This school," he said, spreading his hands, "I founded fifty years ago. It has risen from nothing. Now there are 750 students from kindergarten through high school." He looked at me. "Do you know what they study?" He didn't wait for an answer. "They study the meaning of being a Jew." He smiled and opened his hands. "So," he said, still looking at me, "what is it you want to learn?" "First," I said, "I must thank you for seeing me. I wish also to express my sympathy for your loss." He gave me a curt nod. "I understand," I said, "that ritual slaughter sanctifies an elemental process, that it links what is below with what is above. With your permission, I'd like to witness it."

The rabbi closed his eyes and bent his head. His office was finely paneled, but it was empty except for a bookcase, a desk, and two chairs. Under the glass top of his desk, turned to the visitor, were black-and-white photographs of him standing with three other old men, all of them beaming at one another through their beards. The rabbi leaned toward me, his eyes still closed, his head cocked as if listening to my words. Then, with a jerk, he straightened up and nodded. "Very well," he said. He began to speak then, clearly but rapidly, always looking at me, his glance a test of my comprehension.

"You know, of course, that we are commanded to do this in Deuteronomy, where it is written, 'Thou shalt kill of thy herd and of thy flock, which the Lord hath given thee, as I have commanded thee.' What is important are the words 'as I have commanded.' There is a story about the Jewish people when we stood at the foot of Mt. Sinai. Perhaps you know it?" I opened my mouth, but he wasn't interested. "It is said that Ha Shem lifted the whole mountain in the air and held it over our heads. Then He said, 'Now you can choose. Either you can receive my Commandments and obey them and live. Or you can refuse them and die. Choose." The rabbi's eyes glinted. "So. We chose. We chose to live." He smiled, but it was a smile that could have cut glass. "You understand?" I nodded. He continued like a judge citing precedents.

"The laws governing the process of *shechita* have been elaborated in tractate Hullin of the Babylonian Talmud, then codified by Maimonides and Joseph Karo. *Shechita* consists of a single, rapid, *uninterrupted* cut by a knife across the animal's neck. The cut must be made at a certain point and no other; the knife must be twice as long as the neck is wide; the blade must be sharper than a scalpel, so sharp that if it cuts a man he cannot feel it— because, if a man can feel nothing, neither will a beast. The blade must be without a flaw; its edge must be perfect, since a nick or a tear is always more painful than a cut. The whole purpose is to kill the animal so swiftly that it feels no pain. No pain. That is the principle of *tza'ar ba'alei hayyim*: to avoid inflicting pain on any living creature." I thought of the animals rearing and bellowing in Omaha. The rabbi went on.

"The law forbids an animal be killed in the presence of one that has been slaughtered. And why? To spare it terror and humiliation. The law demands that if, somehow, a wild beast is captured alive and then slaughtered, its blood must be covered immediately. And why? Why is this? Because to kill a wild animal that owes nothing to man is more shameful than to kill one that has been raised by him and owes him its life." "Shame?" I thought. The rabbi leaned over to the bookcase and took out a small black book. He showed the title to me: *Shechita: Religious, Historical, and Scientific Aspects.* "The goyim say we are inhumane. Inhumane?? Listen carefully." He found his place and read: " 'The incision should be carried from the surface of the skin down to, but not touching, the vertebrae. This necessarily includes the severance of the trachea, esophagus, carotid arteries, jugular veins, the pneumogastrics, and the main and upper cardiac branches of the sympathetic nerves. Severing the carotids causes an immediate and acute anemia of the brain, which is followed instantaneously by unconsciousness.' " He closed the book and leaned back. "Do you know what that means? It means that by the time the animal can feel pain, its brain has been deprived of blood and oxygen and it has lost consciousness. All this must be done precisely, without hesitation. Because, if there is a pause, or any sawing or any tearing or stabbing, or if the stroke is too high or too low, or if the blade hits bone or is impeded in any way—then the animal is unfit to eat. And why? Because it may have died in pain."

He stood up. "Come. We'll go to the plant. You'll see with your own eyes." There was nothing I could say. He had religion, law, and medicine on his side. We walked out to the parking lot. I looked around for his car. A Buick? A Chrysler? He walked over to a slate-blue Lincoln Continental, opened the door, and said, "Come!" I was on my way to a slaughterhouse with a pious aristocrat. He drove well and swiftly. I rested in the cushions and listened. "Once," he said, "I was called to testify about *shechita* in Washington. To prepare, I went to a plant where they killed pigs. I wanted to compare. It was a modern plant; the pigs rode up an escalator and at the top a man touched them on the head with an electric prod and they died—but if he didn't touch them in the right place, they screamed. They screamed. This they considered humane. This they ate." I remembered Omaha. The rabbi turned off into a warehouse district that looked as if it had been bombed from the air. Semis roared down whatever side of the road had the fewest craters. The Lincoln bounced along untouched, as if it had diplomatic plates. We pulled up in front of a plant old enough to have supplied beef to troops during the Civil War.

The rabbi jumped out of the car without a word, entered the plant, strode down a corridor and into an elevator. Men stood aside. I followed like an aide. We rode up to the manager's office and were given freshly laundered, newly ironed, light-blue lab coats. Then we went down to the kill floor. It was entirely different from Omaha. It was quieter. It was less congested. There were fewer men, fewer machines, more space, fewer animals. In Omaha, they'd killed 130 an hour. Here, maybe fifty. In Omaha, they'd been driven by the clock. Here they had a quota, but rushing things didn't help. Blacks dressed in bib aprons, boots, and hard hats did the heavy work. Government inspectors stood by, checking as they checked in Omaha, but scattered here and there beside the conveyor belts were bearded Orthodox Jews examining hearts, lungs, stomachs, livers, and spleens, looking for any of the dozens of defects that could have rendered an animal, even if properly killed, unfit to eat. Any evidence that it had been so injured or ill that it would have died in a year made it forbidden. As we passed them, the Jews looked up, smiled, and nodded their respects. The rabbi leaned toward me and spoke in my ear: "The Talmud says, 'The best of the butchers are associates of Amalek.' Do you know what that means?" I nodded. The Amalekites were the cruelest enemies of the ancient Jews. I would have said something, but I knew better. The rabbi answered himself. "It means that even the best butchers are merciless and unfeeling. That is why we require a man, if he is a *shochet*, to lead a blameless life. He must observe the Law; he must be moral. Otherwise, he might sink to such a level, because of his work, that he would become degraded, like a criminal, and whatever he did would be unfit. To be a *shochet* is not just to have a job; it is not just work; it is a service: to be a *shochet*, a man must serve the Law and serve the Children of Israel." I thought of Omaha and Dwight the shitkicker and the Mexican with the ponytails and all the men standing around with their knives, stoned, drunk, or strung out, their faces slack, their eyes dull. I though of McTier and his dirty jokes and what I'd done. The rabbi turned and led me across the floor to the kill.

The *shochet* looked up; the rabbi introduced me. The *shochet* nodded and handed the rabbi his knife. It was perhaps sixteen inches long, perhaps three inches wide, the blade as thin as a bread knife, the end squared off like a cleaver. The rabbi ran his thumbnail straight up it; then he turned the blade to the right and ran his nail down it; then turned it to the left, and ran his nail up it again. He had inspected three of the blade's edges, but all I could wonder was why he hadn't sliced his thumb in half. He handed the knife back to the *shochet*: no nicks. The *shochet* ran his own thumbnail up and down it, nodded his respects, and then stepped back to the kill. The kill was unlike anything I'd ever seen. The animal to be killed had been driven down a chute, then around a corner, into a large metal pen. A black man stood to one side, on a raised platform by a console, operating a set of controls. When the animal entered the pen, the man pressed a button and closed the gate behind it. He touched another button and the gate pushed the animal forward. The animal couldn't see through either side of the pen, but in front of it was a heavily padded opening, about the same size as and at the same level as its head. Hemmed in by darkness, pressed from behind, it stuck its head through the hole to look out. As soon as it did, the man at the console pressed another set of buttons: all at once, the opening closed like a collar around the animal's neck; the back of the pen nudged it even farther forward, and the sides of the pen moved inward, to enclose it. The animal now stood with nowhere to go, staring straight ahead, looking at a blank plaster wall. It could still move its head a bit. To prevent even this, the operator pressed another button and a device that looked like a curved stirrup, made of smooth, tubular, stainless steel, rose underneath the animal's jaw, cupped its chin, and stretched its neck, so that its nose pointed 30 degrees in the air. The animal was still staring at a blank wall, but it was clearly uncomfortable. At that moment, the *shochet* stepped to the animal's side, the knife in his right hand, out of the animal's sight. What he did then looked like a man drawing a bow across a cello, forward, then back. The blade sliced up through the animal's neck to its spine as quickly as if it had sliced through a tomato. The *shochet*'s arm reached out then drew back. There was no noise. Blood spurted, then sprayed. The *shochet* ran his hand between the severed halves of the neck to be sure the cut was clean and complete. The animal stood, perfectly still, eyes open, for perhaps ten seconds. Then its knees buckled, and as they buckled, the man at the console released it and opened the right side of the pen. As it collapsed, a gang of men shackled it, dragged it out, and hoisted it, head down, perhaps three feet above the tile floor. The *shochet* stepped back into a little room adjacent to the kill, washed his blade under running water, washed his hands and dried them, then ran his thumbnail along the blade, from its tip to its handle. The rabbi said goodbye. "See me in the office in twenty minutes," he said. I nodded, and he left me.

The *shochet* and I stood in the little room. He was a middle-aged man with a full gray beard and mild oval eyes. He watched me, calmly. Across from where he stood was a deep vat of hot water that held twenty knives, submerged in a rack, handles up, blunt ends down. "Are these yours?" I asked. "Some are; some belong to others." "But why are they here?" "To keep them ready; there's lye in the water to keep off the rust. When one gets dull, I have another." He stepped out for the next kill. It was just like the other: swift, sure, and quiet. In Omaha, the men had sworn and shouted; the animals had stumbled, kicked, snorted, and died bellowing; here, one animal at a time stood alone, stared at nothing, and died before it knew it.

The *shochet* stepped back into the room. There was enough time between kills for an interrupted conversation. He spoke to me as calmly, as untroubled as a man might chat with a stranger sitting in his kitchen over a cup of tea. He was sixty-three years old, he said. From Poland. He washed his hands. From a town called Pinsk. Now part of Russia. He dried them. He'd been born there, then come to America when he was five. He inspected the blade. How long had he been a *shochet*? I asked. For thirty-three years, he said. Twenty-two here; eleven years in Boston. Now his son was one. He stepped out for the next kill. When he stepped back, he said he'd have a break in six minutes and we could talk. Every hour, he said, they rested, to keep their hands steady. I thought about the frantic factory pace of the kill in Omaha. "A rest every hour for the sake of their hands?" I thought.

Soon, another *shochet* appeared and we left for the locker room. We sat on a bench. The *shochet* leaned back and closed his eyes; his hands lay palms down on his thighs. When he looked at me again, he said, "Do you know what they call the knife?" I remembered the rabbi and hesitated, but the *shochet* waited. "Yes," I said, "a *halef*." "Do you know what that means?" "No," I answered. "It means 'sharp-no-nick.' Literally, that's what it means. But, also, it's called 'that-which-from-life-to-death-transforms.' The knife has physical properties and also nonphysical properties: it is a thing, a no-nick-sharp, but it also has the power to transform." I thought, then, of all the knives I'd seen in Omaha, and how, in the hands of the men there, they'd looked like weapons. The *halef* was a knife, many times sharper, many times deadlier than those other knives, but in the *shochet*'s hands it seemed like a wand or a bow of an instrument. "And what you do," I asked, "what do you call that?" "What I do is a mitzvah, like wearing tallis and tefillin. It is a duty. To fulfill it is a good deed." "But," I asked, "what about the killing? Isn't there a Commandment about that?" "For humans, yes, of course, certainly, but animals have no souls. If they had souls, to kill them would be a sin. Animals are living things; as such, they must be treated with respect, but they have no soul. A steer has more life in it than an apple, but if I went to a tree and picked an apple, it would be no sin. The same with an animal." I thought of McTier and his carrots. I wondered what the animals thought. I wondered what Lord Krishna would say. "Ha Shem gave Adam dominion over the beasts of the field, the fowl of the air, and the fish of the sea," said the *shochet*. "He gave man the right to kill certain of them, 'as I have commanded thee.' So this is what I do."

It was time for him to return to the kill. I thanked him and went to see the rabbi. "They could never sell this as a weekend sport for unhappy accountants," I thought. "There's too much talk of obedience and not enough rage and aggression. It's also more difficult than hitting pop flies to the outfield." I stepped in the elevator and pressed the button for the manager's office. "What an extraordinary set of circumstances," I thought. "In Omaha, the kill was rational and brutal. Here it's religious and humane. In Omaha, the animals and the men were both debased. Here the animals die one at a time, and the men keep clean with holy law." The rabbi was waiting for me and drove me to the train, where I said goodbye. "Warren and the rabbi," I thought. "Different teachers, same lesson. One kills, one dies. Maybe there's a way to do it that doesn't degrade you."

On the flight home, I looked out the window. "Precious but useless knowledge," I thought. "Your teacher's died, you've met the rabbi, you've had lunch with an editor. You know more than you did before, but it's tainted you. It's turned you into a magnet: you attract the darkness as the darkness attracts you. Meanwhile, people play handball and fret about their Saabs. Maybe there's a way to die that's good, and maybe there's a way to kill that's proper, but if that editor's any indication, for most people, what you've learned is nothing but a bunch of words." Three days later, my mother called. "Your father's had an accident," she said. "He was driving and he blacked out. The car's a total wreck. Thank God he didn't kill anyone. He's in the hospital. He wants you to come." I got on another plane. "Ah, Michael," I thought. "Three in a row? Is this what it's about? Warren wasn't enough? Are you trying to speed things up?"

I met my father's doctor in the corridor outside his room. "Your mother's just gone down to get a sandwich," he said. "What about my father?" I asked. "For now, he's okay. What he had was a transient ischemic attack; it's like a little stroke. He'll have to give up his driver's license and he'll have to be watched. This time, he was lucky; but it could happen again, any time. He could be walking and"—he snapped his fingers—"he could blank out and fall. This time he was wearing a seat belt, but next time he could be outside and hit something hard. We'll do some brain scans. He was very, very lucky." When I walked in, he was sitting up in bed, adhesive strips across the bridge of his nose, a gauze across his forehead. I kissed him. "The car's demolished," he said. "I don't remember what happened. I was driving, then, when I woke up, the police were there with an ambulance. The car hit a fire hydrant. It's finished. We'll have to buy a new one." "Forget the car," I said. "Thank God you're in one piece." "Mother will have to drive me from now on. I can't be trusted. It'll put a tremendous burden on her." He put his hands over his eyes. "Dad?" I said. He didn't answer. "Dad?" When he spoke, there were tears in his voice. "I only hope I go before your mother. There's no way to tell." I didn't know what to say. He went on, "Unless you do it mechanically—but that would bring disgrace on the family. I'd never do it." "My God!" I said. "What are you talking about? You had an accident. You're getting old. Mother will drive you. It's not the end of the world." He cupped his forehead in his hands. His shoulders trembled, then he wept. "Why does everything I do go wrong?" he said. I put my arms around him. I'd never held him like that. He'd never spoken like that. All my life, he'd acted as if he were perfect. All my life, I'd believed he was. He'd given advice, healed the sick, comforted the weak; I'd made mistakes, done wrong, and was ashamed. He'd been right; I'd been wrong; he'd been strong, I'd been weak. All my life, until now. Now he wept, and I hugged him. "Precious but useless knowledge," I thought. "Maybe I can use it."

For the next week, my mother and I sat and watched him try to recover. The accident had broken off bits and pieces of him we couldn't see. Arms stiff, legs stiff, fingers splayed, he slid one foot in front of the other, like a man afraid of slipping on an icy sidewalk. Sometimes he'd lean forward, then quickly lean back as if the room had suddenly tilted up, then down. Back and forth, from the bed to the window, he'd feel his way, one step at a time, as if afraid he might fall into a hole hidden under the carpet. When he ate, he ate in slow motion: first the fingers closed on the fork, then the hand raised it to his mouth, then the arm swung it toward his lips, the whole process like a crane lifting cargo into the bay of a freighter. Every gesture he made was tentative; every move, imprecise. Sometimes his words slurred; every once in a while, his mind lost itself. I sat like a man on a beach, watching a sand castle crumble. On the last day I was there, he asked me what I was writing. He'd asked that twice before, and each time I'd told him: a book about people who deal with death. Each time I'd told him, he'd listened but said nothing. This time, though, he replied. "Death means nothing for the people who die," he said. "It's like words on a blackboard: one minute they're written, the next minute they're erased. It's simple for people who die." His eyes were pale gray. "But for the people who live, it's not. They're the ones who do all the writing." "That's me," I said. I kissed him goodbye. He began to cry. "I won't see you again," he said.

I kissed him again. "You'll see me, you'll see me; stop this; you're still alive; stop crying, I'll see you again."

DEATH ROW

"Animals have no souls," the *shochet* had said. Perhaps he was right. But what about other men? There were some in the world whose work was to kill them. What did they believe? How did they do it? When I got home, I called the Georgia Department of Corrections. The state had executed six men since 1983. I asked permission to talk to the prison officials who did the killing. Eventually, John Siler, the department's information officer, said he'd arrange some meetings for me. First with the man who served—to use Siler's words—as "the master of ceremonies," the warden of the State Diagnostic and Classification Center at Jackson, the place that housed the state's electric chair. And then with a lieutenant, a retired army officer, who presided over death row there. "What about the executioner himself?" I asked. "You mean the guy with the hood?" said Siler. He smiled. We were sitting in his office on the upper floor of a brand-new state office tower. "Sorry. We don't have one. It takes three guys to do it, and they change after every execution. Don't worry, though, you're gonna like the lieutenant. Reminds me of the state's first chief executioner. We had one in the old days. A very fatherly man. He built the state's first electric chair. You ever hear about him?" I shook my head. "There're a lotta stories, but the best one's about a lynch mob." Siler leaned back and put his hands behind his head. "See: this mob broke into this jail to lynch a guy, back in the days when the lynch mob was always white and the guy behind bars was always black. They broke in, but the guy broke free and ran for his life. Where do you think he ran?" I shook my head again. "Not to the woods," said Siler. "Not to a church. Oh, no. He ran straight to the house of the chief executioner. Who took him in." "And?" I asked. "That's it," said Siler, "that's the story, you figure it out." I wasn't prepared for a press officer who told riddles. "Was he guilty?" I asked. "Don't know," said Siler, "and it doesn't matter. The point is that a good executioner's better than a mob. The guy knew he was gonna die. He chose between a professional and a bunch of bloodthirsty crazies. I would have done the same thing: at least a professional's gonna get it over with fast." I thought about that for a bit, then I said, "That reminds me of something I just saw." "Oh, yeah?" said Siler. "What?" I told him about the *shochet*. Siler rocked forward in his chair, not taking his eyes off me. I described the swiftness of the kill; I explained how it didn't degrade the slaughterers or their victims. When I finished, Siler was silent, then he said, "Tell you what: when you go down to Jackson, why don't you tell that to the warden. He'd be real interested."

Two days before I met the warden, I started thinking about where I was going. I called Florida and asked for Schultz. "How ya doing?" he said. "I'm okay," I said. "I'm going to visit a prison. What I want to ask you is: how's the dead woman we saw?" "I got twenty-five pages of notes," he said, "but that's it. We lifted some prints, but there're no witnesses. We polygraphed a couple people, but they all passed. Call me in a couple months." "Okay," I thought, "the son-of-a-bitch who killed her is still loose, but the people on death row aren't. If they're guilty, I don't have any problems with them being there. Like Schultz said, murdering people can get to be a habit. If you do it once and get away with it, you'll do it again. Schultz exists so people won't get any practice. The ones he catches go to trial, and some of them even end up on death row. Schultz starts something; the people I'm going to meet finish it."

The meeting with the warden was in his office. A large room with comfortable chairs. On the wall, bad lithographs of standard hunting scenes: pheasants rising, dogs on point, hunters in their skiffs. Scattered here and there were football souvenirs from the University of Georgia featuring the school's mascot—a particularly ugly bulldog striding along with its teeth bared and its fists clenched. Ralph Kemp sat behind his desk, looking like an eleven-year-old who'd lost most of his hair and gained a lot of weight. His deputy sat to his right. His chief of security settled in behind me. Siler, the information officer, took a spot ten feet to my left. They looked in at me from the edge of a cordon. I turned around to check the exit and noticed that Kemp had a hunting trophy on his back wall. It was the hindquarters of a deer, mounted on a plaque, its tail up, its asshole closed, staring him in the eye. "The better part of valor?" I thought.

The meeting began. I gave my standard speech: a book about professionals who deal with death. I added something for the audience: a book about the good guys instead of the outlaws. They nodded. They liked that. We were all on the same team. Kemp offered some numbers: 115 men here at Jackson on UDS. "UDS?" I asked "Under death sentence," he said. Not a bad code word. Next: 1,600 men total, passing through a facility built to process three hundred. Everyone was in transit, except the ones headed for the chair. They stayed; the rest were interviewed, tested, examined, and evaluated, then sent on to facilities designed to hold them for the length of their sentence. I nodded. I asked Kemp how he got started. Studied sociology, he said. Started looking for work as soon as he graduated. Applied to the phone company the same day he applied to the prison system. The prison system called back first. I didn't know what to say. "Tell Ralph about those *shochets*," Siler prompted me. I described the kill but left out the religion.

Kemp took it as a signal to stand up. We were ready to go; a bunch of Georgia bulldogs headed out the door, down a flight of stairs, through a long tunnel that served as a sally port, out into a parking lot surveyed by a watchtower, into a green state station wagon. It was a tight fit: everyone but me had been eating for two for many years. I was squeezed between Siler and Kemp's deputy in the back seat, riding the transmission hump. Every time I turned my head, my chin hit their shoulders. We drove along the periphery. From what I could see, the outside of the prison looked like an electronics assembly plant. We drove through a set of double gates onto an open, grassy field behind a building. A flat-roofed, windowless, brown-painted cinderblock building. The deputy pulled out a set of beautiful flat brass keys that looked like sculptural miniatures designed by Louise Nevelson. We passed through two doors into a large beige room; a half dozen church pews faced a huge plate-glass window fitted into the opposite wall. White drapes had been drawn across it from the inside. "This is for the witnesses," said Kemp. "Church pews?" I asked. "It's all we could get," he said. There were piles of brown paper lunch bags at the end of each pew, stacked up like hymn books. "You know what those are?" he asked. I took a guess: "Air-sickness bags?" "You got it," he said. I wondered about the church pews. When I thought about it, though, I understood. What else could they have used? Theater seats?

Kemp's deputy unlocked another door; the room was pitch-black; Kemp found the lights. There stood the electric chair. High-backed, sturdy, regal, newly made, its wood finished with a clear polyurethane. The natural look. The wall beige; the floor, white linoleum. We stepped around the corner to the equipment room. The main electrical board had two sets of timers, voltage regulators, and amp meters. Made by an electrical engineer in Arkansas, said Kemp. "Man does custom work for lots of places." Coming out of the middle of the main board were three heavy black electrical cords with on-off switches at the end of them. "One of these is live; the other two are dummies. The electricians rewire them for each execution. The leads aren't color-coded, so they don't even know for sure which is which. Three volunteers take them. I give the command; they press the buttons." "Is it wired now?" I asked. "No." I tried one Click-click; like turning on a lamp. Very simple. We went out the door to the next room. There were bars across one end of it: a holding cell complete with a new stainless-steel toilet and sink. Next to it, a separate shower, also barred. "That door over there," said Kemp, "that door connects to the UDS cellblocks. This is H-5. That door leads to H-1, 2, 3, and 4. The regular UDS officers escort the prisoner from his cell to this door. They knock; the door opens; they hand over the prisoner, and a new set of guards takes charge." "One door," I thought. "One side, life; one side, death; everything divided; the milk from the meat."

We walked back, past the equipment room, to the chair. Some-one had pulled the drapes so there was a view through the window to the church pews. They looked at me. I looked at the chair. Silence. Kemp said, "You want to try it?" I laughed. He said, "No kidding. Why don't you sit down, see what it feels like?" I said, "No, really, it's okay." His deputy said, "It's okay. Try it." I said, "Are you sure?" Siler said, "Yeah. Go ahead." I sat down. Just as I settled back, the four of them closed in on me. They had me strapped down in ten seconds. Broad, new leather straps. A strap across the waist. A strap across the chest. Straps on both arms. Straps on both wrists. A strap halfway up my thighs. Straps around my ankles. Nice and tight. They were quick. I couldn't move. I looked up at them. They were grinning. I thought, "If I was into bondage, this would be the happiest moment of my life." I said, "You do this for everyone?" "No," said Kemp. "How do you like it?" "It's pretty tight," I said. His chief stepped behind me then. I felt the back of the chair crank slowly forward, pushing me farther into the straps. "We got a little screw back here," he said. "Uh-huh," I said. "That's great. Now what?" Kemp said, "Now you know how it works." That's when I remembered the steer in the pen at the kosher kill. He'd walked in and the walls had closed around him. "So that's what it felt like," I thought. "I even stuck my head through the hole. Ah! What a fool!" Kemp nodded; the seat uncranked. They unstrapped me. Everyone laughed. I stayed in the chair. I wasn't sure about standing up.

"Come on!" said Kemp. "Let's get some lunch!" I climbed in the car, squeezed in the back seat between Siler and the chief. I was a little dazed. We pulled into a place that looked like a set for a television Western. "Family Gospel Sing Every Friday Night," said a sign. "Family Restaurant and Music Hall," said another. "Lazy Susan Tables," said a third. Inside was a gigantic room lit with fluorescents; huge, round, white Formica tables dotted the floor. They led me to one big enough for twelve people. This was their favorite place. A waitress asked if we wanted sweetened or unsweetened tea. Then she and another woman brought the food. Plates, and bowls, and platters of it. Fried chicken, Brunswick stew, chopped pork barbecue, corn on the cob, collard greens, peas and pearl onions in cream gravy, coleslaw, Jell-O mold, fresh celery, fresh green onions and raw carrots, mashed potatoes, blackeyed peas, boiled white beans, biscuits, butter and honey, and peach cobbler. All of it, as advertised, set edge to edge on a lazy Susan in the middle of the table. The only thing you had to decide was whether to turn it clockwise or counterclockwise. We ate, and as we ate, I wondered: Isn't this all backwards? Aren't you supposed to have your last meal first? I kept eating, and didn't say anything, just in case.

The next day, I went back to the prison to talk with Kemp about himself. I asked him about being a warden. What did it take; what was it all about? "Cutouts," he said. "Cutouts?" "Yeah. The essential element in prison management. I learned it when I was deputy at Reidsville. The warden taught me. I was his cutout." "But what's a cutout?" "A cutout," he said, "is what you do when the shit hits the fan." I remembered the deer's ass: Kemp had just told a joke: I was supposed to laugh. He kept talking. "Whenever someone had to be fired or the whole place had to be locked down, the warden made sure he was unavailable or out of town. He left it to me. I was Dirty Harry. I was his cutout. He stayed clean, I took the shit." "Does that go for everything?" I asked. "Yeah. Everything." "Including executions?" "You better believe it," he said.

I asked him to describe one. By the time he finished, I understood why Siler had prompted me about the *shochets*: an execution in Georgia is intended to be as swift as a kosher kill. Since there's no holy law to protect them, prison officials rely on a system of divided responsibilities. Procedures are so fragmented that no single person remains responsible. All actions are mediated by others or shared with others. Everything is done by administrative decree and court order, conveyed from person to person, down a chain of command and obedience: "I-did-what-I-did-because-he-did-what-he-did." By the time a death sentence is carried out, it's impossible to accuse any particular person of anything. In Georgia, murderers die, but no one man ever kills them.

The process begins, said Kemp, a week before it actually happens. After whatever legal appeals the man has are almost exhausted, the warden sends an administrative assistant and a guard to the man's cell. While the guard listens and watches, the assistant reads the man the court's order of execution. "There's the first cutout," I thought. The assistant sits with the man and helps him make his final arrangements: Who does he want notified; what does he want for his last meal; where does he want his body sent? Does he want a priest or a chaplain? If the man wants to make a last statement, the assistant writes it down and the guard witnesses it. Whatever explanations, accusations, and exonerations the man recites, the assistant records them.

When that's finished, the three of them take an inventory of the man's possessions. He declares whom he wants to have what. He reviews his last statement and the inventory and signs them in the presence of the two witnesses. When the guard and the assistant leave, the men on the cellblock say their goodbyes. After that, they ignore him. "They treat him," said Kemp, "as if he's already dead."

Forty-eight hours before the execution, two escort officers take him to the prison hospital. The medical staff gives him a physical, a shower, and a clean set of clothes. No one's interested in his health or his hygiene: they just want to be sure he lives long enough to die properly. When they're finished, they put him in a cell in the hospital. There, instead of waiting, he's distracted. Distracted by visitors. Whoever he wants to see, he can see. If he wants to talk on the phone, he can talk on the phone. Kemp said he considers it time well spent. Not because it makes the man happy, but because it keeps him occupied. All this goes on until twenty-four hours before his execution. After dinner, he's escorted through the UDS cell block to the door that separates the place where he's lived from the place where he'll die. The escort officers knock; the door opens; he's handed over. "Once," said Kemp, "a man asked the escorts to walk through the door and sit with him. They refused. It wasn't their territory. Their job was to leave him at the door." "There's the next set of cut-outs," I thought. Kemp continued: the man's handed over and locked in a holding cell. Two new guards, guards he's never seen before, watch him as he sleeps. "Another pair of cutouts," I thought. "They keep a death watch," said Kemp. "That's all they do." When the time comes to execute him, they aren't among the six who walk him to the chair. "More cutouts," I thought. "Three pairs this time." The two guards, on watch, keep logbooks. They record whatever the man does. "Once," said Kemp, "one of them wrote that the man woke up, took a piss, and shook his pecker three times." Kemp laughed. In the morning, the man can see more visitors or make more phone calls or spend time with a chaplain. "It doesn't matter to me," Kemp said. "He can spend all his time on the phone or on his knees, so long as he keeps busy."

Five hours before the execution, Kemp and his deputy leave

their offices and check into H-5. "Do you talk with the man?" I asked. "Not if I can help it," he said. "I keep him at arm's length. I keep everyone on UDS at arm's length. From the moment they arrive until the moment they leave. They have a complaint, they have a problem, they have a need? They talk to a guard or a counselor and the guard or the counselor tells me. It's all cut-outs." "What happens to the cutouts?" I asked. "Some crack," he said. "It's happened three times. The first was a young kid, a counselor. A good kid, but inexperienced. He took the man's case to heart. He came in to see me three times. He pleaded his case. He broke down. Here in my office. I transferred him out of H-block. I transferred him right out of the prison." "And the others?" I asked. "They were both in the guard detail that walks the man to the chair. One was black. He said his family and friends were making life hard for him. Making fun of him. They knew what he did. The other one was white. He resigned after we had to give one man an extra jolt. The first didn't kill him, so we had to do it again. When it was over, the officer asked to be relieved."

Kemp went back to the chronicle. Five hours before the execution, he and his deputy check into H-5. They leave behind whatever phone calls, interviews, and controversies have formed around the execution. They settle themselves to their work. They supervise the two electricians who are assigned to the equipment; they search the execution chamber and the witness room; they rehearse the guard detail. Four hours before the execution, the prisoner's given his last meal. One man, said Kemp, asked for lobster. What he got was fried shrimp from the Family Music Hall down the road. At 11:45 p.m., Kemp's deputy opens a phone line to the prison commissioner's office in Atlanta. The line will stay open until the execution's over, the deputy describing it minute by minute. At about the same time, the prisoner's prepared: the crown of his head is shaved; he's strip-searched, given a shower and a new set of clothes. Meanwhile, Kemp's assembled his guard detail in a pew in the witness room. He lets them talk. "About what?" I asked. "About football," he said. Or hunting; or food; or getting laid. Not about the execution. Kemp listens to their voices. He wants to be sure they're ready.

The place begins to fill up. In addition to the prisoner and the two men who've been watching him, added to Kemp and his deputy and the six-man guard detail and the two electricians, a chaplain and two doctors arrive—one a staff doctor, the other a civilian volunteer. "It sounds like Noah's Ark," I said. "You've got two watchers, two doctors, two electricians, three pairs of guards, and you and your deputy." "That's not all, either," said Kemp. "On the other end of that phone, in Atlanta, there's the commissioner, and right next to him a lawyer from the state attorney general's office." "All those pairs," I thought. "Like Tweedledum and Tweedledee, pointing to each other. 'He's the one!' they say in unison."

Kemp went on with his description. At ten minutes after midnight, a guard opens the outer door of the witness room. The witnesses file in, five for the state, six for the press, five for the condemned man. The guard checks their names. The drapes of the big window have been opened. The witnesses take their places and stare at the chair. The window in front of them is bulletproof. They watch Kemp step up to the microphone on the other side of the glass. "A microphone??" I asked. "Yeah," he said, "just like an MC." Kemp addresses the guard who's checked in the witnesses. "Are the witnesses for the state present?" Kemp asks. The guard nods. "For the press?" The guard nods. "For the condemned?" The guard nods. Kemp reads everyone the court order. It's all official. He turns and knocks on the door to the next room. The six guards bring in the prisoner: two in back; two in front; two on either side; one of them holds the man's pants, at the waist, from behind. In three seconds, they strap him in. Belts around the arms and forearms; belts around the waist and thighs; belts around the ankles; a belt across the chest. Just like me. The back of the chair is cranked forward. Kemp leans down and asks the man if he wants to add anything to his last statement. If he does, Kemp holds the mike to him. Like the host of a game show. Once, said Kemp, the man announced he wanted to bless the people who'd helped him and curse the ones who'd stood in his way. He'd looked right into Kemp's eyes when he said the last part. "What did you do?" I asked. "I—smiled," Kemp said.

When the man's finished, Kemp asks him if he'd like the benefit of a prayer. If he does, the chaplain steps forward. When the chaplain's finished, Kemp picks up an extension phone and asks the commissioner in Atlanta if there're any last-minute legal developments. The commissioner confers with the man from the attorney general's office seated next to him. When he replies, Kemp listens to his voice to be certain he's talking to the right man. He acknowledges the reply and announces it to everyone. Then he reads out the complete court order: the charges, the verdict, the sentence. He invokes the text: as found by the jury, as ordered by the judge.

Two guards strap brass plates to the prisoner: one around his right leg, one onto his head. Underneath each is a sponge soaked with water. The plate on his head is held down by a harness crisscrossed over his forehead, his temples, and his chin. That part I'd missed. Each plate has a short metal rod welded to it. An electrician attaches a cable to each rod with a bolt and a wing nut. Then the man's head is tied back with a belt around his chin, and the back of the chair is cranked even farther forward. A guard wipes the man's forehead and then ties a small leather apron over his face. Five of the guards leave the room. Kemp turns off the microphone. He inspects the man's straps. The sixth guard shadows him. After Kemp turns off the mike, the guard checks it; after he inspects the straps, the guard inspects them again. His cutout becomes his fail-safe. The last thing Kemp does before he leaves the room is to turn on the exhaust fan in the ceiling. The last thing the guard does is give the crank on the chair a final turn.

As the guard closes the door, Kemp walks into the equipment room. Three volunteers stand holding the switches. "At my command," he says. On the count of three, they press the buttons. A two-minute timer starts. Two thousand volts at nine amps slam into the man. The first charge lasts four seconds. Then, for eight seconds, a second charge of 1,600 volts at nine amps crashes into him. Finally, for the remainder of the two minutes, two hundred volts at the same amps trickle through him. All this time, Kemp's deputy has been reporting the proceedings to the commissioner in Atlanta. He speaks with the steady, careful voice of Mission Control. For the next five minutes, everyone waits for the man to cool down and the fan to suck the smell out of the room. Then the two doctors, led by Kemp, enter the room and take turns listening to the man's heart. When they pronounce him dead, Kemp turns on the microphone and announces the order of the court has been carried out. Sometimes, he said, the witnesses are upset. Especially the ones from the press. They think they've missed it all, since all they see are the man's fingers jumping around. Kemp orders the guard to escort everyone from the witness room. The drapes are pulled; the man is unbuckled and carried next door to a little room where he's laid out on a morgue table. The two doctors inspect him for any signs of abuse or suffering. "Why?" I asked. "So no one can say he'd suffered 'cruel or unusual punishment,'" said Kemp. After that, a hearse comes and takes him away.

"That's it," said Kemp. "Satisfied?" Again, I didn't know what to say. I nodded. What I was thinking about were all the cutouts, up and down the line. It reminded me of the story of George Washington's ax: an antique dealer hands the ax to a collector. "This is it," says the dealer. "It looks brand-new," says the collector. "This couldn't be the one he used." "It is, it is," says the dealer. "It's had two new heads and three new handles since then, but it's the one." "Just like an execution in Georgia," I thought. Kemp smiled at me. He looked fine. He owned the ax.

"Anything else?" he asked. "That's fine," I said. "But I would like to talk with that officer who runs death row." "You mean our Lieutenant Treadwell?" said Kemp. He keyed his intercom. While we waited, he told me about the man. "He's sixty-three; spent twelve years in the army. Started out in Burma in Merrill's Marauders; fought in Korea. Came out with the rank of major. Been with us for twelve years; been in charge of death row for two." Kemp's secretary opened the door and Treadwell walked in. He was as thin and straight as a pine board. He had a face like the blade of an ax. His eyes were black and gleamed like polished rock. His hair was black and neatly combed. "A military man, an officer," I thought. "He looks like the Minuteman statue up in Concord." Treadwell looked at me, then at Kemp. "Warden?" he said. "Meet our Lieutenant Treadwell." Kemp beamed. "We call him the Father *and* Mother of death row." Treadwell smiled, embarrassed. Kemp introduced me. "Lieutenant, I want you to show Mike around. He's a writer, but he's

okay. Answer his questions; tell him what he wants to know."
"Yes, sir," said Treadwell. "Glad to." I thanked Kemp, and we
began our tour.

We entered a windowless corridor, as wide as a two-lane road,
barred by a gate that slid open without a sound, then slammed
shut behind us like a hammer hitting an anvil. Lines of men in
prison uniform stepped back against the wall and looked at us
as we passed. I began to grow uneasy. "There're only two of us,"
I thought. Treadwell walked beside me, proud, calm, and digni-
fied, describing the prison like a Texas gentleman describing his
ranch. As we turned down another corridor and passed through
another portcullis, I began to sweat. Treadwell strode along as if
marching in a parade, with music in his ears. I began to wonder
how I could get out. "The key word is 'rehabilitation,'" I heard
him say. I nodded, then caught myself: I hadn't been listening.
Had he said "rehabilitation"? "Our job is to turn them into men,"
he said. He sounded like a preacher. "What was he talking about?
Boot camp or death row?" I looked at him. His eyes glowed like
an evangelist's. "I must not be paying attention," I thought. "He
couldn't be talking about death row." He turned and put his hand
on my shoulder. His voice grew soft, his eyes gentle. "Mike," he
said, "I *am* sorry. I should have asked. Are you hungry?" He
spoke kindly. "Yes, Lieutenant, as a matter of fact, I am." "Well
then," he said, grinning, "let's get you something to *eat*."

We walked past a line of seventy men waiting to be given
aptitude tests. He touched my arm and gently turned me through
a door into a small cafeteria reserved for staff, operated by prisoners. Country fried steak, greens, sweet potatoes, iced tea. And
for dessert, a square of white cake covered with a film of vanilla
frosting and sprinkled with peanut crumbs. We sat at a table
with two black escort officers dressed in freshly laundered uniforms. Treadwell eased himself down, leaned back, then straightened up. "Sergeant Lewis." He nodded. "Sergeant Grimes." He
nodded. He smiled at them as if they were parishioners. "These
are *my* men," he said. "Two of the *best*, two of *the* finest officers
I have ever had under my command." His eyes sparkled. "These
men here," he said, "they can do anything I can do. They're
too good to be sergeants. They don't need me. They don't need
me *at all*. They know what to do without me." They were both

big, solid men. One of them ducked his head and tittered; the other looked at me, very pleased, and grinned. They'd heard this before, but they weren't ashamed to hear it again. "*This* is the finest facility in the state," said Treadwell, with the conviction of a man who believed in the power of faith. His nostrils flared. "These two men could go anywhere and *take command.*" He looked down at my plate and his voice grew soft. "Mike? Are you *sure* you don't want another piece of cake?" he said. "Go on now. Don't be shy. Go get yourself another." "Jesus!" I thought. "No wonder they call him the Mother of Death Row."

I came back with another piece, then changed the subject. I told them about what I'd seen in Florida. I told them about the guy with the chicken knife. I asked Treadwell about the men in his charge. "Are they evil?" I asked. "Some are," he said, "and some were just left holding the bag." His voice changed again. He drew himself up. "But they're all guilty." He looked straight at me. He spoke very carefully and very gravely, like a man reciting a creed. "*None* of them are *ever* going to leave here. We'll never, *ever* let them out. No sir. Not even if someone swung the door wide open and said they *could* go. I wouldn't let them out." He swung his eyes across the faces of his men. "My men wouldn't let them out. They'd have to walk over us." He looked at me and nodded. "Yes sir," he said. I finished my cake and he led me to death row.

He walked me down the tiers of three of the four cellblocks. The place was as pale and lifeless, as barred, barren, and constricted as a nineteenth-century asylum. No sunlight, only shadow; no breeze, only a windless heat. Tiny cells, and inside each cell a man sat reading or lying on his back or listening to the radio on a pair of earphones. I thought of hamsters in a cage. A group of five men stood outside a row of cells, dressed in gray sweatpants and faded T-shirts, aimlessly talking, leaning against a bare metal railing; two other men sat on the concrete, legs stretched apart, facing each other, toe to toe, playing checkers, their hair shaved so close their skulls looked gray. A single man stood alone in his cell, rearranging a Styrofoam cup, a tube of toothpaste, and a bottle of mouthwash, stepping back and looking at what he'd done, like a man studying a furniture arrangement. Several others sat on their bunks, backs against the wall, heads down, knitting. Knitting? I looked again. These men were murderers; they'd committed the fiercest human act and now— what were they doing? Treadwell and I were on a walkway protected by bars and steel link fencing, twenty-five feet from the men in their cells. Treadwell called across, "Larry! Larry! Let me see that church you made! Hold it up!" Treadwell turned to me. "Will you look at that!" he said, loud enough for Larry to hear. The man held up a church with an eight-inch steeple made entirely of yarn, knit with a plastic needle, stretched over pieces of thin plastic. "Isn't that something!" said Treadwell. "Eighty-five-cent hobby kits. They get them once a month, then at the end of the month we collect them. But isn't that something!" All this Treadwell spoke loud enough for the man to hear. Then to me, in a theatrical aside, in a voice low enough to be considered confidential but just loud enough for Larry to catch, he added, "There's so much talent here going to waste! So much potential! Look at what these men can do!" Then, louder, to Larry again: "Son! You still got that yacht you made?" By God, Larry did. A whole motor launch made of yarn. He took it down from his shelf and showed it to us, smiling. "Look at that!" said Treadwell. "Just look at that! Larry, I'm *proud* of you." We walked on. "Five or ten years of this," I thought, "and I'd ask for the chair."

To every man we passed, Treadwell spoke. Men looked up and smiled. Not grinned like prisoners, but smiled like men. One man called across and complained about the TV reception. Treadwell told him he was working to get it fixed. "We'll have it done. I am doing my best, Jerome, I'm doing my best." Another man called across to complain about wet food trays and cold meals over the weekends. Treadwell stopped and listened. When the man repeated himself, Treadwell stopped him. "Herold! I *said* I would talk to Captain Russel and I have. I *have* talked to him. I will bring it up again. I *have done* what I can. I know there is a problem. I have told Captain Russel and I will tell him again . . ." The man interrupted. Treadwell stopped him. "You just quiet down, Herold. I have done what I can, so you quiet yourself." "The Father of Death Row," I thought. We walked on. Past one man, Treadwell said quietly, who'd murdered his wife and two daughters. Past another who had to be regularly X-rayed because he ate whatever pieces of metal he could find. Past one who'd killed the wife of his minister in the middle of a Sunday service. Past another who'd tortured a woman, then cut her legs off to fit her into a trunk.

We strode along through double-locked steel doors, concrete embankments and blockhouses, past one tier of pallid men and tiny cells after another, while Treadwell marveled out loud at their cleanliness, their quietness, and their decorum. To me, he spoke more quietly. "Eighteen months ago," he said, "there was none of this. Eighteen months ago, they would have shouted and spat at us. They would have thrown their own urine at us. There were rapes; there was a suicide. It was so noisy all the time, if a man wanted to read or study, he couldn't. They weren't living like men. But that changed. It changed. And do you know why?" he asked. I shook my head. I was prepared for the name of the Lord. "I'll tell you why," he went on. "Because we made them understand that we intended to be *fair*. It's not for me to question the man who was here in command before me. He was a fine officer, a fine man, but we made some changes. First of all, I let my officers know that I stood behind them. Then we told the inmates we were going by the *rules*. We told them: if they break the rules, we *will* punish them. But if they obey them, we will respect them. The inmates learned they had to *earn* our respect. That's our policy: *Fairness. Firmness. Respect.*" Treadwell spoke those words in cadence like a man reciting a litany. "They know I'm fair, and they know I'm firm. They can depend on that. They also know that I don't *mind* being friendly. We have rules. If they do what's right, I'll *treat* them fairly. And—if there's room— it doesn't take anything away from me to be friendly." He smiled at me when he said that last word. I didn't know what to think. It all made sense, but it was all a deception. The men weren't raping or killing each other, but they were all terminal.

We kept walking, through one bulkhead to another, down one passageway to the next, until we reached an upper tier of cells that were all empty because the men were outside in the exercise yard. At the end of the tier was a barred window. There was no one but the two of us there. Treadwell motioned me to the window without a word. He pointed outside. He nodded for me to look. I saw a flat roof with a ventilator cowling in the middle of it. It was the roof of the execution chamber. Treadwell looked at me again, then put a finger to his lips. He took a pen out of his pocket, and wrote "H-5" on his palm. Underneath that, he wrote "electric chair." He pointed at the words, then out the window. I nodded. He nodded. He rubbed out the words and we continued. He acted as if he'd just let me in on a Big Secret.

That's when I wondered if he was a little crazy. I knew the place was. Anyplace where grown men sat in cells and knitted and rearranged tubes of toothpaste and swallowed spoons was crazy. Anyplace where men who'd murdered their families played checkers, toe to toe, with men who'd sawed the legs off their girlfriends—that place was a madhouse. Until we'd stood at the window and Treadwell had done his pantomime, I thought he knew that, too. Understood it and acted accordingly: praised the inmates, boasted of their potential, listened to their grievances, insisted on order, obedience, and respect—all that, I understood, kept the madhouse from turning back into the bedlam it once had been. But the show at the window had been unnecessary. He could have spoken; no one could have heard us; no one could have seen us. There was no Big Secret. The place was a dungeon, full of men who were as good as dead. He told me that while I finished my cake. He looked me straight in the eye and said they were all guilty and he'd never let any of them out. I understood that it was only polite to lower your voice and whisper about funeral arrangements in the presence of the dying. That was good manners; it was good policy; it helped morale. But Treadwell and I had been alone. Treadwell was like a doctor in a cancer ward who dispensed hope and praise like opiates. The question was whether he'd swallowed some of his own medicine.

We turned and he walked me back to the warden's office. As we walked, he talked, but I had stopped listening. All I could think about was the pantomime at the window. "Treadwell's an actor," I thought. "He knows the truth but he works hard to help his audience deceive itself. ('Gosh! Maybe no one's really gonna die!') Treadwell intensely believes in what he's doing. Because of that, the place is clean and quiet, and orderly. The question is: To fool his audience, does he have to fool himself? Has he gotten so good at the deception that he can't stop, even when it's not show time? Or is the whole place a stage set, so that, to break character, even in front of a stranger, might reveal it to be as hopeless a trap as it truly is? Illusions keep the lid on. The Germans knew that when they killed the Jews. 'Be sure to remember your number,' they said. 'Many people, after their showers, forget their numbers and cause needless confusion by donning the clothing of others.' Under the circumstances, Treadwell's doing what's necessary. But maybe not. How can a man in charge of death row talk about rehabilitation? How can he say all his prisoners are guilty and still be thoughtful enough, even when they're not around, to avoid using words like 'electric chair'? The only answer is that he's capable of being in two mental places at the same time. That's either the mark of a very special sanity or a remarkable craziness." When we reached the warden's office and Treadwell turned to say goodbye, I asked him if I might talk with him again. "It'll be my pleasure, Mike." We shook hands. "You take care, now," he said. I could hardly wait to see him again. I'd always wanted to watch someone resolve a paradox.

The next day I came back and was escorted to a locked corridor, adjacent to death row, where Treadwell, his sergeants, and the row's psychologists had their offices. Treadwell's office was only a little bigger than a cell; a desk, a chair, a file cabinet, and a red wooden chest filled it. Treadwell sat at his desk, smoking Pall Malls. I sat on the chest, facing him, bumming cigarettes. We talked for four hours, occasionally interrupted by brief reports from his officers. He talked in a calm, quiet voice, the voice of a gentleman of modest good sense, very different from the evangelical uplift of the day before. What he said, though, was no more reasonable and even less predictable. What he told me were war stories. I'd encouraged him by asking how he'd reached the rank of major. What he answered, I could never have anticipated.

It began, he said, when he'd enlisted in the U.S. Cavalry in 1941. "The cavalry?" I asked. "Why, sure," he said. "I grew up on a farm; I've loved horses all my life; the cavalry was my choice." He spent his time grooming polo ponies under the eye of a parade ground sergeant. Then one day his unit boarded ship and sailed to India. From there they were sent to Burma to join Merrill's Marauders to fight the Japanese in the mountains. "But why Merrill's Marauders?" I asked. "They used mules," he said.

"That's the way they carried everything; it was the closest we ever got to a horse for the rest of the war." I knew a little about what had happened there. In Burma, the Allies fought to keep the Japanese out of India; the Japanese had an airfield up north; the Americans fought to capture it; all sides were badly supplied; the fighting was prolonged and vicious; in the end, the Allies won, only because they managed to stay alive longer than their enemies. Treadwell talked of constant attacks and counterattacks: the Japanese at night; the Americans during the day. He spoke of air drops always lost in the trees, and rations that tasted like rust. He mentioned a man who'd died in his arms, and two others killed by artillery; the one on his right lost his legs but "died without a groan"; the one on his left turned gray and died "without a scratch." Many men died of disease; many others went crazy. Treadwell came out of it a first sergeant. When the war ended, he was sent to Japan. He bided his time on garrison duty and rose to lieutenant. Then the North Koreans took Seoul and everyone who could ran south.

His commanding officer called him in. "Treadwell," he said, "I'm sending you to Korea. You'll be in command of a company." "Thank you, sir," said Treadwell. The officer waved him away. "Save it," he said. "They're 'undesirables.' We would have discharged them, but we need every man we've got. They're in a compound under guard. They're all yours. If you can't handle it, let me know. Assemble them, draw your equipment, and board ship." Treadwell went to inspect his men. What he found were two hundred discipline problems. None of them had committed any crimes, but none of them could stand garrison duty. "They were some of the best *soldiers* we had," said Treadwell. "They were real men, men's men, but if an officer told them to pick up every cigarette butt in a five-hundred-yard radius, they wouldn't do it. They were tough, but they couldn't take the spit and polish." Treadwell called them together, read them their new orders, and a week later they set sail. His men may have been real soldiers, but what happened to them happened to everyone who was thrown into the rout that began the war: only seventy were left by the time the Americans held at the Naktong River.

"There were so many bodies and so many flies," Treadwell

said, "a man could slap his arm and kill a dozen of 'em with one blow. We had everything you'd ever want: mosquitoes, leeches, mud, and bad food—if we could get it." The North Koreans would attack and break the American line; the Americans would draw back around the pocket, counterattack, push them out, then straighten the line again. In the middle of that first summer, the Americans pushed the Koreans out of a pocket and discovered the bodies of fifty men who'd been captured, shot and left behind. They'd been left in the sun, on a hill. Treadwell was ordered to load some men on a truck and bring the bodies down. They parked by a stream bed and walked up a mile of trails to the top. The North Koreans had tied the men together with telephone wire. Treadwell said the bodies had "puffed up so big they looked like balloons, with arms and legs sticking out." He told his men to cut the wire. Then he ordered them to carry the dead down to the truck. No one moved. Treadwell bent down and threw a body over his shoulder and started walking. He never looked back. One by one, his men each took a body and followed. By the time he got down the hill, the body on his back had split open. "Juice ran down like a rotten cantaloupe." He heaved it into the truck and went back for another.

When he got back with the next one, the truck had filled up. He had to lean forward and pitch the body in. As he did, the dead man's finger broke open and he saw he was wearing a wedding ring. "A lot of thoughts went through my mind then," he said. "I saw the ring, and the first thing I thought about was the man, then his wife, then his kids. And I asked myself, I said, 'Bill—is this man in heaven or hell?' I asked myself that, then I said, 'That man's not in heaven and he's not in hell. He's just lying in the back of this truck.' I went down to the stream then. It was about dry, except for a muddy little trickle. I lay down and put my face in the mud, and I thought, 'Why don't you just stay here, Bill; why don't you just stay here and breathe this up your nose and die.' I thought about that. It was the first time I'd ever thought anything like that. I lay there a little while. Then I got up. From there on in, I decided, I *knew* there was no way I'd ever leave Korea alive. The odds were too great. Too many men had died. I decided, though, that I wouldn't tell my men. I wouldn't let them know. From there on in, what I decided was to be a sportsman." "A sportsman?" I asked. "What do you mean?"

"In Burma," he said, "I'd just been a good soldier, fighting for my country. But in Korea I became what you might call a 'professional.' I decided I would *destroy* as much as possible. I decided that was why I was there. I would do it, though, at the time and in the place of my own choosing. We started to accumulate a lot of heavy weapons, .30-caliber and .50-caliber machine guns. All that, plus buckets and buckets of ammunition. More than we should have had for a company our size. Because we decided that if anyone shot at us, we'd fill the place with lead. I refused to fight the enemy on his terms—only on mine. That meant that at the end of the day we were all alive. We could come back, and light our fire, and drink our coffee. That's what I did: I attacked and *destroyed* as much as I could." He paused. He leaned forward and looked at me. "I've probably killed more men," he said, "than all the men on this death row put together. But"—he started counting on his fingers—"I never shot a man coming toward me with his hands in the air. I never allowed a rape. I never shot a child. I never shot a woman. I never shot any old people. That's how I got to be a major.

"When it was over, I came home, and I bought seven hundred acres and planted it with milo for cattle feed. I rode my tractor and raised the crop, and thought about the war. I thought about it for a whole year. Then I asked God. I asked Him, 'What do you want me to do?'" Treadwell glanced at me. "Do you know what He said?" I shook my head. "He said, 'You just be yourself, Bill. It's not for you to know the truth about things. Just do your best.' That calmed me down. But one thing I know for sure: there isn't any heaven, and there isn't any hell. There's just this earth, the way it is."

He told me other stories after that. About how he'd worked for the FBI as a counter-espionage agent, about how he'd run training programs for the Army Signal Corps at the Redstone Arsenal, and about the years he'd spent working for the telephone company in Florida. He told me about his auto-parts business, and his real-estate ventures, and about his father, who was eighty and rode motorcycles. He told me enough stories, as we sat in his office, to have filled the lives of two other men. It grew late, and my mind was so full that when I stood up to leave and he handed me a card with the name of his farm on it, I couldn't quite make it out. "Casa Valhalla," I recited, like a man reading an unknown language. "This your milo farm?" I asked. "Oh, no," he laughed. "I lost my shirt on that years ago. No, sir. This is my horse farm. I raise Arabians now. Tell you what: this weekend, why don't you come and visit." That last detail snapped my head back like a punch. I let myself be escorted back to where I'd parked, but my brain didn't start working again until a few hours after I got home. I was just as amazed as I'd been the first time I'd met him. "He runs death row and raises Arabians? You talk about paradoxes! And all that stuff about Korea and the bodies and the stream bed and being a 'sportsman.' He may have talked softer, but he preached a goddamn sermon. He's sunk deeper in death than any of the men I've met. He's been soaked in it, bathed in it. He's lived through more fear than anyone I've talked to. So—he can run his death row with as much discretion and uplift and denial as he likes. He's earned the right. He's been deep into the darkness. If he wants to whisper about it, that's fine. But the Arabians: what about the Arabians? How do they fit?"

I understood as soon as I saw them. That weekend, I drove down a long dirt road, past padlocks and exercise rings, to Tread-well's house, a two-story chalet built into the side of a hill, over-looking a stream that ran through forty acres of forest and pasture. Treadwell came down the stairs to greet me, dressed in Levi's, as lean and fit as a man in his thirties. "Mike," he said, grinning, shaking my hand, "come on and meet the boys and girls." I knew he had a wife, but I didn't know he had a family. Then I saw them, galloping in the pasture. There was one of a startling white-ness, and others light brown with a white blaze between their eyes, eyes dark and responsive, set wide apart on elongated heads held high on graceful necks. Treadwell called and they turned and ran toward him, ears pointed, tails high, strong, long-legged, beautifully configured. I thought of dancers leaping, bounding across a stage. They came to him, and he touched them and spoke to them. "These are my babies," he said. "These are my little boys"—they nodded. "These are my little girls"—they nuzzled him. He turned and spoke to me. They butted him like impatient children. They were bred for intelligence and good nature, he said. He bought them as colts and fillies and sold them as three-year-olds. Last year, he'd sold eighteen and won an award. He raised them to be steady and gentle, ready to learn polo or the steeplechase or race long distance. I understood then: he wasn't just the Father of Death Row; he was, as well, the father of this herd of living creatures. One balanced the other. Exuberance against hopelessness; freedom against captivity. At home, Treadwell presided over life; at work, he kept watch over death. The balance seemed so perfect, the poison of one matched by the antidote of the other, that, as we turned back to the house, I asked him about it. He answered with a question of his own.

"Mike," he said, speaking steadily and deliberately, "if you had a rattlesnake in your back yard and you knew it—because you'd looked and made sure it wasn't a king snake but a rattlesnake—if you had one, what would you do with it?" "I'd catch it and kill it," I said. "Of course you would. That's what I'd do if I found one in my back yard. I'd catch it and kill it." He paused. "Well, then," he said, "now you understand." "You mean you've got four cellblocks full of rattlesnakes?" "That's exactly right," he said. "But it all depends on how you handle them. If you know how to pick up a rattlesnake with a forked stick, there's no need to be afraid. The same with a horse. I've never been *kicked* by a horse, because I've *never* walked on the *wrong* side of a horse. I know about horses, and they know about me. I can raise a horse for three years and that horse'll come when I call. I can lead a horse out of his stall and I can lead him back without a bridle because he *knows* that I'm his *friend* and I know that he's *my* friend. When he hears my voice, he doesn't remember the feel of the *bit* up in his mouth. He remembers that I'm his friend. It's the same with the men. My attitude is: I'm not their enemy. And they're not mine. I know *exactly* who they are, and they know who I am. They know I'm fair and firm. If they obey the rules, they know I don't mind being friendly. They also know what happens if they break them." "Which is?" I asked. "Cuffs," he said. "Cuffs, leg irons, and isolation. Then, when the time comes, Sergeant Lewis and I escort them to H-5. We hand them over. One man asked us to sit with him. We said no. That wasn't for us. Our duty was to guard him. We'd done our duty. I've known some of the men who've volunteered to push the buttons. They were corrections officers and they were weaklings. They got a thrill out of it. They did it to prove how tough they were." He stopped and looked at me. "No man should be allowed to volunteer to execute another man. No man's worthy. A real man should have to be ordered to do it. He should *have* to do it because it's his *duty*. There's something wrong if a man *wants* to do it."

We reached the house and I met his wife. We sat and talked and drank iced tea and looked out through a wall of glass at the stream and the woods beyond it. Treadwell talked about Burma and he talked about his family. I listened and nodded and said the proper things, but what I thought about were the snakes and the horses and what Kemp, the warden, had called cutouts. Treadwell used them all. The guards on the other side did the dirty work; Treadwell did his duty. He obeyed the rules. He kept clean and trained the animals. He kept the snakes until the time came. Then he handed them over and went home to his little boys and little girls. Long ago, in Korea, he'd crossed over into the other room. Now he refused. If I wanted to learn more, I'd have to meet a man who'd stepped through and stayed.

A MAN-KILLER

I spent the next two months making phone calls. I wanted to meet a professional killer who wasn't a liar or a lunatic or a criminal. Since there was no way to verify a man's credentials, let alone his sanity, on the phone, I relied on introductions and recommendations made by mutual friends. Everyone I talked to claimed to know someone who could help me. After six weeks, though, all I had were promises: this one said he'd call that one, who said he'd have to call someone else, who'd call the man who'd call me. Good manners and discretion and some version of the Neutrality Act kept me from ever calling the man himself. Finally I lost patience and began to call the editors of mercenary magazines. I started with *Soldier of Fortune*, a monthly whose editorial content is a mélange of weapons tests, alumni news, and eyewitness accounts of undeclared war. I introduced myself as an author, asked for an editor, and found myself talking to a man with a finicky voice. I gave my little speech: "I'm writing a book about professionals who deal with death," I said. "Oh, *really*??" "I want to talk to a man-killer who isn't a criminal." Silence. "I want to talk to someone on our side, someone who does things for us that we'd rather not know about. I want to talk to a warrior." The "warrior" must have done it. Bells and buzzers sounded. "*Of course*," said the man. "I *understand*. I know *just* the *one*. I know him *myself*. What is it that Don Juan said? An 'immaculate warrior'? He's *perfect*. He's spent years in a communist prison in Angola. He could be a Zen master. How he survived is a story in itself. Hold on. Just a minute." He put his hand over the mouthpiece and spoke to someone. "I'll have him call you in thirty minutes." I'd never heard that one before. A Zen master? Until now, I'd been dealing with ex-Green Berets. I agreed and hung up.

The phone rang exactly on time. The man's voice was young and gentle. I explained and asked him his story. He'd been a machine gunner, he said, in the Marines in Vietnam. He'd gotten out, but wanted some action. He'd answered an ad in the back of a magazine. He'd wanted the job so much he'd paid his own way.

He got off the plane in Angola, in the middle of a civil war. A week later, they arrested him. "You were in jail?" I asked. "Yes," he said. "For how long?" "Seven years." "My God! When did you get out?" "Two weeks ago," he said. I took a breath. "Then you've been in jail all this time?" "Yes," he said. I stumbled. "Well, then. Are you—ah—working now?" "I'm between jobs," he said. Between jobs? I didn't know what to say. I apologized: "I don't know if I have the right words, but—ah—when was your last job?" "When I was arrested." "So—you haven't worked for seven years?" "That's correct," he said. I took another breath. "I don't want to hurt your feelings. That's the last thing I want to do. You've suffered; I'm sorry. But—I'd hoped to talk with someone who was—I don't know the word—more 'current.' I don't mean to insult you, but . . ." "It's okay," he said. "Thanks," I said, and hung up.

Six weeks of nothing and now this. "What are you?? Some kind of connoisseur?" I thought. "More 'current'!!! Jesus Christ! What do you want? Blood on their pants and notches in their gun? If they're current, they aren't going to talk to someone like you. And if they're not, who in hell cares. A Zen master who's worked for one week!! Sweet Jesus!" The next day I called *Eagle* magazine. Of all the mercenary magazines, *Eagle* seemed the most reasonable. It read as if whoever edited it paid more attention to facts and sentence structure than to cliché and innuendo. The receptionist answered with the last four digits of the phone number. Fine, I thought, nothing like a little discretion. I asked for the editor. The man who answered had the voice of a talk-show host. I asked for the editor again. "You got him," he said. I introduced myself. I gave my speech. A phone rang. "Hang on," he said. "Listen," he said. "Now's not a good time. Call back this afternoon. I've got a Rolodex full of names—this'll take a while." "If you've got the Rolodex, I've got the time," I said. "Fine," he said.

For some reason, he liked my voice and I liked his. We spent two hours on the phone, him dictating, me scribbling. "Let's see now," he said. "Okay. Here's one. This guy rode horses and killed commies in Rhodesia. Looks like Gene Autry. A little eccentric, though. The only military forces he admires are the Israelis and the SS. Always has Jewish girlfriends, though. The last one walked out on him in Salvador. A real beauty. Everything was okay until

he put on his record of Waffen SS songs. She nearly killed him."
"He sounds too complicated," I said. "All right," he said. "How
about this one? A photographer. Remember *The Killing Fields*,
the movie? Remember the photographer in it? This guy was the
real thing. They did open-heart surgery on him with no anesthetic.
He survived, but—I don't know, I mean, if you want someone
firmly packed . . ." "No, I need a combatant." "All right, all right.
How about that guy in the photo they took during Tet, the one in
Life where the guy blew the brains out of that VC in front of the
camera. He's in San Diego now." "No, thanks," I said. "He has to
be an American." "An American, huh? I got plenty of Falangists.
How about a Falangist? I got a Christian Lebanese Freedom
Fighter here. He was in on the Sabra and Shatilla massacre. He's
in Boston." "No," I said. "Too many dead civilians." "Okay," he
said. "I got an ex-Selous Scout. Did consultant work with Chuck
Norris. You remember *Invasion, U.S.A.?* He did the shaped
charges. No? I got an Iroquois Indian here. A crack shot, a great
take-down man. Damn! He's in Belize, though. Hang on. I got a
Brit here, ex-Special Air Service, does corporate work, just got
back from Oman; he's in L.A. Wait a second! I got a bodyguard,
ex-Marine, Force Recon, worked for Somoza, then told him to
shove it. And—hang on! I got it. Goddamn! I got just the man
for you. I don't know why I didn't think of him! You want a hero?
This guy's a hero. Captain D. L. Hicks. Everyone called him
'Pappy.' Carried a kukri knife in Vietnam, one of those big Gurkha
knives. He worked for a forerunner of the Phoenix Program." "You
mean the one Colby ran, the one that took out Vietcong infrastruc-
ture and political cadres?" "Yeah. That one. He worked for the
one before that. They gave him lists; he went down the lists. This
guy's for real. A warrior. Part Cherokee. He's a writer, a good
writer; he's written novels. He knows what he believes. The
Montagnards made him a blood brother. He's been there. He
knows things. He can talk." "All right," I said. "He's the one.
Thanks."

I called Hicks and introduced myself. He said he'd have to check
with the man from *Eagle*. An hour later, I called him back. He
was very cordial; the editor had said I was fine. We talked. Hicks
had the voice of a cowboy. He called himself a " 'breed Cherokee."
He said he'd been a Special Forces captain. During the day, he'd

done one thing. At night, he'd done something else. He'd done it so quietly that the only white people who knew about it were some staff officers close to Westmoreland. Every week, he said, he'd been given a list compiled by South Vietnamese intelligence. He and a small band of Montagnards—men he called "my fellow warriors"—either captured or killed their targets. I asked him about his kukri knife. It was his favorite weapon, he said. Curved, well balanced, heavy, it could chop wood or take off heads. He called his the Great Silencer. He said I could come see him any time I liked. I thanked him. He said, "Hang tough."

That night, I had a nightmare. The next night, I had another and then another. I dreamed the whole world had been poisoned. Innocent acts bred evil. In the dream, I planted a seed. Instead of a plant, a serpent grew. When I started my car, its wheels blew off, its engine blew up, and the front of it burst into flames. Everywhere, there were bombings, hijackings, and the murder of innocents—and all because someone had planted a garden or gone to the store or answered the phone. Simple gestures bred carnage and suffering. Nothing good or safe was left in the world. Everything was poisoned, bloody and lethal.

I called Robert Lifton. I told him about my dreams. He listened, then he told me about his. He said that when he'd first thought of writing his book about Nazi doctors, he'd discussed his plans with a philosopher who'd survived the camps. The philosopher had been very pleased and very encouraging. Lifton began his research. He began to read the accounts. As he read, he began to have bad dreams. He called the philosopher and they had coffee. He said to the man, "You didn't tell me about the dreams. They would have been bad enough with just me behind the barbed wire. But my wife and kids are in them." Lifton said the philosopher had listened and then looked at him. He looked at him without surprise or sympathy or pity. He said, "Good. Now you're ready to begin."

"The dreams," said Lifton, "come with the territory."

The next day, I flew to Dallas, then to Tyler, and checked into a fake Mexican hacienda. After dinner, I called Captain Hicks. His voice was a low, steady rumble, his accent as dense as hickory smoke. "It takes me time to get my legs going in the morning. Why don't you come at 9:30 and we'll have some coffee. I ought to be loose by then." He hadn't mentioned his legs before. "Did you have an accident?" I asked. He barked a laugh. "You might say so," he said. "I stepped on a little something in Vietnam. See you tomorrow. Hang tough." I hung up and turned on the TV. The ground blew up and Gene Hackman jumped out of a helicopter, firing bursts as he ran. "Oh, shit," I said. It was the same thing as in Omaha, only this time it wasn't the *Titanic*, it was MIAs in Laos. I grabbed the TV listing. "*Uncommon Valor*," it said. "A mission of mercy and revenge in the jungles of SE Asia." I sat on the bed and watched. The listing was right. Hackman and his men fought their way into a prison compound full of captured Americans. One by one, they sacrificed their lives, killed the guards, and freed the prisoners. They were fearless, merciless, and tender. Nearly all of them died. I watched and was thrilled. "Is this the man I'm meeting?" I wondered.

The next morning I drove to Troup, population 1,911, named after a Confederate general. The water oaks and crepe myrtles made me think of Georgia. I bumped over the tracks in the center of town and headed east, until I found Hicks's place, a big, plain, solid old house on a quiet street. Hicks came to the door dressed in a tailored Western shirt and freshly pressed gabardines. He was in his fifties, strongly built, no more than average height, the face handsome and relaxed. "Good to see you," he said, and shook my hand. The grip was steady, bigger and beefier than I'd expected. "Nice old place you got here," I said. He turned and led me back through to the kitchen. "Doctor built it in the twenties during the last oil boom; lost it in a poker game." He introduced me to his wife and one of his sons, poured us some coffee, and led me through a breezeway to a garage he'd turned into a study. "I do my writing here," he said. "What sort of things?" I asked. "I've done a couple of historical novels, and I send a piece off to *Eagle* every once in a while." He turned on the lights. "The stuff you want to talk about"—he motioned me to a chair—"is stuff I don't talk about in the house. My wife and I don't have any secrets; we've been together through a lot, but it's not something you talk about in the kitchen along with the weather." He sat down stiffly and leaned back carefully, like a man who knew about pain. The light was bright enough for me to see him, but not much else. I could make out a couple of file cabinets with pint bottles of Maalox on them, a pool table draped with a sheet, four or five rusty old revolvers and carbines resting on it, and here and there, on one wall, small, garish paintings of spindly little brown-skinned men dressed in ragtag uniforms. Hicks followed my eyes. He turned his chin and nodded at the weapons. "I just got those out of an old family cabin that burnt down. It's a damn shame: there're some nice old pieces there." Then he looked up at the paintings. His voice went down deep in his throat. "Those are my fellow warriors," he said. He looked back at me. "All right then," he said. "I kinda know what you're after, but why don't you ask. There're some things I can't talk about because they're still classified, but otherwise I'll tell you what you want to know. Go ahead and start."

"I've never talked to a professional soldier before," I said. "If I don't use the right words or I say something really stupid, tell me, okay?" He nodded. "That's affirmative," he said. I went on. "I don't know about you, but I write books to learn things. You know a lot more than I do. I'm here to listen." Hicks nodded again. "Okay," he said, "shoot." "To begin with," I said, "I'd like to know about your ancestry, your history." He shifted his weight in the chair. "You asked the right man. I've got a bachelor's degree in all that stuff. I can tell you more than you'll ever want to hear." He grinned. For the next four hours, I sat back and listened. Sometimes, as he spoke, I thought about the rabbi in New Jersey, sometimes about Lieutenant Treadwell in Georgia. Mostly, though, I kept quiet. I kept quiet, because I'd never heard stories like his before. I was afraid that if I said something I'd lose track of where he was and where he was taking me.

To begin with, he said he was a Tsalagi, a Cherokee. He wasn't a pure-blood, he reminded me, but he could trace his line back to Sequoyah, the great chief who'd devised a written alphabet for his people. The Hickses had married into the tribe in the 1760s; by 1810, part of the family had been baptized; by 1830, one of them had risen to the rank of Principal Chief of the Cherokee Nation. All this was on his father's side. His mother, he said, was one hundred percent Texas white. Her side went back to the 1820s, to a powerful man named George Thorne, the first millionaire Texas had ever seen. Both sides of the family had fought in the Civil War. All the way back to Sequoyah, there had been warriors. And all the way back to the Hickses there'd been Christians. Hicks's Indian grandparents were teetotaling churchgoers. The only things Hicks's father kept of the old ways were some lullabies and some animal stories, the Indian equivalent of fairy tales. Hicks said he would have grown up to be a Baptist if it hadn't been for his Uncle Charlie. Uncle Charlie, said Hicks, saved his soul.

Uncle Charlie was his grandfather's brother, Hicks's great-uncle. Charlie lived in Oklahoma and only came to visit. When he did, Hicks's grandparents pretended he wasn't there. They did that not only because Charlie was a "heathen" who believed in Asgaya Galulati, the Man Above, but because Uncle Charlie was a drunk. The combination made him invisible, which gave him the chance to tell Hicks the way things really were. To begin with, when Hicks was eleven, Charlie told him he had another name besides the one his parents called him. David Larry was his Christian name. His Indian name was Panther Follower. He was destined, said Charlie, to follow in the footsteps of a wildcat. By following, he would grow strong and learn cunning. When he was twelve, Charlie sent him out on his quest. Armed with a shotgun, alone, he tracked and killed a mountain lion. He cut a piece from its hip and ate it; then he buried the body and chanted his thanks to the animal for its spirit. I knew the rabbi would have scoffed, but I kept listening. I'd wanted the pathologists to say the same sort of thanks just before they'd opened up Al.

When Hicks turned sixteen, Charlie told him another secret. Hicks's father had fought in the Second World War; Hicks's grandfather had fought in the Spanish-American. Both had talked about being soldiers, but Charlie taught Hicks about being a warrior. First, he sent him out to find his war song. "What's that?" I asked. Hicks paused, considering his words. "It's like a chant," he said. "Every warrior has one. When he 'finds' it, he composes it, and then it's his for life. He says it just before battle. It draws up his spirit." "It sounds like a mantra," I thought. "Captain," I said, "I may be about to make my first big mistake—but can you tell me what your song is? I mean—if it's not a secret, and if telling me won't do you harm." Hicks took a breath and held it. Then he let it out and said, "It doesn't matter: Charlie 'fixed' it so no one could steal it, even if they heard it. You can't use it; for you, it'll only be a bunch of words." He took another breath and recited the song, his voice flat and uninflected, like a bad actor's. "Enemy beware I came," he said. "Enemy beware I came / I have never failed / My knife is always thirsty." He looked at me and rubbed his hands on his knees. "That's it," he said. "Thank you," I said. I remembered, then, about his knife, his kukri. I thought about the *shochet* and his *halef*. Hicks went on.

If a man was born a Cherokee, he said, the finest thing he could hope to be was a great warrior. A man could do other things in his life; he could be a shaman, or a hunter, or a bow-maker, but if he wouldn't learn to fight, and if he wouldn't go to war, he was banished from the tribe. Cherokee women were as fierce as the men. Women warriors formed a separate group called the Long Hair Society. Any of them who wanted could join a war party; if captives were taken, it was the women alone who had the right to torture them to death. The tribe's law was blood for blood. Torture was how widows evened the score. All this, said Hicks, Charlie explained. Then Charlie showed him how to "go to water."

"What is it?" I asked. "It's a purification before and after battle," he said. Four days before a war party set out, the men crawled down a tunnel into a windowless lodge built below ground. They sat in a circle around a war fire and drank 'black drink,' an emetic brewed from yaupon leaves, a kind of holly. For four days, they sweated and vomited and fasted and told stories of war, killing, and death. Then they came out into the light, re-formed, and went off. Every war party included a shaman, a leader called a "Raven," and a second-in-command, called a "Man-killer." Charlie told Hicks that after he'd killed his first enemy in battle, he'd have that rank. "How straightforward," I thought. Just before the fight, a war party always paused. Each man chanted his war song, faced east, and "went to water." In peacetime, each man would have found a stream, faced east, and dipped himself seven times. "Why seven?" I asked. "It's a sacred number. It's so sacred no one could say it. It's made of all the compass points and directions, up, down, and center, north, south, east and west." "And the water?" I asked. "It's a sacred substance," he said. "It can heal and purify. Running water's best, because it's a sacred messenger that leads to the Underworld." On the edge of battle, the beliefs held, but the ritual was abbreviated: each man faced east and smeared his face and chest seven times with his own spit. After the battle—if it was successful—the men returned to the sweat lodge, stripped off their clothes, burnt them, then crawled back inside to drink the black drink and purify themselves. Four days later, they crawled out again, went to water in a proper fashion, dressed in new clothes, and returned to the tribe. I interrupted Hicks. "You said something about 'if it was successful.' What if it wasn't?" Hicks grinned. "Then, if they wanted to, they could head straight for the tribe's War Chief, the one who'd declared the war, and they could kill him." Hicks let loose a laugh. "Kept everyone on their toes. Eliminated the incompetents." He laughed again.

Everything he'd said, so far, made human sense: a warrior culture had developed a way to send its men (and women) into battle, then readmit them after they returned. Their beliefs gave them a way to focus their energies, cleanse themselves, and integrate what they did with a divine order. Even the torture made sense as an act of revenge: if a woman lost her husband, let her kill another. What the Cherokees did in battle may have violated the Ten Commandments, but David had killed Goliath and Samson had buried the Philistines. Men had always kept the law for themselves, and murdered their enemies. "So, Captain," I said, "how'd you become a Man-killer?" "I enlisted in the army just before Charlie died. They sent me straight to Korea." "Another Treadwell," I thought. "What happened?" I asked.

"What happened," he said, "is that I got angry." He looked at me. "I used to hear these guys, veterans I mean, when I was growing up—they'd been in World War II, and if someone asked them what it was like, they'd say how sad they'd been when they saw their first dead American, or how ashamed they'd felt when they killed their first man. I used to hear all that when I was growing up. But let me tell you something"—he glared at me—"when I saw my first dead American, all I wanted to do was go out and kill the son-of-a-bitch who did it. I didn't need a shoulder to cry on. I wanted revenge. Cherokee law wasn't 'turn the other cheek.' The old guys in my outfit gave me some advice. They said, 'Son, when you walk through a field of dead men, you just be sure not to turn your back on them. Because some of them are just waiting to get up and shoot you. You just take your time and shoot 'em again where they lay. If they're dead, they won't feel a thing. It

never hurts, and you won't get surprised.' So that's what I did."
"You mean you killed the dead?" I asked. He looked at me and
paused. "Yeah, you could say that. I killed the dead. Then, one
day, I lined up a man in my sights and I shot him. I saw him go
down. Then I went out and shot him again. I made sure."

"Before a fight, I'd go off a little ways and chant and go to water.
People thought I was crazy, but I didn't give a damn. Because
they knew that when things got hot, I stayed where I was. I started
off as a rifleman. Most everyone in my platoon got killed. So I
traded in my M-1 for a BAR." "A what?" I asked. "A Browning
automatic rifle. A heavy automatic. Then I traded the Browning
for an A-4. It's a .30-caliber machine gun. It takes three men to
handle it. By then it was February 1952 and we were way up on
a hill, way past the thirty-eighth parallel. Hill 1243. It was so far
north it felt like the North Pole. Two other guys and me sitting in
a bunker with our A-4, freezing. One morning, just before the
sunrise, the bugles started blowing. The Chinese always blew goddamn bugles before they attacked. The gunner heard them and
started firing and wouldn't stop. He cracked. I had to beat his
hands off the trigger with the butt of my .45. I picked him up and
threw him back into the sleeping hole and took over the gun. I
ordered the other man to come up next to me and feed the ammunition. He wouldn't move. The gunner going crazy with the
bugles blowing got him so scared he was paralyzed. I told him to
go outside and clean his rifle and pull himself together. What he
did was go outside and shoot himself in the foot. So there we were:
bugles blowing, one crazy man, one wounded man, and me. The
medics came and they took the two of them away. That left me,
sitting all alone.

"In the middle of the morning, they started to shell our position.
I stuck my head out to see if there were any troops coming up
behind the barrage. I looked out and I saw two army forward
artillery observers coming up a defile toward me. I waved them
away, but they kept coming. I kept waving; the barrage got worse;
they kept coming; then a shell landed between us. It landed closer
to them than to me, because it cut one guy in half and blew the
other guy up in the air and broke his leg. It blew me down.
Shrapnel went up my foot. Tunnneled right in." Hicks stuck out his
right leg and pulled himself up. He walked over to the desk in the

corner of the room and came back with a long shiny metal icicle. He handed it to me. It was flat, thick, heavy, and sharp, two inches long. "That's the biggest piece they could find." I bounced it in my hand. He'd been lucky. I handed it back to him and he went on.

"I couldn't feel anything. I couldn't hear anything. I woke up, flat on my back, staring up into this big, clear, perfect blue sky. And you know what I thought?" I shook my head. "I thought the Black Man from the West, the one who collects men's spirits, had come to get me. I thought I'd be going up to see my Grandfather in the Sky, the Man Above. It was so quiet, I thought I was dead. Then my ears started working again." He laughed. "The shells were still coming in. I got myself up and ran for cover. The medics came and took me and the man with the broken leg down to an aid station. They took out that piece of metal and stopped the bleeding. They asked if I wanted to be evacuated. I just laced up my boot and went back up the hill. My foot hurt like a son-of-a-bitch. It started bleeding again. I changed my socks. It got dark. It was just me and the A-4. I sang my war song and I waited. The Chinese came charging up the hill in the middle of the night. They ran right over me, right on top of me. I climbed out and killed two of 'em with my .45. The next day, my lieutenant said he'd recommend me for a Silver Star. He never did, though, 'cause a sniper shot him.

"I stayed put for three or four weeks. My damn foot started coming apart on me. I kept changing the dressing and changing my socks, but the meat started coming off the bone. A patrol went out right in front of me and walked into a minefield just beyond the wire. I organized a human chain to get them out." I interrupted him. "You carried them out?" He nodded. "Like a bucket brigade, hand-to-hand." "But your foot was coming apart. How could you walk? How could you stand it?" Hicks folded his arms. "What are you asking me?" "I'm asking you how you did what you did. Your foot was a real mess. You must have been in a lot of pain. How did you do it?" He dipped his head and shoulders forward, then straightened up and looked at me. "Charlie taught me." He spoke slowly. "It's hard to explain, but you can put the pain outside yourself. You can learn to do it. You can put the pain somewhere else while you stay where you are and do what you need to do. It's not easy to explain: the pain's one place; you're another;

you keep it away. It takes practice, but I had four weeks before they evacuated me." "Jesus Christ," I thought, "this guy's got a solution for everything." "What did they do with you?" I asked.

"They put me on a hospital ship and sent me back to the States. I was in and out of the VA for the next four years while they worked on my foot. I got married to the finest woman in the world. I went to college, got a bachelor's degree, got an ROTC lieutenant's commission. In '61, I got myself posted to Fort Bragg, Special Forces. That's where I met General Stilwell." "*The* General Stilwell?" I asked. " 'Vinegar' Joe Stilwell, our man in China?" "No," he said. "Not him. His son, 'Cider Joe.' We used to call him 'Papa.' Papa Joe changed my life." I was going to ask how, but Hicks kept going. "Papa Joe never made it beyond brigadier general, but that suited him fine. You ever heard of STRAC?" I shook my head. "STRAC was the Strategic Army Command / XVIII Airborne Corps. It was headquartered at Fort Bragg and Papa Joe was its chief of staff. STRAC commanded two airborne divisions, *plus* the Special Forces. In other words, STRAC had worldwide contingency plans and Papa Joe was in charge of operations. Papa Joe was interested in two things: Southeast Asia and Latin America. The more he knew, the happier he was. He had teams out all over the place, gathering information. Some were old China hands, China–Burma OSS. He had one special group he called 'the Game.' " "What was it?" I asked. "The Game was four or five guys, all combat veterans. You ever heard of 'Bull' Simons?" "Sure," I said. "Ross Perot made him a star. Perot hired him back in '80 to go to Iran and get his executives out. Simons was pretty old by then. Was he in it?" Hicks nodded. "Were you?" Hicks nodded again. "Oh, yeah. We all knew each other and we all knew the Game, but no one else did. We worked for Papa Joe, Papa Joe worked for General Trapnell, General Trapnell worked for the Joint Chiefs. It was all legal. We all obeyed the Constitution. But if Papa Joe wanted us to go somewhere, he cut the orders and we just disappeared for a couple of weeks." "Where'd you go?" "All over. Some of it's still classified. It was all covert. We gathered intelligence; we acted as couriers. One thing for sure: it was dangerous: you could end up in jail or you could end up dead. We operated in Africa, Eastern Europe, Latin America, Cuba, Laos. We extracted agents. We trained insurgents. The main thing is that we worked for Papa Joe and we *took care* of each other." "The Game sounds like a tribal band," I said. Hicks stopped and looked at me and didn't say anything. Then he nodded. "You are a perceptive son-of-a-bitch, aren't you? That's exactly what I liked about it. When I was in ROTC, I had to pretend I wasn't an Indian. My fellow officers didn't want to hear me talk about the Cherokee way. I'd say something and they'd make some joke about taking scalps. I had to close it up, put it away. Papa Joe wasn't like that. The people in the Game weren't like that. What we were doing wasn't called 'unconventional warfare' for nothing. A Tsalagi warrior fit right in. That's where I first learned about the Rhades."

"The what?" I asked. "Not what," he said. "Who. The Rhades are Montagnards, mountain people native to the Central Highlands of Vietnam. Their tribal lands extend into Cambodia. They're racially different from the Vietnamese, originally Malayo-Polynesian. They speak a different language. The Vietnamese considered them animals. *They* called the Vietnamese *yawns*. That's something so dirty there's no translation. They've been at war with the Vietnamese for hundreds and hundreds of years. They're a lot like the Cherokees: the same sort of matrilineal descent, the same sort of medicine men, the same reverence for the land. The more I learned about them, the more I liked them. They were familiar to me." "But why did you learn about them in the first place?" "Because of Papa Joe. We'd been in Laos for a while, gathering intelligence. It was a covert, long-term operation called 'White Star.' 'Bull' Simons led that. Papa Joe knew things were heating up. Hell, everyone did. He'd heard a lot about the Vietminh. He wanted me to go into the Central Highlands and look around. He said there were some policy changes in the works about Vietnam. I could speak Rhade. He wanted me to meet some people, pick up some reports, keep my ears open.

"One day I was in North Carolina, the next I was in Thailand. I was supposed to be good old plain Dave Hicks, a farm-animal expert from Texas, sent to help the Montagnards breed better hogs. I flew to Saigon, then up to Nha Trang on the coast, then over to Ban Me Thuot in the Central Highlands. The Rhades were glad to see me. They knew I wasn't there to talk about pigs. They didn't like the Vietminh. For that matter, they didn't like *any* Vietnamese, but the Vietminh were beginning to lean on them pretty hard, and they wanted us to help. I was going to tell them how much good the Americans had done the Indians, but I decided it wasn't the right time. They held a rice-wine ceremony for me and gave me a brass friendship bracelet, a *kong*." As Hicks said that, I looked at his wrist. "Is that it?" He held it out to me. "No. This is something different. See those three cuts in it? They're from an initiation. One cut for each day of the ceremony. The *kong* they gave me then was just a get-acquainted present. We sat around and drank for a while, then they took me up the road to see a *song*, a longhouse built on stilts. The Vietminh had commandeered it. They did that a lot: they'd take a longhouse and use it as a billet or a depot. They'd booby-trap them. When they were ready to leave, they'd blow everything up and set half a village on fire. When we got there, two Vietminh came out on the porch and started shouting at us. The Rhades yelled back. All of a sudden, the guys on the porch went inside and disappeared. It got real quiet. One of my friends was standing in front of me, one behind. I turned around to say something and the longhouse blew up. Something hit me in the back and I went sailing through the air. I landed on my belly. I couldn't move. I figured I was back-shot, paralyzed. I turned my head. That's when I saw what'd hit me: it was the head of the Rhade who'd been standing in front of me. 'Goddamn!' I thought. 'Welcome to Vietnam.'"

"You went back?" "To Vietnam? You're goddamn right. In '66 I got recruited into the ICEX program. It preceded Phoenix, the program everyone heard about. *No one* talked about ICEX. Officially, I was a Special Forces advisor, assigned to help the Rhades with civil defense and nutrition and all that other stuff. My commanding officer thought that; my fellow officers thought that. Really what they thought was that I was shacking up with someone, 'cause every night I went up to the village. What I was doing was hunting. ICEX was a joint U.S.–Vietnamese intelligence operation. The Rhades did it because, for the first time in history, one group of Vietnamese was giving them weapons and money and telling them it was okay to kill another group of Vietnamese. Killing Vietnamese was fine with the Rhades. Our targets were VC and North Vietnamese political cadres; we were supposed to bring them back alive. Sometimes that wasn't possible, and sometimes people got in the way and lost their lives." "Where did all this happen?" "In the Ninh Hoa district, north of Nha Trang, in a fifty-kilometer radius, in a valley." "How long did this go on?" "A year, '66 to '67. Ten big missions, more than a hundred little ones." I took a breath. "Captain, I've got another one of those questions for you. I don't know quite how to phrase it, and if I get it wrong, you've got to understand it's out of ignorance, not anything else." "Okay," he said, "what you got?" "My question has to do with what you did." "Okay," he said. "What I'm wondering is: exactly how many people did you kill?" "Personally? In that year? 1966–67?" I nodded. "Officially, South Vietnamese intelligence credited me with three kills with my hands, twelve with my knife, and 120 to 130 with small arms. That's official, you understand. My team captured eight people in our district, and eleven more north of us. Our targets were assigned by joint agreement between South Vietnamese intelligence and the CIA in cooperation with the Special Forces Command. Our missions were well defined: what we did, we did according to orders. If I was ordered to kill someone, I'd kill him. Unless it violated the Constitution. I killed a lot of people, but I never killed anyone I wasn't supposed to. If you do that, you're a murderer, you're an animal. I've killed people in every way you can imagine, up close and far away, with every kind of weapon you can think of, with my knife, with my hands, but I never killed a child, and I never let the Rhades kill a child, even though the VC used to kill their children all the time, used to bayonet them and slam them into trees. I never killed unarmed women or old people or children, and I never tortured anyone, because if you torture someone, it'll affect you, it'll cost you in the long run. I knew one man, he was a friend of mine, he used to have an orgasm every time he killed someone. Whenever he had a choice between a kill and a capture, he chose the kill because it gave him more pleasure. That man had a problem. Other men I knew had problems. A lot became drunks. A lot didn't. They had their own ways, their own understandings. Some did it for God; some did it for God and country, the red, white, and blue. The only difference between them and me was that they had to talk about their reasons all the time and I didn't." "Why not?" "Because I knew who I was and what I was doing. If you're a soldier in the army, you better understand that the only reason the army exists is to train to kill and to kill. I was a Man-killer. I was a warrior, in a tradition of warriors. I fought the enemy; I served my country; I obeyed the Constitution; I led my fellow warriors. They made me their brother. I helped them defend themselves and their families. I had a code. I had a motto: I can *die* with honor, but I cannot *live* with dishonor." He stopped talking then and we both sat and listened to the room.

I looked up at the paintings on the wall, then back at him. "Vietnam sounds like the place where one part of your life came together with the other part. You could be an Indian warrior and an American officer; you could serve your country and help people who could have been your own." He looked at me. "They were my own. They initiated me. That's what this *kong's* about. They initiated me into their warrior society. They gave me a name. They called me E-Among. It means Tiger-Man. My Tsalagi name was Panther Follower. They never knew that. I'd never told them. When that happened, I *knew* I was where I was supposed to be." He stopped again and once more we sat and listened to the room. He shifted in his chair and his face contorted. "Listen," he said, "my bones are getting stiff. Sitting like this isn't as easy as it used to be." He looked at his watch. "Let's call it a day. You're welcome to come back tomorrow." He'd told me a lot, but there was something I still needed to ask him.

"I've got one last question," I said. "Everything you've said makes sense. I want you to know I admire you." He nodded, gravely. "Thanks," he said. "You're a special sort of man, but you're also human. I understand, I think, how you did what you did. But —what were the aftereffects?" His voice grumbled out of him. "You mean nightmares and that kind of shit?" he growled. I nodded. "I never had any. Except one. It's a dream. I've had it every once in a while. I've had it on and off for years." He leaned forward toward me, bent stiff at the waist. "This man comes up behind me with a knife. I guess he's got a knife because I've killed so many people with mine. He comes up behind me and"—he jabbed the air—"he sticks his knife into me, into my back, between the fifth and sixth ribs. That's a good place to kill a man; it's the place to choose because it leads right to the heart. I know that place very well. He sticks it in and I feel it, but as he does it I reach"—he gritted his teeth, growled, and threw his arms back over his head—"I reach back, and with all my strength"—he threw his arms forward, back over his head, down toward his feet— "I pull him over my shoulder and"—he chopped down with both his hands—"I *kill* him. I kill him before he can kill me. But I'll tell you something: one day I'm going to have that dream and I won't be able to stop him before he gets the knife all the way in. I won't be able to stop him. And I know that the day that happens"—he looked at me—"I'll wake up and I'll die." He pulled himself painfully up, out of his chair. "Come on," he said, "let's call it a day. Come back tomorrow and we'll talk." We shook hands. He opened the door and I walked out to my car. I didn't realize what he'd told me until I got back to my motel. It was Jacob and the Angel. Except the Angel was Death. In Korea, Hicks had shot the dead. Now, when he dreamed, he killed Death.

I found someplace to eat, then I took a walk, and as I walked I thought. Everything Hicks had told me, I could understand, but not quite comprehend, as if I'd been listening through earphones to a translation of a barely familiar story being told in a foreign language. When I was twelve, I'd prepared for my bar mitzvah, not gone on a quest and killed a mountain lion. My Hebrew name had been as different from Michael as Panther Follower had been from David Larry. My Uncle Ed had probably been as much of a drunk as Hicks's Uncle Charlie, but Ed had never revealed the secrets of a hidden religion or laid out my destiny as a Man-killer. When it came time for me to be drafted, the army doctor had examined my eyes, expressed his sympathies, then classified me 4-F. I'd never manned a machine gun, or chanted a war song, or learned how to circumvent pain. I had no way to verify Hicks's exploits in the group he called the Game, but I could sympathize with his finding a home among strangers, helping them defend themselves while becoming more of himself in their presence. His strength, his endurance, his courage I admired. But most of all I admired how his religion filled his life. I was a Jew, not an Indian, but he seemed to pay as much attention to the sacred and the profane as I did. As much as I admired that, I also admired the dream he'd confessed. If all he'd told me were war stories about how he'd killed and others had died, I might have stopped listening. His willingness to talk about a dream that was a prophecy of his own death, his ability to describe his thoughts and not just boast about his actions made me want to hear more.

The next morning Hicks met me at the front door, carrying a cane. "I tell you," he said, "after you left yesterday, I lay down on the bed in my wife's sewing room and I didn't get up until this morning. All that talk tired me out. My bones aren't what they used to be." "Are you okay now?" I asked. He turned and led me through to his study. "I've been better, but it doesn't matter. You got me stirred up." He turned on the light, lowered himself into his chair, and looked at me. "It's better to talk about this than let it simmer. I had myself a dream last night. It must have been because of all that about Korea. I've dreamed it before. It's a true memory, but last night it came out different." He paused. "You know, Cherokee people have always believed in dreams; they always told each other their dreams; their medicine men interpreted them. If a man had a dream and it told him to do something, no matter what, he had to do it." He stopped, then began again. "Last night, I dreamed I was back in Korea. It was during an artillery barrage. This did happen. They started shelling us, and I dived into a bunker full of dead Chinese. I knew it was full of 'em, but that was the only place to hide. They'd been napalmed. They'd burned to death. When the shells started coming, I dived in, head first, and slid across 'em on my belly, with my arms straight down"—he pushed out his arms and pulled back his head —"and my face up so they wouldn't touch my skin." He stopped and looked at me. "You ever felt the skin of someone who's burnt to death?" he asked. I shook my head. "It's sticky," he said. "It comes off and sticks to you like flypaper." He began again. "I dived in and skidded across 'em and their skin stuck to my belly and legs, and my chest, but I managed to keep my face clear. After the barrage, I climbed out and rubbed myself off with dirt. Last night, I dreamed all that. But last night"—he looked at me again— "I couldn't keep my head up. The skin stuck to me. It stuck all over me. Now—what do you make of that?" I remembered Lieutenant Treadwell. I remembered how he'd carried the bodies down the hill and been soaked by their juice, and then how he'd lain down in the stream with his nose in the mud and thought about not getting up. I remembered something else, too, a phrase Robert

Lifton had used in one of his books to describe what happens to soldiers in battle. Lifton had called it "death immersion." It had happened to Treadwell, and last night it had happened to Captain Hicks. I told him about it, and then I told him about Jacob and the Angel of Death. Hicks listened and nodded and said, "I think you got that right. You got that right."

"What I still can't understand," I said, "is how you sustained yourself. I remember what you told me yesterday. But the dreams alone would have finished me off. How could you keep it up?" Hicks didn't stop to consider his answer. "It's the adrenaline," he said. "In battle, a man's got a mix in him between fear and excitement, and if the excitement's greater than the fear, he can do it. That old adrenaline starts pumping, and you're *different*. I mean even your piss smells different. You're not gone, though. You're very clear. I'd sing my war song and the adrenaline would start through me and—oh boy—I'd be *ready*." "Yesterday, when we met, I asked you what your song was and you told me. It was probably the wrong question at the wrong time. You answered me and I listened, but—I don't know how to put it—when you told me, it sounded like something was missing. Am I right?" "You sure as hell are," he said. "You want to hear me? I'll *sing* you my song." He stood up, took a breath that filled his chest, and began. His voice rose deep out of his belly, the sound syllables punching out of him like small, rapid explosions. "*Hey!*" came his breath, "*Hey*, yah-yah-yah-yah-yah-*yah*! / Enemy! *Beware*! I *Come*! / Hey, yah, yah, yah, yah / Enemy: Beware I *Come*! / Hey, yah, yah, yah, yah / I-have-*never*-failed / Hey, yah, yah, yah, yah, yah / *My-Knife* is *Always-Thirsty* / Hey, yah, yah, yah, yah." He stopped and ran his hand over his forearm and let out a hoarse Rebel yell, "OO-EYYY!" he said, "Feel it *pumpin'*!' My hair's standing up and I got goose bumps!" He wasn't the only one.

He settled back down in his chair. "What else you want to hear?" he said, smiling, "I'd like to hear something about Vietnam," I said. "Not everything, though. You said you went on more than a hundred missions, big ones and little ones. How about describing a big one?" "All right," he said. He leaned back and drew himself up. "This was a big one, but nothing special.

"The scouts in my band spotted a VC safehouse inside a woodcutter's compound. The compound was fake. If it'd been real, it would have been used seasonally. Woodcutters would have used it as a camp, gone out, cut their wood, hauled it to market with ox teams, and then abandoned the camp until next season. The VC had found the camp and taken it over. It'd originally had nine huts; they'd added eleven more, and surrounded it with a palisade; they'd even brought in a herd of water buffalo and put 'em in the corral. All to make it look like the camp was real. What it was was a rest stop for traveling VC political cadres. At the time we spotted it, there was a VC political officer with a seven-man escort resting in the main hut. Our scouts spied on the camp for three days and learned the routine. Then they bribed one of the guards and came back and told me. We got permission to go in and capture the political officer. We were supposed to bring him out alive. If we couldn't, we were to bring back documents.

"We left in the middle of the night, during a heavy rainstorm." "How were you armed?" "I had an M-1, four grenades, and my kukri." "Why the M-1?" I asked. "Why not an M-16?" He hobbled over to his desk and brought back two rounds. "The big one's from an M-1"; he handed it to me. I could feel it in my palm. "You hit a man with that and he's dead." He handed me the other. It looked tiny next to the first. "The whiz kids who worked for McNamara thought it was better to produce wounded, since wounded cost the other side more money. But a wounded man can come back, madder and wiser. The best thing is to kill him the first time. Especially if you're doing what we were." "What were the other people carrying?" "The men with me?" I nodded. "They had M-3 grease guns—they're suppressed automatics that fire .45s. There were six people on my team. Two carried Thompsons and suppressed .38s; their job was to watch trails that led in and out of the compound. The three with me had the grease guns. We were going in after the target. We were the hunters." He smiled.

"Before we left, I went to water. Then I painted my face, like I always did. If I would have had my own colors, I would have painted my right side red. The right side's the killing side. Red's the color of the east; it's the symbol of the rising sun, the source of power, all strength and success. Since all I had was standard army camouflage colors, I painted my right side green, the color of the center, one of the seven directions. My left side I painted black, the color of death and defeat. After that, we started out.

After two hours, we heard three people coming toward us. We stepped off the trail and let them pass without their knowing we were there. Four hours later, we sighted the compound. The front gate faced east; the exit was to the west; the corral with the water buffaloes was to the south, along a stream. We stood in the dark; it was raining; we waited. I sensed a man coming toward us." "You heard him?" I asked. "No, I *sensed* him. In battle, you can do that. It's a sixth sense. You can develop it. I could feel the adrenaline pumping. It makes you more alert. I could sense him coming. I stood on the west side of a tree by the trail and waited. He came from the east. I reached around and . . ." I watched as Hicks demonstrated: he cupped his right hand and swung it out like the ball of a mace. He explained: "I hit him below the sternum as he passed. That—then the suction of the hand as I pulled it away— stopped his heart. He went down without a sound. I stepped behind him, caught him, picked him up, and slammed him feet first into the ground. That broke his back." I cut in. "Can you show me how you did it?" "Sure," he said. "I can show you. But there're some other things I won't. There're some things you shouldn't know." He stood up. "Okay. Come over here and stand with your back to me." I did, and as I did, he slipped his right arm around me, below my diaphragm, and pulled me back hard against him; at the same time he slipped his left hand under my armpit, then up, flat onto the back of my neck so my head bent. As he did all this, I felt his knees press in and bend mine. "There," he said, "that's it. I pick you up and drive you down and your back breaks in maybe four places. Satisfied?" "Yes," I said. "Thanks." We both sat down. He continued.

"I laid him down and we all stood and listened again. We were waiting for guard dogs, but there weren't any." "What would you have done if there were?" "Scared the shit out of them. I would have gone down on all fours and huffed myself out and started growling. I've done it. You learn. You huff yourself out and growl mean enough and you can scare any son-of-a-bitch." He laughed. "But I didn't have to. All we had to do was signal the guard we'd bribed and he opened the gate. There were fifty men sleeping in the compound. Plus seven in the officer's escort; plus a woman with him in his room; plus an old crone sleeping in a lean-to next to the hut—she was the cook and housekeeper. There was a guard standing watch at the foot of the stairs that led to the hut. It was just after two o'clock in the morning. The guard was fresh. I'd have preferred taking him out at the end of his watch, but we didn't have a choice: the guards changed every two hours; the next one would have been at four. That wouldn't have given us any margin, but it would have been easier. "Why?" I asked. "Sleep's deepest then," he said. "Between four and five is the low point of the sleep cycle. It's one of the best killing times—then and midnight, at the beginning of the cycle. This guard was alert. It was dark and still raining, so he wore a poncho over his weapon. I used my Great Silencer. I took off his head. It was a selected, swift stroke." I thought of the *shochet* and his *halef*. " 'A selected swift stroke,' " I repeated to myself. Hicks continued. "His head came off; he slumped; I caught him and laid him by the side of the steps. Then the four of us went in. One Rhade went to the room where the officer and the woman were. The rest of us went to the escorts. We opened the door and things happened fast. I slit the throat of the man sleeping closest to me. One of the Rhades fired a round into another man. The weapon was suppressed, but it still woke up the man next to him. He sat up and I took him out with a bare-handed chop to the neck. The Rhades killed the rest with single rounds. As we came out, the man who'd gone next door led the political officer out with a wire noose around his neck. He'd left the woman asleep in the bed next to him. The old crone in the lean-to never made a sound.

"We came down the steps. It was still raining; it was very quiet. No one had heard us. We went out the east gate and hid close by. We waited." "Why?" I asked. "Why didn't you keep going?" "Because we wanted the payoff." "What payoff? You had the officer." "That was fine for the people we worked for. We wanted something else." "What?" I asked. "We wanted to hear the screams when the guard changed and they discovered the bodies. We wanted to hear that. We wanted to enjoy that. That was our payoff. The screams were our bonus." He looked at me. "The Rhades weren't doing this because they believed in the Republic of Vietnam," he said. "They were doing it to even the score. What the VC did to the Montagnards was bad. They used terror selectively. They used it to control villages. Terror was policy. They'd take a village, assemble everyone, and lead out the family of the headman. First they'd rape his daughters and his wives while everyone watched. They did this to women who'd been raised in a puritanical culture that forbade premarital sex and punished extramarital sex with death. They'd rape the women in public, then kill them, then execute the chief. Then they'd do the same thing to the chief's assistant and his family. Then they'd ask if anyone wanted to be the new chief. When no one spoke up, they'd say 'Fine' and install one of their own. All this sounds familiar, right?" I nodded. "All that's *nothing*. That was just for openers. They'd take the kids and pick 'em up by the feet and swing 'em into trees. They did this to people who *loved* children. We walked into a village once, on patrol, and found a man standing all alone. Everything had been burnt. Everyone had been murdered. They'd left him. First they'd cut off his nose, his ears, and his balls, and cut out his tongue. Then they'd driven long, thin slivers of bamboo into his eyes, his ears, and up his cock. He couldn't do anything about it because they'd cut off his fingers. They'd left him standing there. The Rhade who found him was the same man I said who slipped the noose around the political officer's neck. He walked up to the man, took out his .45, and shot him between the eyes. It was all he could do for him. The next thing we saw was a woman. They'd cut off her breasts and shoved a big piece of bamboo up her vagina, all the way up into her womb. She'd been pregnant. They'd impaled her baby. They'd split her open and left her." "Stop," I said. I felt sick and scared. "That's it; that's enough." "No, it's not," he said. "You asked why we waited, and I'm here to tell you. Compared with what the VC did, what we did was nothing. We never raped women or killed kids or murdered noncombatant females. But—I'll tell you this—if we caught a VC patrol, we left our signs." I swallowed what was in my mouth. "What do you mean?" I asked. "We marked them. My custom was to shoot or slit the throats of the dead. That was from Korea. The Rhades adopted that. But they had their own customs." "Which were?" I asked in a very quiet voice. "Their custom was to cut off a dead man's cock and balls and hang them out of his mouth. That was their message. It was their calling card." Suddenly I remembered some of the homicide reading I'd done, months before in Florida. "Captain," I said, "I understand this was war, plus a blood feud, but I swear to God it reminds me of some of the stuff I learned from detectives. All the sexual mutilation reminds me of serial murders committed by psychopaths. The FBI calls them 'lust murderers.' What you're telling me is crazy. Killing in combat I can understand, but the stuff you're talking about is evil lunacy. That valley you were in sounds like it was inhabited by lunatics killing lunatics." Hicks looked at me very level and very steady. "Yeah," he said. "That's what it was."

We sat for a while. My mind felt full of water. "How long did you last?" I asked. "A year," he said. "I stepped on a land mine outside a VC compound. The charge blew me back off my feet. It gave me a concussion and damaged my heart. I woke up with a cloth over my face, lying on my back. The Rhades' medicine man was sitting next to me, beating a death drum. He took the cloth off my face and I asked him, 'How bad?' He said they couldn't find anything except some bruises on my leg and back. I hurt bad, everywhere. Everything hurt, all of me. I asked him if I had a fever. He said yes. I pulled myself up and told them to get me back to the Special Forces compound. When I got there, I went in my room and locked the door." Hicks shifted in his chair. Something must have caught, because he grimaced, then his face went slack. He took a fluttery breath and began again. "I used to do that a lot toward the end of the year." "Do what?" I asked. "Go back and lock the door. I'd stay inside. I'd read trashy novels and drink too much Jack Daniel's. It got so I couldn't stand the smell of fresh blood. I used to smell it so much it stuck in my nose, I couldn't get rid of it. The Jack Daniel's took it away. Then I'd stick my head out the door and get a whiff of the smell from the mess. I'd smell that overcooked, greasy meat frying on the grills and I'd want to heave. I'd shut the door and take another drink to settle my stomach." Hicks shifted in his chair and grimaced again. "Anyway—I got back in my room and lay down. I knew I had a fever. That's the last thing I knew. I must have gone to take a shower because my friends found me lying there, bleeding from my rear end, in a pool of blood. I had amoebic dysentery and didn't know it. That was the fever. It has a two-day incubation period. It hit the same day I stepped on the mine. These amoebas were eating their way up through my colon, headed for my liver. My friends packed me in ice and called a medevac. They put me in some hospital, propped me up, and pulled everything out of my rear end. They cut out the bad stuff, sewed together what was left, and stuffed it all back in. I nearly died. Not just from the land mine and the dysentery. I'd lost a lot of blood, and the fact was I hadn't been eating much for about five months. I was in pretty bad shape, but what just about killed me was the medicine they gave me to treat the dysentery. It killed the amoebas, but it damn near took me along with 'em. They sent me back to the U.S. in '67.

"By '68 I was out of the hospital, walking around Fort Bragg. One night I was standing in my bathroom and it felt like my whole head exploded. I tell you, I'd never felt pain as bad as that, ever. A blood clot had come loose from somewhere and got stuck in my brainstem. I felt myself float up out of my body. It felt very peaceful after all that pain. I looked down: I was way up over my house, and I saw my wife and one of my sons bending over me. I could have kept on going, but I decided I didn't want to: I didn't want to leave my wife. I felt like I'd died and come back. If you count the time in Korea and the Rhade medicine man beating his drum, that was my third time. It took me four years to get over it. I couldn't talk right; I couldn't walk right; I couldn't think right. The VA gave me some medicine for the pain, but all it did was scare the shit out of me. That was one of its side effects. I'd wake up in the middle of the night. I'd sit straight up in bed, and I'd be *scared*, pure scared, but scared of nothing. The worst part of it was that the stuff was addictive. In those years, I wasn't worth the powder it would have taken to blow my damn brains out. One day I just flushed all the pills down the toilet and from then on I started feeling a whole lot better. I decided to go back to college. I had to learn how to think and write all over again, but it healed me. Now all I take is Inderal for my heart, Tagamet for my stomach, and Persantine so I don't get another clot."

Hicks talked about other things after that: his wife, his sons, the junta's war against the Indians in Nicaragua. He told me he was tired and he looked it. He pulled himself up and opened the door to his study. I wished him well. "Hang tough," he said. I drove back to my motel, lay down, and stared at the ceiling for the rest of the day and part of the night. I began to realize how badly Hicks had been damaged, not just his body, but his soul. Even though he'd had rituals to cleanse himself; even though his endurance had been remarkable and his reflexes extraordinary; even though he was a warrior in a tradition of warriors; even though he accepted what he'd done and could talk about it—none of this had protected him. What he'd done had poisoned him. Neither his ancestors nor his chants nor his reflexes had protected him from the toxins released from his kills. The effects had been cumulative. He was proof a man couldn't kill other men and walk away unharmed, no matter how well protected he was. The world he'd inhabited, that thirty-mile radius of valley in Vietnam, was a place for psychopaths. In a year, he'd lost his health and his sanity there. His skills and his rituals had helped him endure it longer than most. Eventually, he succumbed.

The *shochets* had had the word of God and their victims had been animals. Ralph Kemp, the warden in Georgia, had had a judge, a jury, and any number of cutouts. Lieutenant Treadwell had had his horses, his rattlesnakes, and his firm refusal to cross the threshold into H-5. All these men had had their duties and evasions, their antidotes and rituals. Captain Hicks had had his rank, his tribe, and his knife, but eventually the not so simple facts of killing all those men had almost ended his life. Ten years later, he was still breathing, but there were large parts of him that were missing.

All that might have been obvious to anyone who'd been to Sunday school or been the victim of a bully during recess or survived a nearly homicidal love affair. Everyone knew by analogy: thou shalt not kill because you'll be punished. But Hicks had not lived by analogy. When I'd first met him, I'd thought I'd met a man whose experiences had made him exempt from peaceful clichés. Since the world was full of wars, and those wars were conducted by man-killers—I'd thought Hicks might tell me the secret of how men could keep killing other men. The secret was that even warriors can't. There're no exemptions: one way or the other, even if you do it properly and for all the right reasons—if you kill other men, you'll die. Not immediately, and not all at once. But as Hicks learned in his dreams: the skin of dead men does stick to you and the knife will eventually make its way to your heart.

AIDS

I had to recover fom Hicks and prepare myself for the people I was to meet next week—the people who comforted the outcasts dying of AIDS. Hicks had been marked by being a killer. In trying to understand him, so had I. The people I was going to meet presided over the deaths of men who might have been me. I'd been less frightened before I'd seen Hicks than after I came back. Before I saw him, I'd kept replaying the last movement of Moussorgsky's *Pictures at an Exhibition*, riding the last wave of the climax, from threat to transcendence, up and down, over and over again. Hicks had been hard to bear. I'd been hoping to meet someone who'd discovered an antidote to the fear of death. God, justice—anything at all if it counteracted the poison. Some American Indian version of Zen and the Art of Man-killing. I'd been hoping for something like that since they'd strapped me in the electric chair in Georgia. Death had marked Lieutenant Treadwell in Korea—not as deeply as Hicks, but deeply enough. Treadwell had made me start looking for an antidote. I'd turned to Hicks, and now I was going to talk to people who helped men who might have been me. What I needed to understand was why —if I was so frightened by all this—I kept doing it. I stayed at home for a week and thought about it.

I discovered that what sustained me was something Hicks had described: in the contest between fear and excitement, exhilaration was more powerful than terror. Both are stimulants: if one wins, you stay; if the other wins, you run. In either case, the pupils dilate and the heart quickens. Whether the risk was real or not, I imagined I was the star and audience of a high-wire act: I swayed suspended above my head; I applauded as I grasped the bar of the incoming trapeze; I sighed as I landed safely on the far platform; I turned and looked down as one part of me cheered the other who stood high above, out of breath, acknowledging the other's praise. Before every encounter, whether with Hicks or Treadwell or the rabbi or Schultz the detective, I'd expected to be turned to stone by the horror of what these men would show me. What I learned was that they were as human as I; what they could bear, so could I. Each time, when I'd returned, I'd touch my face and sides, and when I felt my skin, its warmth exhilarated me. "I'm not stone," I'd say. "I'm still alive!" I'd shout. "I made it! I made it! I'm back and I know more than I ever did. I've lived to tell the tale." And the tale? Death, I learned, was a colossus that lay on its back like Gulliver, sprawled across the horizon. The men I met were like the men in the story: they'd thrown ropes over the giant; they'd stretched and twisted and tied them down to keep him there, and then, like ants, they'd scurried up and scampered about to survey the length and breadth of the monster. All I did was scurry up behind them. We all knew, though, that sooner or later Gulliver would wake up and the ropes would snap like the strings they were, and the monster would rise, and those of us who were lucky would tumble off and run away, brave men that we were.

Brave man that I was, I almost didn't go up the next set of ropes. The people I was to see worked in hospitals and hospices in San Francisco. All of their clients were young, dying men. Until now, the professionals I'd met had had clients or victims or targets who were already dead, or were animals, criminals, or the enemy. The detectives and slaughterers and prison officials and man-killers had all thought of their "clients" as "them." That had helped them keep their distance, and that, in turn, had helped me keep mine. If the clients of the people I was to meet in San Francisco had been old, infirm, and dying, I might have had trouble, at first, not imagining that every white-haired old man lurching down the corridor wasn't my father. With practice, though, I could have controlled that projection. Unfortunately, the people in the hospital beds in San Francisco were about my age, dying in the prime of their lives, ages twenty-five to forty-four. I was almost forty. Twenty-five years ago, when I'd gone to an all-boys boarding school, I could have acted out my infatuation with a wonderful kid who was a terrific athlete and a fine painter. I could have declared my love and the two of us might have groped our way into bed. If I had known enough then about my own heart and hungers, I might have made the first of a series of moves that, over time, would have put me in one of the hospital beds in one of the AIDS wards I was going to visit. The men who were dying had been a little more precocious than me. Twenty-five years ago, I'd hesitated and they hadn't. They'd turned one way; I'd turned another, but not so long ago, we'd all stood in the same spot. If I was going to talk to the people who took care of them, I'd have to consider the possibility that I might have been one of their clients. I'd have to admit something I'd avoided until now: I'd have to acknowledge my own death.

I spent three weeks making calls to the Coast, trying to set up appointments. The disease had become epidemic. The health professionals there had better things to do than talk about death with someone from Atlanta. The harder I tried to talk my way past their secretaries and assistants, the more upset and agitated I became. Why was I trying so hard? What was I trying to prove? That I was fearless? That I was an outsider? That I was gay? That I wasn't?

In the evenings, I read Solzhenitsyn's *Cancer Ward*. As I watched his patients walk across the screen in front of me, I thought of myself, "That could be you: that could be you. Your father's dying; your time will come." One night I dreamed I was an archaeologist. There was a guide. We were in India. We were going into a set of deep caves carved into a granite mountain. They were vast, perfectly smooth, of rectilinear purity. Deep chambers of pure darkness. As we entered, the guide said, "There are scavengers and treasure hunters here; we must be careful." He shone his light in front of us. There, on the floor, was a bedroll. The sheets had a starched, white crispness; the blankets were clean gray wool. I bent down: they smelled of sleep, not mildew. Whoever had been there had just left. This was not a site abandoned years before. This was the bed of a grave robber, armed and dangerous. Just as I felt the danger, someone beside me threw a blanket over my head. As the guide's light failed and the gray darkness came down on me, my eyes rolled backwards, and I fell, head-first, in a swoon, into an abyss. I knew, then, it wasn't a blanket that had come over me but a sickness, and I was falling into a grave. I woke and I thought, "That's what you are: a grave robber. Not a death defier; not a daring young man on a flying trapeze. You're a grave robber, and where you're headed is a place full of freshly made, empty beds. You claimed you were an archaeologist engaged in research, but you're not; you're a scavenger in business for himself. The man who ambushed you—he was a sick man, risen from his bed, and that darkness and sickness, that ecstatic fall into the abyss—that was you falling into his bed; that bed was your own bed; it was; it could be; it will be; you're headed toward it as surely as any dying man is headed toward his own grave." I nodded and fell asleep again, and this time I dreamed I was talking to Robert Lifton, the way a man talks to his mentor. I told Lifton I could fly. He was interested. "Really?" he said. "When did you learn?" "Right after I finished *Death Trip*," I said. "Want to see?" I rose and hovered in the air above him. I soared and swooped and thought, "Like a bird; like a soul; like an angel." The wind, the height, and the light—I could see it all, everything, everywhere. I woke up happy. I thought, "You rise only as far as you fall."

A week later, a policeman knocked on my door. He said my phone was off the hook; he'd been sent to tell me to call home. My mother answered. She said the paperboy had found my father, in his pajamas, lying in the street outside their apartment. Sometime in the night, he'd gotten up to go to the bathroom, but when he'd gone back to bed, he'd turned right instead of left. He'd stumbled down the hallway, found a door, and opened it. He thought it led to the bedroom, but it was the front door and it led to the corridor. His legs gave out, so he crawled along the carpet, trying all the doors, until he found one that would open. That led to another and then another. Still looking for his bedroom, he finally locked himself outside. It was dark and windy and he didn't know where he was. He pulled himself up, but his legs folded. This time, though, there was no carpet. When he fell, he broke both his arms and fainted. The paperboy found him at dawn. He told the super; the super called the police. The police woke up my mother. Did she know where her husband was, they asked.

My mother told me to get on a plane and meet her at the hospital. I was there in five hours. My father was lying on his back with his arms in casts. The morphine they'd given him had scrambled his brain. He looked at me and spoke gibberish. For five days, my mother and I took turns sitting with him. At night, when we weren't there, he tried to find us and had to be tied down. He kept talking nonsense. His chart read, "Acute confusion." His doctor thought he had Alzheimer's. Since there was nothing else to do, they discharged him after a week, and we took him home. He sat next to me and looked out the window as I drove. "Does the world look any different?" I asked. I didn't expect an answer. "It does," he said. I was encouraged. "How?" I asked. "It's gotten bigger and I've gotten smaller." It was the first coherent thing he'd said in seven days.

His mind began to clear as soon as we got him through the front door. Within two days, his reason returned. Then he realized what he'd done and took to his bed. He was ashamed. I sat next to him as he lay staring at the ceiling. He turned and looked at me. "I don't want to lose your love," he said. "I know you don't think much of me now. But it's time to repay me. Give me back what I gave you." He turned and looked up at the ceiling again. He waited.

All I had were words. "I love you," I said. I took a breath. "I still love you, but . . . Do you remember when I was a kid and I was crazy and I did everything wrong? You didn't like it, but you still loved me. Now it's reversed. You're the one who's acted crazy, and I still love you, but I don't like it any more than you did." He drew in his lips. He shut his eyes. His face grew stern. It wasn't enough. I'd said it wrong. Clichés. All I had were clichés. I tried again. "Do you remember when you were little and you went to say Kaddish for your father and you got stuck in the snow but you lived long enough for that man to rescue you? Do you remember?" His eyes flicked at me. "Do you remember when you were older and the boys chased you and wanted to kill you because you were a Jew?" His eyes flicked again. I was telling him the story of his life, the story he'd told me night after night after dinner, the story of his triumphs. "Do you remember when you were in London, all alone with your mother, pushing a cart, peddling in the streets? You survived that. Then you came to America. Do you remember?" He nearly turned and said something. "You couldn't speak English, but you told everyone you wanted to be a doctor." He turned and looked at me. "Then you got rheumatic fever and almost died. No one thought you'd live long enough to be anything, let alone a doctor. But you *lived*. You lived and became a doctor and saved people's lives." His face grew soft. My words had touched him. "Now you have to heal yourself. You've lived a long time. You're a man of will. You've triumphed over many things." I looked into his eyes. "Now. *Listen*. It's the *same*. You've got to learn to live with what's wrong with you. It's very hard. You're eighty-five. You've got to find a way to live through all this until you die." He kept looking at me. "Your life's not done. Your job's not done. You've got another problem to solve. You've got to live until you die. You've got to figure out how to live as completely as you can until the moment of your death. Then you can die. Do you understand?" "Yes," he said. His voice rose out of him like a door opening.

I said all this to comfort him and it did. The next day, he got out of bed and I bought him a new recording of Beethoven's *Ninth Symphony*, his favorite. That night, after we listened to the "Ode to Joy," he said, "When you're old enough, you'll understand how much is in there." The next day, I left for California. I looked out at the clouds over Oklahoma and thought about what I'd learned. Not much. Not very much. Barely enough to repay my father. But enough. From all the men I'd listened to—from the pathologists and detectives and slaughterers and *shochets* and man-killers— I'd learned something. A very little kind of wisdom, but enough to get my father up out of bed. What I'd learned was how to comfort him and, by comforting him, I'd comforted myself. I had no medicine and no money. All I had were words, but sometimes words were enough. I hoped they'd still be when I landed.

I'd made appointments with half a dozen clinicians, hospice and psychiatric workers, all of whom cared for men who had AIDS. The clinicians practiced at a variety of public and private hospitals in the Bay Area, but chief among them was an oncologist named Paul Volberding who headed the AIDS ward at San Francisco General Hospital, and who, at the age of thirty-five, had become an internationally recognized clinical authority on the disease. Of all the hospice and psychiatric workers, the most intriguing was a man called Jim Geary, the director of an AIDS hospice and counseling organization called Shanti. Months before I'd contacted him, I'd heard an extraordinary set of radio interviews conducted with a number of Shanti's counselors. These interviews had been remarkable not only because of the power of the emotions the counselors expressed—feelings of intense empathy and sorrow— but because of the candor with which the counselors confessed their motives. From what I could gather, there were many among them whose friends, relatives, or lovers had already died of the disease; as survivors, they used the aid and comfort they gave others to reexperience, understand, expiate, and dissipate their own grief and guilt. There were many as well who in their counseling experienced an intensity and variety of emotion that they had despaired of ever feeling. Many confessed they had been able to meet the emotional and moral needs of their clients only by reaching so deeply into themselves that they'd opened up their own hearts and souls. Some described feelings of intense, selfless love that verged on *agape*; others spoke of a clear-minded delight in the simple pleasures of being alive that came close to a state of *satori*. The existence of an activity that appeared, from the outside, to be self-sacrificing and morbid, but was, from within, seen to be life-giving and self-enriching, made me anxious to meet the people at Shanti. After dozens of phone calls, I'd been given an appointment to meet with Jim Geary the morning after I landed, and then, that afternoon, I'd been invited to San Francisco General to meet Dr. Volberding.

I expected the day to begin with something close to a performance of Verdi's *Requiem* and end with the equivalent of excerpts from *The Magic Mountain*. I was in for a surprise. I took a bus to the Shanti Project. It occupied three floors of a monstrous Victorian stone ruin that had once been a convent and now housed a variety of homosexual service and political organizations, as well as a neighborhood day care. The neighborhood itself was one of the places in San Francisco that remain fogbound while other districts sparkle in the sun. On every corner, poor little groceries sold cheese crackers, cheap wine, beef jerky, and loose cigarettes, "your choice, menthol or regular," fifteen cents each. I was early, so I sat and looked through the Project's newsletters and pamphlets. All bore a black-and-white logo of a solar eclipse ("From light to dark to light again" was the motto); some had pink valentine's hearts inside pink triangles; many had two cute little teddy bears, one with its arm around the other's shoulders. There were lists of rental videotapes with titles like "How to Avoid Burnout" and "Facing Death and Dying"; there were stapled handouts "To all Emotional Support Volunteers" with memos about "Volunteer Conflict Resolution Procedures" and "Healing Ourselves Through Laughter," and back issues of the Project's newsletter, *Eclipse*, with articles headlined "The Spirituality of Resistance," "Gentle

Brother, Gentle Friend," and "Hour by Hour," illustrated with photographs of men and women smiling sincerely and fondly embracing. The articles themselves elegiacally described various states of dying, grief, and transcendence experienced by a variety of patients and counselors. Except for the teddy bears, the pink valentines, and the "Healing Ourselves Through Laughter," it was what I'd expected.

A half dozen men walked past me, nodded or said hello, and kept walking. I wondered which one was the director. Finally a middle-aged man wearing jeans and a plaid flannel shirt walked up and said, "Mike?" Was this Geary? "I'm Skipper Hobbs." I rose. Skipper took my hand; he put his left hand over my right hand and we shook. "I'm so *glad* to meet *you*," he said. He looked into my eyes. The handshake, the tone of voice, and the eye contact reminded me of the way a visiting minister had said goodbye to me and everyone else as we filed out of vespers one Sunday at boarding school. "Call me Skip," he said. He guided me back to his office like a shepherd. We sat down. He drew back and sighed. "*Mike*," he said, "Jim had something come up just now and"—he nodded at an appointment book on his desk—"it doesn't look like we'll be able to see you at all for the next two or three weeks." Skip sighed again. He was a man who carried a heavy load. "I *know* how inconvenient this is, but it was just one of those things. I *want* you to know, though, that I'm here for you, to *help* you in any way I can. *What* can I do? *How* can I help?" He looked into my eyes again. Geary must have walked by me while I was reading about the Spirituality of Resistance. He must have taken one look and canceled. Not our kinda guy, he must have said.

"Skip," I said, "I've had this appointment for weeks. It took a long time to get it. I just came in from Atlanta. Isn't there anything you can do?" "Mike," Skip said. He crossed his legs, folded his hands over his knee, and leaned forward so that his face was close to mine. "*Mike*, I just wish there was, but"—he sighed— "Jim's just got so *many* things . . ." There was a pause. "Okay, Skip," I said, "can *you* tell me about the Project, how it works, who volunteers, how they're trained, that sort of thing?" "*Of course*, Mike, but do you mind if I start by asking *you* a question?" "Sure, Skip, shoot." "Mike, what do you call someone who has AIDS?" "Gosh, Skip, I don't know." I thought for a bit. "A 'patient'?" I

said. "An 'AIDS patient'?" "Would you call him anything else?"
Skip asked. "Would you call him a 'victim'?" I thought again.
"Well, sure, Skip, I suppose you could. I mean, they're smallpox
victims and cancer victims and typhoid victims. Sure. Why not?
An 'AIDS victim.' You could call him that." Skip unclasped his
hands, drew himself up straight in the chair. He sighed again;
then he said, "Mike. We *never* call anyone a victim." He sounded
disappointed in me. "We call someone a 'pwah.' " Skip never took
his eyes from mine. "A what??" I asked. "A 'pwah,' " he said. "A
Person with AIDS, a PWA."

"Sorry," I said. "I'm sorry I didn't know. Look, Skip. Maybe I'm
going about this wrong. Maybe it would be better if you could
introduce me to a counselor, someone who's had direct experience
with being a, ah . . . with someone, I mean, with a pwah. Because,
I mean, I'm sure you're up to your neck in . . ." "That's not possible,
Mike," Skip said. "That would be a breach of our policy of con-
fidentiality. We couldn't allow that." "But, Skip," I said. "I'm sure
you know I'm writing about people who deal with death, and if I
can't meet and talk to someone . . ." "Mike, it's not possible. We
have a *strict* policy of . . ." "But, Skip," I said, "I'm not interested
in people's names, ranks, and social security numbers. I'd just like
to get a sense of the experience itself."

Skip rocked back and put his hands behind his head. He looked
away and then glanced at me. He smiled. "Mike," he said, "there
is something. It's not something we generally do." He looked very
serious. He lowered his voice. "I can let you have a copy of our
counselor's training manual." "That's *great*, Skip!" I said. "Thanks!
I really appreciate it." Skip grinned like a kid who'd just let me in
on a secret. He reached forward and slid open the door of a
cabinet. Inside, there were stacks of thick, spiral notebooks. "What
color do you like?" he asked. I thought, "This could be a test.
Choose blue; it's very spiritual." "Blue," I answered. "Right you
are," he said. "Blue it is." He handed it to me. It must have
weighed ten pounds. "Gee, Skip! Thanks; this is great!" I said.
"That'll be $35," he said. "Oh, sweet Jesus," I thought. "This is
just like a church, except no one's singing." I paid. Maybe he'd let
me meet someone.

I tried again. I opened the notebook and looked through the
table of contents. It read like "Everything You Always Wanted to

Know About Death but Were Afraid to Ask." "Skip," I said, "this is wonderful. This is a real treasure. But, Skip, a writer needs more than words; he needs real experience; he needs to talk to *people*. I'll take this home tonight and study it, because the last thing I want to do is ask you guys any stupid questions. But, Skip—what do you think? Tomorrow? Is there anyone . . ." Skip put his hands together in front of his face as if he was praying. He touched his forehead to his fingertips. He didn't say a word. He was thinking. Then he leaned back, opened his hands, and arched his fingers, tip to tip, to make the vault of a church. He looked down through the rafters at me. He considered my plea. "Mike," he said, "why don't you come back tomorrow and we can show you some of the videotapes we use in our training. We have some of encounter groups; we have some guest lectures." Then he took a sharp breath. "There's *one* in particular." He leaned forward. *"That's* an *amazing* one. It's with Gary Walsh, a doctor, who was one of our support counselors and board members. He died. He made the tape with Jim Geary just before he died. Gary *shared* so much. He died so *beautifully*. I wasn't with him, but Jim was. Jim said, 'Gary's last words . . .'" Skip put both hands on the arms of his chair; he looked straight at me. Then he looked up at the corner of the room behind my head and said, "His last words were, 'I am the Christ. I am the Christ.'" Skip's voice fell to a whisper. He looked back at me; his eyes were wide and fixed on mine. "Can you imagine!?" he said. Then he whispered again, "'I am the Christ!'" "Terrific," I thought. "What is this? A counseling organization for a seminary? Who does he think he is? Who does he think I am? I'm a goddamn Jew. 'I am the Christ!!'"

There was silence in the room. Skip looked at me and slowly shook his head. "Amazing," I said. Skip stood up. I stood up. Skip walked me to the door. We stood there. Then he put his arm around my shoulder, just like one of those teddy bears in the pamphlets. "Mike," he said, gazing into my eyes. He sounded tired. He looked as if he was in pain. "Mike," he said, "always remember that the lives of *millions* and *millions* of people depend on what you write. I'd feel as if I'd *failed* if you *ever* used the word 'victim.' Will you *promise* me not to use it?" "Of course, Skip," I said. We looked into each other's eyes. He took my hand in his, left hand on top of right hand. We shook. It was a touching moment. "See you tomorrow," I said. "Ciao," he said.

"Shit!" I thought. "First he stonewalls me, then he asks me for money, and then he sends me out the door feeling guilty. 'The lives of millions and millions of people!' If that was true, why didn't he help me?" The worst part was that I felt like a white liberal who's just been robbed and then hears himself calling the man who did it a nigger. Skip had behaved like a caricature. He'd given new meaning to the word "smarmy." I'd walked in feeling full of "there but for the grace of God go I." Now I wanted to strangle the son-of-a-bitch. "Hi, Mike! Welcome to the wonderful world of homophobia!" "Who? Me??" "Yes, you." Next?

Next was San Francisco General. I got off the bus in front of a massive red brick annex with limestone, Art Deco capitals, and a vaguely Assyrian bas-relief of some bearded men above its entrance. Inside, on the facing wall of the elevator were signs in English and perhaps Thai or Laotian that instructed all Mong refugees to get off at the fourth floor. I was headed for the fifth. The fifth was a busy place, the place where most people in San Francisco who had the first signs of AIDS came to get the bad news. It was here they were tested and treated as outpatients for as long as they could walk. In another building were the beds where they lay when their lives became a matter of serious doubt. I made my way to Volberding's office and gave my name to the receptionist. She had no idea who I was or what I was doing there. Just then a voice called out from over the partitions, "Michael? I'll be right out." The receptionist shrugged. Volberding appeared, followed by a bearded man with a Nikon around his neck. Volberding grinned and shook my hand. I liked him at once. Tall, boyish. Women would have called him cute. A man without a spot, a wrinkle, or a gray hair, untouched and eager, the perfect man to preside over a plague.

He waved me to follow him and the man with the camera. As he walked, he talked. "Look, I'm sorry; I'm running late. Oh! Excuse me! This is Arny Bolling from *Time*; he's here to take some pictures, but I got hung up on the phone, and now you're here, but come along and we can talk a bit, and then when he's done, we can find a quiet place and talk some more." I drew abreast of Bolling and we shook, just as Volberding excused himself "for one minute," and left us standing in front of the elevators as the doors opened to reveal a Mong grandmother. Bolling said something to her in French; she nodded and bowed as the doors closed; Bolling said he'd spent some time in Vientiane. "What are you doing here?" I asked. He shrugged. "They want pictures of AIDS. The scene's changing: the bathhouses are closing; now there's safe sex and the antibodies test. They want pictures; I'll give them pictures: Volberding with a patient; 'the compassionate physician,' that sort of thing." Volberding reappeared. "Okay!" he said. He grinned and waved us into the elevator like an eager first lieutenant. When it stopped, we swept out, past a neonatal clinic, down a hall, around some hairpin turns, out into the sunshine, across a street, up some steps, down a corridor, into a new elevator, out into a ward.

Volberding waved us close, dug his hands into the pockets of his lab coat, stared down at his shoes, and began the briefing. "This is 5B; this is the AIDS ward. The man we're going to see is in the last stages of Kaposi's sarcoma. We discharged him so he could be at home. He was under the care of his aunt. He was doing fine. The pain was under control; he was comfortable; it was all we could expect. We just readmitted him for a drug overdose. It's a little touchy. He and his aunt are very close. He's had a history of drug abuse. The morphine may have been too much of a temptation. He may have talked her into something, but we don't know; she's a little wound up. So. He's back; his brother's here from St. Louis, and his aunt's here, and . . ." Bolling interrupted, "It sounds pretty touchy. I don't know if they'll let me take any pictures or even sign a release. If we all go in, it might spook them." He looked at me. "Would you mind waiting in the hall until I'm done?" "Are you kidding??" I said. "Of course not. You've got a deadline; I don't. Go on; I'll wait. Good luck."

I stood in the hall and they went in. They left the door open and I heard Volberding say hello and ask how the man was doing. Just as he began to introduce Bolling, a heavily perfumed, middle-aged woman wearing a blond wig, designer jeans, cowboy boots, and a strawberry-colored satin blouse embroidered with bucking broncos over each breast rounded the corner, carrying a bouquet of red roses in a spray of baby's breath. She walked straight into the room and let out a little shriek. She must have been the man's aunt. "What?! What are you? Who are you?? What's going on?!" she said. Then she fainted at Bolling's feet.

That's when they closed the door in my face and left me staring at the Day-Glo pink placard pinned to it that listed the twelve rules all staff had to observe when treating a patient with AIDS. I'd reached number 6 when I heard laughter and apologies and explanations coming from behind the door, followed by Bolling's strobe leaking around the edges. I'd reached number 12 and was headed back to number 1 when I felt someone standing behind me. I turned and saw a little man dressed in a brown tweed suit standing on his tiptoes, looking over my shoulder. "Hello?" I said. He came down from his toes but kept reading the placard. He didn't say anything. His hair was combed and plastered to his skull with sweat; his skin had the color and texture of a navel orange; he had a thin mustache like a French waiter in an old movie. "Who are you?" I asked. He answered with a question, just like Skipper. "Who's in there?" he asked. "What do you mean?" I said. "I *said*," he said, "who's in there? Who's in there?" He sounded exasperated; I hesitated; he grew impatient. I'd made one mistake already that day. I tried to remember the right words. I decided to be cautious; I began rhetorically. "Who's in there?" I said. "There's a man in there," I said. "A human being," I said. I tried to keep it general. "He's sick. He's got AIDS. He's a patient with AIDS." I knew I hadn't said it right but the little man didn't care. He noticed the light from Bolling's strobe. He looked at me as if he couldn't decide whether I was too dumb or too smart for my own good. "How come there's a photographer? Is Burt Reynolds in there?" he asked. "Who??" I asked. He repeated himself. He'd decided I was a fool. "I *said*, 'Is Burt Reynolds in there?'" "Are you kidding??" I said. "What are you talking about? There's a guy with AIDS in there? Who are you??" "I'm a reporter," he said. "I'm with *The National Enquirer*, okay?" "*The National Enquirer*?" My voice rose. "What are you doing here?? Have you checked in with the nurses' station?? What the . . ." He put his hands out and backed away from me. "Take it easy, okay, take it easy. I've been to all the hospitals, okay. I'm a reporter. Don't get excited." He edged backwards down the hallway. Then he turned and disappeared through a set of double doors.

Just then the door to the hospital room opened and a man I'd never seen before stepped out. I introduced myself; he introduced himself: he was the dying man's brother. He said he sold TVs; I said I wrote books. We talked a little about St. Louis as compared to Atlanta. I said I was sorry his brother was so ill. "Yes," he said, "we never knew until . . ." The door opened again and Volberding stepped out. Bolling was still in there, chatting happily with the man and his aunt. The salesman's face lit up. "Dr. Volberding!" he said. "I nearly forgot! I saw you last Sunday on *Face the Nation*." I almost missed it, but my wife called me in and I saw the last ten minutes. You were *great*." Volberding ducked his head. "Thanks," he said. He looked embarrassed. The man went on. "I saw you on Donahue, too. It was a shame the way that other guy took advantage of you. That smartass. Donahue should have shut him up and let you talk." Volberding blushed.

I stopped listening. *Face the Nation*? Donahue? *Time*? *The National Enquirer*? Burt Reynolds?? What the hell was this? This morning it was "I am the Christ." And now? The Plague vs. Falcon Crest? What was I doing here? This morning, they wouldn't talk to me because I wasn't pure enough. This afternoon, it looks as if I might have to go through Volberding's agent. I was wrong, of course, but by the time Bolling had said his goodbyes, thanked Volberding, and headed off in the same direction as the man from the *Enquirer*, I'd decided to try my luck another day. Volberding agreed. It was late; he had to attend a staff meeting to review new drug protocols. I had a dinner engagement with a psychiatrist. "How about lunch tomorrow?" Volberding said. I was due back at Shanti then. "How about lunch the day after?" I asked. "Great," he said. He grinned, gave me a jaunty wave, and walked off like a man with a future.

The psychiatrist I was to meet for dinner had been recommended as one of the brightest young doctors on the staff of Langley Porter, one of the country's finest psychiatric institutes. A graduate of Yale and Stanford, Neil Whitehead had an extensive practice that included all elements of the city's homosexual community. If there was anyone who could give me a sense of how a group of human beings collectively dealt with epidemic death, it was Whitehead. While I waited for him, I looked through the obituaries and classified ads of the *Bay Area Reporter*, the city's major gay weekly. On one page were photographic portraits and life histories of the newly dead; on another were line drawings and beefcake shots of various male models. "Handsome Young Man, Rock Hard Body, Ex-Football Player Who Loves to Ride On Top" followed the photo obituaries of architects, stage managers, and medical illustrators, all of them killed in the prime of their lives by what was sometimes described as "a lengthy illness," sometimes as "pneumonia," and sometimes as AIDS. On the page facing the obituaries was a Hollywood studio portrait of Rock Hudson, illustrating a guest editorial that decried the actor's deathbed refusal to admit his sexual preference. The combination of career summaries that ended with lines like "He lived with style and died with grace," sex ads for "Teddy Bears" and "Ass Masters," and editorials that equated sexual candor with civil rights made me feel as if I'd been hit on the head with a blunt instrument. I was relieved when Whitehead sounded his horn to take me to dinner.

Whitehead leaned over to open the door of what he called his "standard-issue BMW," and we drove across the Golden Gate to Sausalito. He smiled. A scholarly-looking man with glasses. "So," he said, "how do you like it here?" "I don't know what's going on," I said. I told him about Shanti, and the man from *The Enquirer*, and the articles I'd just read in the *Reporter*. I was still talking when we were seated by the maître d' at our table. "Is this crazy or am I missing something?" Whitehead laughed. "It's both," he said. He ordered veal Marsala and scampi for us, then folded his hands under his chin, leaned forward, and began a lecture that would continue with few interruptions through the English trifle he ordered for dessert.

"Seven years ago," he began, "if you opened the papers or the yellow pages, what you found were row after row of ads for sex therapists and sensitivity encounter groups. This was the center for all sorts of self-actualization movements. Now, when you open the papers or the phone book, the sex therapists and sensitivity trainers have been replaced by grief therapists and thanatologists. This place is still the same, but it's changed. It's always been the end of the rainbow, but now, instead of looking at that arch of brilliant light, people have noticed its end plunges into the earth.

"As far as what happened to you at Shanti—it's true you weren't, as you said, 'pure enough,' but look at all that's happened: a group of people who were outcasts left their places of birth, left their pasts behind, and came here to 'be free'; these people founded a politically powerful movement, based in large part on the free expression of sexual appetite. Then, suddenly, these people found themselves in a town where a man could shoot a mayor and a city councilman—men these people had elected to represent them— could shoot them in cold blood and then get off by claiming to have eaten too many Twinkies! After that, almost on cue, an epidemic broke out among them, and the outcasts became pariahs. People started shouting about 'God's wrath' and 'unnatural acts.' Then someone said the word 'quarantine.' Maybe where you come from, 'quarantine' is an innocent word. But here people still re- member what happened to the Japanese. The gay community's natural reaction was to circle the wagons. That's what you walked into. You're from the South, so—pretend it's the sixties and you're a white boy and Stokely Carmichael has just made his speech about Black Power. If you want in, you're going to have to offer more than curiosity and good intentions. You've walked into the middle of a fire storm! People look around and see other people's whole lives going up in flames. Out of a gay population of seventy thousand, maybe half will test antibody positive, and 25 percent of them stand an excellent chance of dying. If there's the slightest inclination toward paranoid suspicion or denial or magical think- ing, the situation amplifies it. My patients talk to me about CIA plots to spread the disease. One of my colleagues claims there's no such thing as an HTLV virus, that the entire epidemic is a form of mass hysteria, the result of collective guilt and depression, a state of mind engendered by being historically outcast, a whole community whose immune systems have finally collapsed due to an overwhelming, cumulative burden of guilt and self-hatred. If ordinary people can believe in government plots, and highly trained professionals can entertain ideas of an entirely psycho- somatic epidemic, then what happened at Shanti shouldn't sur- prise you. This whole city has always teetered on a fault line. The 1906 earthquake let loose a horde of bubonically infected rats from the broken sewers of Chinatown. It's taken eighty years, but that plague has spread to rodents as far east as the banks of the Mississippi. This city has always sat on top of earthquakes and epidemics. But this time! This time the fault line runs right down the middle between Love and Death! Pleasure turned into pain, delight into disease, Eros into Thanatos. What happened to you today is just the beginning. If you're smart, you won't get used to it."

The next morning, I staggered out of bed and presented myself to Skipper. "Ready for those videotapes?" he asked. He smiled brightly. He looked glad to see me. He reminded me of a cruise director recruiting another hand for bridge during a storm. "All set?" he asked. After everything I'd heard and seen the day before, I wasn't sure. "Absolutely, Skip," I said. "Well, then," he said, "let's go up to the chapel. I have it all set up for you." "He has to be kidding," I thought. He wasn't. The building *had* been a convent, and there had been a chapel. Everything but the altar and the confessionals remained. On the ceiling were frescoes: a cross of gold surrounded by a garland of red roses and ivy; a sheaf of wheat draped with a blue ribbon; an anchor graced with an olive branch, floating on a cloud; a white swan feeding her babes, floating on another. Every ten feet along the wall, just beneath the ceiling, carved plaster angels knelt in prayer, each behind a shield emblazoned with a cross. Lilies, white and yellow roses, and morning glories wound around the room, just above their heads. On the ceiling in the alcove where the altar must have been floated the radiant white dove of the Holy Ghost. The room itself must have been eighty feet long and thirty feet wide, its ceiling twenty feet above our heads. It was empty except for a video monitor on a stand, circled with garlands of bright red foil-wrapped prophylactics. "Here we are!" said Skip. "Here are the tapes; here's how to load them; get yourself a chair, and just yell if you need anything."

I sat down and looked around. "Laudate Domino," it said at one end of the room. "Trojans and morning glories?" I thought. "Okay. Let's see what we got." There was an "Introduction to Grief," something called "Fishbowl Roleplays," and something else called "How to Avoid Burnout," and as promised, the Gary Walsh tape. I decided to save Walsh for last. The burnout tape sounded like a perfect way to begin. For the next few hours, I sat through a series of candid lectures and heartrending improvisations. In the lectures, a psychologist told of what he'd learned from sitting by the deathbeds of three hundred people. "To be with someone who's

dying," he declared, "is to be with someone at the most emotion-
ally powerful point in their life cycle . . . It is, to witness it, a
transpersonal experience . . . There is no such thing, though," he
continued, "as full-grief resolution for someone who stays in
hospice work for any length of time . . . They experience mini-
griefs," he explained. "Not one significant one with an eventual
resolution over time, but repeated griefs, one following the other,
some more meaningful and felt than others, but all in a succession,
week after week." The long-term effect of such "little deaths"
could be damaging. "To be a helper is an empowering mission," he
said, but "if you suddenly gain sixty pounds, stop talking to your
wife and kids, and start avoiding your friends, it might be time to
find another line of work." I nodded. "A sensible man," I thought.
I played him again, took notes, and went on to the "Fishbowl
Roleplays." They were called "fishbowl," I discovered, because
volunteers, two at a time, took turns being a patient or a counselor
while an audience of other volunteers looked on. One woman
stuck a tube in her mouth and pretended to be dying while on a
respirator; one man pretended to be a dead man's lover, suffering
from survivor guilt; another man pretended to be a newly diagnosed AIDS patient, angry, alone, and afraid in a strange city,
without friends. The effect of these rehearsals, played through
twice, was like sitting through a crazed adaptation of the *Oresteia*,
inspired by *Uncle Tom's Cabin*. I kept looking up at the angels
along the wall. I was confused. I'd never learned how to laugh and
cry at the same time. "One thing for sure," I thought. "Whitehead
was right: this town's doing its best to learn as much about death
as it knows about sex." I stood up and walked around the room,
did a couple of deep knee bends, took a good look at the white
dove in the alcove, and loaded Gary Walsh into the machine.

Walsh looked like a concentration-camp inmate who'd just gotten a good haircut. He sat in a chair, dressed in a black T-shirt
with the Shanti eclipse logo on it, his arms as thin as the limbs of a
sapling. Next to him sat Jim Geary, a long-haired, heavyset man
with acne scars at his temples, dressed in a kind of scooped, V-
necked shirt decorated with concentric sunbursts of colored gem
shapes—the kind of shirt that had last been seen at Be-Ins during
the city's Summer of Love. The two men sat facing each other in
one of the corners of the chapel, close to where I sat watching

them. As the interview began, Geary reached across and took Walsh's hand and held it. Geary spoke very briefly, only at first, to summarize the circumstances: Walsh's doctors had given up all hope; he was thirty-nine years old, a psychologist; he was dying of AIDS; he wanted to say some things that might help others. For the rest of the interview, Geary let Walsh talk, holding his hand and keeping in touch with little "uh-huh"s that purred out of him like the voice of a mother comforting a child. Walsh began with his own summary. His voice was clear, but with a slight tremolo. He'd been in practice for fifteen years, he said, always working for someone else; a month after he'd finally opened his own office, he was diagnosed; he closed his practice within a week and began to look for a cure. He smiled at the ironies and escapades that had followed. His eyes twinkled. First he went to Mexico for amino acids; then he tried megavitamins; then he went on chemotherapy. He'd had Kaposi's sarcoma and pneumocystis carinii. Now he was dying. His doctors gave him two months. He could feel the changes in him already. He felt many things: he was relieved because his fight was over; he was overjoyed because he knew his soul would leave his body and be more peaceful than it had ever been before. As he spoke, his voice filled with tears: he was sad, he said, so sad that his death would hurt the people he loved. He was so sad they were afraid. Their grief hurt him the most. The worst thing was saying goodbye. He almost wished they could go with him. He sobbed. I swallowed hard. He took a quivering breath and resumed. When he'd first been diagnosed, he'd been terribly afraid, he said. Now, though, he was at peace. Now he knew that when he died, he'd "just stop living on *this* planet, not just *stop* living." Geary interrupted. "How do you know?" he asked. "Two of my friends told me. They appeared when I was wide awake," he said. One was an older woman who'd died four months before. She'd stood across from him, her arms outstretched, dressed in a long white robe. Walsh's eyes gleamed. He looked at Geary and gave him a brilliant smile. "She just stood there and gave me such a *spectacular* smile. She said, 'Don't worry, honey, I'll help you over the line.'" Then he'd seen a writer he'd known who'd died of leukemia. "'There's a passageway,' the man said. 'You have to go through it. I'll help you. Don't worry.'" Three days later, Walsh called him back. "Now what?" the man asked. "I'm scared," Walsh said. His friend got upset. *"Don't worry,"* he said. "I told you not to worry. I'll help you. Now leave me alone. I've got to go back to work. I've got writing to do." Walsh laughed and shook his head and smiled. He took a breath like a winded runner. "So it's nothing?" Geary asked. "Nothing at all? Just leaving the planet?" Walsh looked up at the ceiling. Up at the swan or the anchor or the cross. He looked back at Geary. His eyes glistened. He smiled happily. "I'd stake my life on it," he said.

I shut off the machine. I didn't feel like laughing anymore. Ghosts—he'd seen ghosts. I reran the tape. He'd called them visualizations, wide-awake visualizations. A woman and a man standing there; she'd looked terrific; he'd been busy. There was life after life. First you died and left the planet, then you went on a working vacation. I kept thinking about the ghosts, though. He'd seen them with his eyes open. There must be a lot of them in this town. I went downstairs and thanked Skip for everything. "If there's *anything* else I can do," he said. "No, Skip, thanks. You've been great. Stay well." He shook my hand and I left. And now what? Volberding and I were supposed to have lunch the next day. There was still time to see someone else, but the question was who. I had a few more names. One was a senior fellow in oncology at one of the city's largest private hospitals. He'd told me he had some things to say, some "astounding things," but only if I didn't identify him. I'd said "Maybe" to that. After what Whitehead had said about everything being a bit crazy, and after hearing Walsh talk about ghosts, I'd changed my mind. If the man wanted to astound me, I'd listen. I called him up, and he invited me to his office.

"You won't identify me, correct?" he said. I agreed. He settled back into his chair. "I want to tell you some stories," he said. "Fine," I said. "I love stories." "Stories about AIDS," he said. "That's why I'm here," I said. "A lot of my friends are patients, and a lot of my patients are friends," he began. "First—this is about a woman I knew, a friend of mine; she died of cancer. I wasn't her primary physician, but I was always available. Her doctor told her there was no hope. She and her boyfriend began to save her pills. She didn't want to die inch by inch; she wanted to go out as soon as she could. She asked me for help. I said, 'I can't do that. But if you need something at the last minute, all you have to do is ask.' A month later, they decided to do it on a Friday night. They told me. I said, 'Okay. I've got my beeper. If you need anything, let me know.' Three o'clock in the morning, I get a frantic call from her boyfriend. 'It's not working!! Come quick.' When I arrived, I found her in bed, laughing and singing, stoned out of her mind, the life of the party. She'd swallowed all the pills, but all they'd done was made her high. She was cracking jokes, telling stories. I asked them, 'What do you want me to do?' She shook her finger at me. 'Come on, you *promised.*' I looked at her boyfriend. He looked worse than she did. I had something with me. I ground it up, mixed it with some honey, and gave it to her." "What was it?" I asked. "Morphine. She took it and her boyfriend and I sat down by the bed. She got funnier and funnier. Then, in the middle of some song or something, she started coughing. She coughed and she vomited; she aspirated it and inhaled it, and that's how she died." "On her own vomit?" I asked. He nodded. "You and her boyfriend watched?" "Yes," he said. I let out a breath. "What's this got to do with AIDS?" I asked. "It's what happened afterwards," he said. "I saw her again. She was the first." I shivered. "You did what?" "Not exactly 'saw' her," he said. "Let me go on." I took a breath. Gary Walsh in the morning and this guy in the afternoon. "I'm sorry," I said. "Go ahead."

"She wanted to be cremated," he said. "She wanted her boyfriend and me to rent a balloon and scatter her ashes over this one particular vineyard. So we did. Most balloon ascents occur here just before dawn, to avoid the wind shifts and currents that come with the sun. Very early in the morning, we were in the air over the vineyard. The sun was just coming up; the balloon operator asked us if we wanted to stay low or go higher. We said go higher. We went up and up, and just as the sun rose, we scattered her ashes. But, instead of blowing away, they formed a vortex and the sun shone through them. That's when I felt her." "What was it like?" "Like a wind," he said. "Except it blew in me and through me and I could feel *her.* It was physical but it wasn't, and she was there. The sun shone through the ashes and she was there." I shivered. This man was a senior fellow in oncology. He'd had his passport stamped; he had all the right credentials. And what he tells me is a story that begins with euthanasia and ends with a spirit?

"That's a remarkable story," I said. "But . . ." "What happened next is a little crazier," he said. I was glad he used that word. "I had a patient who was a naval engineer. Very famous. Very, very famous. He was diagnosed as having AIDS. He was very sick. I treated him. I kept him alive. Then his lover was diagnosed. I treated him. They were both my patients. We became friends. They owned several houses and moved between them. The house they owned in the city was a mansion. An antiques dealer rented one wing of it. One day, he got in the bathtub and blew his brains out. When it was over, they said to me, 'How'd you like to move in? We need someone to occupy it. His furniture's still there. If you want to, go ahead.' I was a little uneasy, but it was a magnificent place. I moved in. Things started happening then. First, the downstairs tenant left on a trip to Chicago. He was going to meet an old friend and they were going to drive back across the country. Somewhere in Iowa, they got hit head-on, and his friend was turned into a vegetable. Then the next-door neighbor went into the hospital. He was a severe alcoholic. He suffered from delirium tremens. Somehow or other, he was overmedicated and he died. Then the engineer's lover got pneumocystis and he died. Then the engineer got very, very sick. I told him there wasn't much I could do. He was from Charleston. He wanted to go home to die. He asked me to make arrangements to transfer him to a clinic there. He knew the doctor. He checked in; they put him on a morphine drip and he was dead in two days." "What's a morphine drip?" I said. "It's an intravenous solution of morphine sulfate. You slowly increase the flow rate. Very slowly. The patient goes into a deeper and deeper sleep, until finally he just—forgets to breathe. It happens all the time. It's not something that people talk about. It takes the cooperation of not just the doctor and the patient, but the nursing staff. It's common. Much more common than you'd think. It's been part of oncology for years, and now it's part of AIDS." "Ah, my," I said, "I didn't know." "But that's not the end of the story," he said. "Before he died, the engineer offered to leave me the house and everything in it. I was very tempted, but too much had happened there. Five deaths in one place is a bit much, don't you think?" I nodded. "Then this peculiar thing happened again: I was in the supermarket shopping, not thinking about anything. I was in the snack-food section and I felt that wind again. Passed right through me. Like a wave. Only this time it felt like the engineer. It was as if he were there. I couldn't understand it. But then I remembered: he'd *loved* pretzels. Just like some people love jelly beans and some people love almonds. He always had this big bowl of pretzels he'd offer you when you walked in." The doctor looked at me expectantly. Who did he think I was? A casting agent for *Ripley's Believe It or Not*? The first ghost had been over a vineyard; the second in the snack foods. Where would the third one be? By the cheese? "Doctor," I said, "I've never heard anything like this before." He smiled; he took it as a compliment. "Those are remarkable stories. I'll have to think about them." "You won't identify me?" he asked. "Certainly not," I said. I thanked him; he thanked me, and I left.

Four ghost stories in one day. It was early evening. What I needed was a quiet night without apparitions. What I got was a sandwich followed by a few hours with the notebook from Shanti. Somewhere between a chapter on Denial and an essay on Pain Control, I fell asleep with my clothes on. I woke just after sunrise. I thought about leaving the city. I could call Volberding's office from the airport. If his secretary asked for an explanation, I could offer the Book of Genesis, the story of Sodom and Gomorrah. Whitehead had been right: a plague ran down the city like a fault line. AIDS produced all the ill effects of an archaic disease: helplessness, premature death, and superstition. Volberding served at the center of it. I'd liked him at first sight, but what if he had his own set of celebrity ghost stories and famous morphine drips? When the time came, though, I took the bus to his office.

"I have only one meeting today," he said, "and, if you like, you can come along. A law firm's just learned one of its clerical employees has AIDS. They want to know what to do. They've asked me to brief their senior staff. We get these requests all the time. If you want to come, it'll be fine." "Sure," I said, "thanks." He stood up, turned his back, then faced me. "I need to tell you something," he said. "Sweet Jesus," I thought. "What's it going to be? A personal message from Rock Hudson?" "What is it?" I said. He looked very serious. "I smoke," he said. "One cigarette three times a day. It's a habit, but . . . Do you smoke?" "Only when I work," I said. "Do you want to?" he asked. "Sure, if I can bum one." He smiled. He took a pack of Marlboros out of his desk. "You have any matches?" he asked. "Yeah." He handed me a cigarette and he slipped his into his pocket. "Okay. Let's go." I followed him down the hall. He opened the door to the stairwell. "Up here," he said. We walked up to a landing. There were two old school desks surrounded by cigarette butts, next to a small open window. "The smokers' lounge," he smiled. "Smoking in the boys' room," I said. We lit up.

"What do you want to know?" he said. "I want to know why you do what you do. No one's forcing you. I want to know what you know about death. Ninety-eight percent of the population would turn and run. You stay. Why? What do you know that the rest of us don't?" "I'll tell you one thing I know," he said. "I know I'm going to die. You don't have to be a philosopher king to know that. You can't see as many deaths as I've seen and still think it won't happen to you. The average age of the men in the ward is thirty-five. I'm thirty-five. I'm not going to die of AIDS; I know that; that won't kill me. But something else will. It's been four years since I thought I was immortal." "What happened then?" I asked. "That's when I began to practice oncology. That's also when I became the director of the clinic. All that was about two weeks before my son was born. The *birth* of my first child more or less coincided with the first AIDS death we saw here. That was four years ago, when no one knew; no one knew what caused the disease; no one knew how contagious it was; no one knew its incubation period, or the range of opportunistic infections associated with it. No one knew anything. I'd go home at night and think I was a dead man. I'd go home and think, 'You're a carrier. You're going to kill your wife and you're going to kill your son.' My wife and I had dreams about that, night after night. And the phone calls! Everyone who was treating the disease, all over the country, we used to call each other, day or night: 'Do you have a rash? I have a rash. Do you have a sore throat? What do you have?' Clinicians calling each other to compare their own symptoms. Was it the beginning of the flu or the beginning of the end? No one knew, so we consoled each other: 'It's just the flu; it's nothing; take it easy.' Now we know. Now, once a month, the entire staff is tested for AIDS antibodies. Four years after we started, we're all okay. But four years ago we were walking in the dark."

"My God," I thought. "This one sounds like a human being. He's telling me he thought he was a dead man and he hasn't even said PWA yet." I didn't understand why he hadn't made some excuse and left. Something like, "I'm an oncologist and this looks like an infectious disease. That's not my specialty. If you'll excuse me, I think I hear the sounds of private practice." He could have said that, but he didn't. I wanted to know why, but I didn't want to rush him. After two days of magic tricks, I'd met someone who didn't claim to hear voices. I decided to ask him how he got started. That made him stand up, grind out his cigarette, and suggest lunch. Three hours later, he was still talking and I was still listening. Sometimes he'd describe something so clearly—a state of mind or a motive—that I'd get excited and we'd volley back and forth like players at a net. We talked through lunch and then took a break while he briefed the lawyers. After he reassured them (in so many words) that they had little to fear unless they drank coffee from a machine with which their employee had just had sexual congress, we resumed our conversation. Part of it happened inside his car; part of it happened out on the sidewalk. I remember the down ramp of a parking garage, the sight of a gigantic radio pylon on a peak, and an avenue of buildings faced with marble and limestone. I remember so little of the settings because the conversation filled the space where we spoke.

His father, he said, was a dairy farmer who couldn't afford his own herd. Whether he worked for someone else or leased their animals, I didn't understand. The fact was the man lived a life controlled by the eating, sleeping, and milking habits of a herd of cows. He made so little money at it that, eventually, he became a baker. The family lived on the edge of town, sent their children to Lutheran schools, and got by. Volberding looked in toward the center of things like a poor kid pressing his nose against a store window. What he stared at were the towers of the Mayo Clinic that rose above the town of Rochester, Minnesota. It was a company town, where doctors, not businessmen, were the rich, the wellborn, and the able. They were the gentry, and the men out in the fields were the clods, no matter how many herds they owned. Since Volberding's dad didn't own any, the family came close to being invisible.

I don't know exactly how many brothers and sisters Volberding had; he said he was a middle child. The important thing, though, was that two years after he was born, his mother gave birth to a baby boy with Down's syndrome. The doctors advised her to give up the baby. The child was an idiot, they said. His condition was chronic; he might live, he might not, things would only get worse; the best thing to do, for everyone concerned, was to put him in a state institution. Volberding's mother said no. The doctors explained: the baby was brain-damaged; if she brought him home and something happened, she wouldn't be able to help him; if she brought him home, his needs would rob her of her strength, and rob her healthy, normal children of the love and care they deserved. It was best for everyone if she gave up her baby. Volberding's mother refused. "He's my son," she said. "We understand," the doctors said. "That's a natural reaction. We know how you feel, but you'll get over it. You'll have other children. Many women find it difficult to adjust to the loss, but . . ." Volberding's mother wouldn't listen. "He's my son. I'm going to take him home and we're going to raise him." Of course, they let her. They knew she was wrong. Soon enough, they thought, they'd get a call. The delay would only make the final decision more difficult to bear. She never made it, though. She raised that boy, and he grew and grew and he didn't die, and it didn't hurt her and it didn't destroy her family. In fact, said Volberding, it changed her. She changed from being the wife of a failed dairy farmer into a woman with a mission. She proved those doctors wrong. Her son didn't die, curled up in some back ward of a state hospital. He lived; the family loved him, and she joined a group of people who'd not only refused to listen to their doctors but had finally convinced them to change their policies.

Volberding loved his brother, but sometimes he was ashamed of him. When he was fifteen, he didn't want to be the kid with the idiot brother. He wanted to be as good as everyone else. For a kid like him, from a family like his, that meant trying to be even better. His parents said, "Paul, do good, be great, we love you." His high school guidance counselor said, "Are you kidding? You'll never get into those schools. Harvard? Stanford? The University of Chicago? Be realistic: the best you can do is four years at a state school and then back home. Get yourself a decent education and then come back and settle down. If you're lucky, you might even get yourself a steady job." Volberding didn't listen, any more than his mother had. He applied to the University of Chicago and was admitted. He'd never been anywhere but Minneapolis. When the time came, he packed up his things and moved to the big city.

He studied biology for four years and then applied to the University of Minnesota for medical school. After that, he went to Salt Lake for his internship and residency. That's where he decided to be an oncologist. "Why there? What happened?" I asked. "I saw a man there," he said. "He was a faith healer. He was dying of cancer." Volberding named the cancer, cancer of the pancreas or thyroid, a very deadly cancer, swift and intractable. "Until then," he said, "I couldn't decide between oncology or psychiatry. The man decided me." "Wait a second," I said. "Psychiatry and oncology? That's like saying physics and metaphysics. What does one have to do with the other? Isn't that a bizarre set of alternatives?" "They're not," said Volberding. "Many people I know, oncologists my age, considered them." I couldn't understand that, but I wanted to know about the faith healer. "The man knew he was dying," said Volberding. "He accepted it; his wife didn't. He remained steadfast in his beliefs; his wife panicked. She brought in one faith healer after the other to pray over him: laying on of hands, anointing, 'In Jesus's name we pray,' kneeling by the bed. The man knew he was past help, but he couldn't tell his wife. He didn't want to question her faith, didn't want to upset her more than she was. So he kept quiet, and the faith healers paraded in and out, and his wife did everything she could to deny his death. She thought she was preventing it, but it wasn't prevention, it was denial. She trapped him: he couldn't talk to her, he couldn't say goodbye, couldn't die in peace, lived out his last days in a lie. That's when I decided, 'If I can prevent that from happening again, I will.' Medically, there was nothing I could do for that man. I couldn't have cured him. All I knew was a way to comfort him." I understood then about the psychiatry.

All that may have been said before lunch. Some of it may have been said while we ate; some of it while we stood outside, before Volberding briefed the lawyers. I remember, though, that when we began again, I asked him, "What have you learned? You've seen a lot of people die. What have you learned?" He didn't say anything at first. He may have been edging his way into traffic. "What I've learned?" he said. "I've learned that what we were taught to say and do with a patient who's terminal is nonsense. We were taught to sit down with the patient and explain exactly what was wrong with him, what the course of treatment would be, what the side effects would be, what he could expect. We were taught to spell it out: the whole truth and nothing but the truth. Based on the assumption that the patient was a responsible member of the middle class who wanted to understand and participate in his course of treatment, who wanted to know because he was accustomed to being well-informed and in control. That's standard medical practice, and standard medical practice, in this case, doesn't have much to do with dying people. Dying people want to know the truth, but only at certain times, in certain ways. I tell the truth, but only as much of it as they let me know they want to know. People have many ways to tell you, without saying it, when and how they want things explained. The art is to sense what part of the truth the patient wants to hear, and to give him that—no more, no less, at the right time, in the right way. Answer him, not tell him. That's the art. Otherwise, a doctor's like a policeman reading a man his rights."

"What else?" I asked. "Do you want to know how people die?" he said. I nodded. "Most people don't die very well," he said. "What's 'well'?" I asked. " 'Well' is reconciled," he said. "Most people don't accept their fate. Some are very bitter: they behave as if they've been cheated. They go over the edge kicking and screaming, grabbing at anything." The worst, he said, is when they die unreconciled and alone, when they don't have anyone they love or even know. "Very few people die peacefully," he said. "How do you define a 'peaceful' death?" I asked. "A peaceful death is when a man *lives* out his time, from one moment to the next, because he actually knows who he is, where he's been, and where he's going. That doesn't happen very often." "How often?" I asked. "I've seen it once or twice," he said, "but that doesn't matter. No one's keeping score. What matters is helping people get there." "Have you ever seen anyone just give up?" I asked. "Once or twice," he said. "It's as rare as dying peacefully." Nearly everyone, he said, hangs on until the last minute. No matter how painful or bloody or dirty or swollen or ravaged they are. They hang on; they set goals; they do what they can to stay alive for as long as they can. They act as if life was precious; they refuse to abandon it.

"What about people who want to be put out of their misery?" I asked.

Until I asked that, Volberding had remained calm and very steady. Until I asked that, he'd spoken to me without flinching, without hesitation, as a man would speak of anything serious and important. Now he looked dismayed. He sounded alarmed. "You mean 'put to sleep'?" he asked. "Yes," I said. "What about euthanasia?" I asked. "It's *very* rare, *very* rare. Once or twice, I've had a patient who's asked to be sedated or asked their friends or family to do something to stop the pain and speed their deaths. But it's *so* rare. Most people *don't* want to die." He hesitated. "This week, two of my patients, one after the other, spoke to me about that. Both very ill, very weak, both in a lot of pain. One of them has to sit upright in a chair when he sleeps, and he can't sleep more than an hour at a time. He can't tolerate any of the analgesics we've been giving him, so he's in constant pain. The other one is terribly debilitated. The other morning, he said, he woke up feeling terrific. He felt so good, he said, he decided to take a shower. The effort of turning on the water and climbing in so exhausted him that, five minutes into it, he barely had enough strength to climb out and crawl back to bed. Neither of these men know each other. They're two very different men. They both said to me, in private, 'Look, we put our pets to sleep when they get sick. We don't like to, but we do. What about us, when our time comes?' They both used the same words. They both talked about their dogs. I was very shaken; I just don't know; I hope, when my time comes, I'll have the courage to ask for that, but I doubt it." "I'm sorry," I said, "I have to ask you something else. I have to ask you about morphine drips." "They're *so* rare," he said. "I've seen that done once or twice, in one or two instances. But—do you know that line from Dylan Thomas: 'Rage, rage against the dying of the light'? That's how it is. Very few people go quietly."

He didn't say anything for a while and neither did I. I began again. "What about you? What do you get out of this?" He smiled. "You saw part of it, the other day." "Do you mean *Time* magazine?" I said. "All that," he said. "The attention, the travel, the prestige. I have an ego. The attention feels good. It's different from what happened to my father. It's not exactly what my high school guidance counselor had in mind." I thought about the little kid on the edge of town, looking in at the towers of the clinic, pressing his nose against the glass. At least he was honest. He'd earned it. "The rewards," he said. "They're not just rewards. They're antidotes; they're escapes; they're ways to balance the pain and the dying. I need them; I use them, the way I use the administrative work of being the director to keep a distance. But the only time I feel I'm working is when I'm with a patient. That's the only real privileged moment. To have the chance to be present, to talk to someone candidly about the meaning of their life or death—that's a privilege. The best is when there are no evasions. Things can get very clear." "But most people don't die very well," I reminded him. "That's true; that's true," he answered. "If you're hysterical when you're healthy, you'll be hysterical when you're dying. You die the way you live. There are very few last-minute transformations. But the process can be very powerful." "The process of dying?" I asked. "Not dying. The process of trying to understand your life. If you choose to. If you can. To understand it and to leave it. The process of making amends, or acknowledging your weaknesses and failures; the process of reconciliation, settling scores, ending feuds, dissipating whatever poisoned the life you lived with the people you knew. A kind of clarity can set in. Clarity, reconciliation, confession, forgiveness. You lighten your load and then you go. If I can help that happen, or at least prevent people from trapping each other in lies, then the dying's easier, and I'm satisfied. I'm more than satisfied. I feel privileged. Being there gives you a vantage point. It's like being up on a cliff: you look one way, you see a valley; you look the other, you see a plain; one side, life; one side, oblivion. In college, we used to call it Edge City. Up there, you think some unusual thoughts."

"Such as?" I asked. "Now's the time for ghost stories," I thought. "You want to know?" he said. "If you don't want to tell me, don't tell me," I said, "but you've been there, I haven't. If you don't tell me, no one's going to know." "All right," he said. "I'll tell you what I think about: I think about energy, life energy. I imagine it's a gigantic pool, a mammoth lake. We're all part of it. Human and inhuman, animate and inanimate, we all live in it. If we leave it in one form, we return to it in another. Water vapor and rain, neither created nor destroyed. Forms change; they live and die; beneath them, the energy remains constant, ongoing, continuous. We rise out of it; we sink back into it; our forms mutate; the life beneath them is immortal." He looked embarrassed. The words he'd used before had been Christian. What he'd just said sounded Asian. I'd almost expected him to speak of *maya*. I still expected him to talk about ghosts. He didn't say anything, though. He still looked embarrassed. I prompted him. "All these deaths, these privileged moments, these thoughts. Have you ever seen anything unusual?" "Like what?" he asked. "Like ghosts," I said. He looked at me as if I was crazy. "Like what??" he said. "Like ghosts," I said. "Are you kidding?" "I'm sorry," I said. "People have been telling me strange stories." "Not in this hospital," he said. "We're not haunted."

The day ended like that. "Come back tomorrow," he said. "People don't talk very much here about their thoughts. I miss that. It can be very mechanical: we add one drug; we take away another. We tinker, but we don't talk. Come back and we'll talk. I enjoyed it." I didn't tell him how happy I was. I was amazed. Maybe I'd met a hero. If not a hero, then at least someone who behaved like a man, someone who persisted, without the help of ghosts and morphine drips. Who did something very dangerous without reference to the Mysteries of the Rosy Cross or the Seven Last Words of Christ, or the Journey of the Spirit After Death. I remembered a story about a Zen master named Bankei. He was challenged to debate a priest who believed that salvation could be had by repeating the name of the Buddha of Love. The priest said to Bankei, "My teacher has miraculous powers: he can stand on a riverbank with a brush in his hand and write the name of Amidah Buddha on a piece of paper on the opposite shore." "Maybe your master can really do that. My miracle is different. My miracle is that when I feel hungry, I eat, and when I feel thirsty, I drink." Bankei's miracle was to be alive. Eat when you're hungry; drink when you're thirsty. Live in the present. No chants, no ghosts, no mysteries. No mysteries except one—the one I'd noticed at the beginning. I still didn't understand why Volberding had persisted. Why had he kept going back in the beginning? He'd told me about the rewards. But the fame had come later. Why had he stayed? He was a well-trained clinician, but the disease had turned him into an overqualified hospice worker. If and when the researchers discovered a cure, Volberding would be one of the first to test it. To see a man live instead of die—that would be his revenge. He could climb down from Edge City then. But why was he there? If he was a hero, what sustained him?

The next day, I asked him. We were sitting in a small room with a couch and an easy chair. "What is this place?" I asked. "It's where we talk to patients and their families," he said. "This is where you do your counseling?" I said. "Sometimes." He reached around and closed the door. "I have to ask you something stupid," I said. "I'm sorry, but I still don't understand some things." "Okay," he said. "What I don't understand is why you kept coming back in the beginning when you thought your life was on the line. I don't understand that. And I don't understand something else: why are you still here? All your patients are dying. There's very little you can do but talk to them. You said yourself: all you do is tinker. This isn't exactly a place full of success stories. And something else: the people who are your patients: they're outcasts; if there wasn't a fear that the disease might spread to the rest of the population, most people would say, 'So what?' Some people might even say, 'Good riddance.' " That last line made his eyes wide and his nostrils flare. "That may be true," he said. "Maybe, in the beginning, when I came here, I could distance myself. I could say, 'That man's gay; that man's queer.' But very soon you stop thinking that way: the man in the bed is a man. What you say, though, is true: the medical establishment still considers AIDS a somewhat 'dirty' disease. The profession finds it distasteful: a sexually transmitted disease, more or less confined to a deviant risk group. But"—his voice rose—"if you went by standard medical practice or commonly held opinion of any kind, I wouldn't be a doctor and my brother probably wouldn't be alive. According to accepted medical opinion, my brother didn't stand a chance. My brother didn't stand a chance; my family didn't stand a chance; my mother was making a terrible mistake; my father was a failure, and none of us would amount to anything. If my mother had believed everything she heard, she would have left my brother propped up in some hospital bed. And if I had believed everything I heard, I'd be lucky if I was a baker or a fertilizer salesman by now."

I felt exhilarated. "That's it, then, that's it!" I said. "That's why you're still here. That's why you came back. You know that, don't you? You couldn't leave these men any more than your mother could have left your brother. You're here because of what she did. The doctors told her to leave him, but she wouldn't. She risked herself and her family and she won. Your brother lived and she was changed for the better. You're here because of her fortitude. And because of your brother. Down's syndrome is chronic, isn't it? He's never going to get better? You lived with him, didn't you? You lived with an outcast. You lived with him and you loved him." "Wait, now," he said. "I lived with my brother. That's true. And I loved him. But sometimes I wished he wasn't my brother. I remember when I was a teenager. One time, at choir practice at Christmas, my brother came up on stage and I had to leave, in front of everyone, and take care of him. That was the *last* thing I ever wanted to do. I loved him, but . . ." "That's the point!" I said. "You experienced it: love, anger, shame, guilt. You climbed down off the stage and you took care of him. He was your brother. I mean, it was Christmas, wasn't it? Wasn't Christ born in a barn? Didn't he die along with two thieves? Wasn't he an outcast? You were raised a Lutheran, weren't you?"

"Okay, okay," he said. "Maybe that's true. I'd never thought of it. Maybe you're right. But I have a question for you." "Okay," I said. I'd forgotten about what had happened with Skip. "What I want to know," said Volberding, "is whether you're really a writer." "How come?" I said. "Because you sound like a psychiatrist." I grinned. He laughed. We stood up and he walked me to the elevator. As we stood there, one of Volberding's assistants walked up. She glanced at me and whispered in his ear. He laughed again. "You want to hear the latest rumor?" he said. The elevator opened and I stepped in. "No, thanks," I said. "Come on," he said. "You'll love it." "No," I said. "I've heard enough." The doors began to close. "It's about Dolly Parton," he said. He was just starting on her and Burt Reynolds when the doors shut.

UNDERTAKERS

I came home in time to celebrate the New Year, but it wasn't January; it was the month of Tishri and it was Rosh Hashanah, the first of the Days of Awe, the time when God and his angels reviewed their records and decided everyone's fate. On Rosh Hashanah, the decrees were written in the Book of Life; on Yom Kippur, the Day of Judgment, the decrees were sealed. In between, for ten days, human beings held their breaths and prayed. I found a dark suit, dressed, and went to the synagogue. "Let us read together," the rabbi said. "The decree is inscribed," we repeated, "who shall live and who shall die; who shall perish by fire and who by water; who by sword and who by beast; who by hunger and who by thirst; who by earthquake and who by plague; who by strangling and who by stoning; who shall have rest and who shall go wandering . . ." On and on, we recited the alternatives, asking forgiveness, promising piety, begging for mercy, until finally, together, we admitted who we were: "Man's origin is dust and he returns to dust . . . like a fragile potsherd, as the grass that withers, as the flower that fades, as a fleeting shadow, as a passing cloud, as the wind that blows, as the floating dust, as a dream that vanishes." "A wanderer?" I thought. "A cloud; like dust, like a dream? That sounds familiar, and I'm tired of it." I walked out of the service, went home, and called the undertakers. There were two of them, both friends of friends, residents of Charleston, and rivals. One was a Russian Jew named Daniel Feld; his grandfather had started a hardware store; now the family owned seven funeral homes. The other was Phillip Lazar, a descendant of French Huguenots; his family had been undertakers for four generations. The House of Lazar buried only the finest of Charleston's dead; Feld's firm buried nearly everyone else. Feld was a rich man with a passion for sailboat racing. Lazar's father had been a painter, a friend of Franz Kline, an associate of Motherwell's; Lazar's aunt was an art patron, and Lazar himself was said to have studied the classics and fancied himself a rhapsode, a reciter of the epics. When I called him and explained my interests, he said he'd be happy to see me. "I even have an epigraph for your book," he said. "What is it?" I said. "It's from the *Odyssey*, Book Nine, line 134. Do you know it?" "I'm not sure I do," I said. He recited it then, in ancient Greek. On the phone, it sounded like a man imitating the love song of a fish. "What does it mean?" I asked. "It's Tiresias prophesying Odysseus's death to him," he said. " 'And death shall come to thee . . . far from the sea, a death so gentle, that shall lay thee low when thou art overcome with sleek old age. . .' " "How nice," I said, "but actually I had something else in mind, a postscript." "And that is?" he asked. "From the *Aeneid*, Book One, I believe. They've just been shipwrecked and blown ashore; Aeneas goes off and kills some deer; he returns and his men cook the meat. As they eat, Aeneas consoles them. '*Haec olim meminesse iuvabit,*' he says. 'In the future, the memory of these things will be sweet.' That's my attitude." "Very good, indeed," said Lazar. "Come and we'll talk." When I called Feld, the response was a bit different but just as cordial. "I have a *terrific* story for you," he said. "A friend of mine just died. He collected African art. We laid him out in the room where he kept his masks. We put him up on a marble table, with two rococo candelabra, one at his head, one at his feet. Then we carried him out and buried him under a live-oak tree in his back yard. It was so dramatic, you would have loved it." "Sounds great," I said, "but why don't you save it until we meet?" "Super," he said. "Come see me."

I drove to Charleston the next day, found an inn, and called Feld. "It's been a crazy day," he said. "We were closing on a new property, but the son-of-a-bitch backed out at the last minute. He said he just didn't want to sell his funeral home to us. Now we're back to square one. What can I tell you? It's a crazy business. Listen: why don't I pick you up tomorrow and we'll go sailing. It'll give me a chance to get away and we can talk." "Fine," I said. I was still getting over San Francisco. A day on the water would help. I changed clothes and took a walk. Charleston was a city of mansions, churches, and graveyards. I watched a busload of English tourists fan out across a cemetery looking for ancestors, and listened while a woman from Boston made outraged noises when a black man told her the price of one of his rice fanners. "Three hundred dollars?" she said. "For a basket?"

The man muttered something and I decided it was time for dinner. "Living well's the best revenge," I thought. "There're no plagues here, just tourists. I'll have a good meal and go to bed early. Then I'll go sailing and listen to stories." I found a restaurant that was playing an aria from *Tosca* when I walked in. The maître d' was a wonderfully bearded man dressed in a Harris tweed coat. He looked very pleased to see me. He led me to a table near a row of French doors that looked out onto a patio. We smiled at each other. Everything seemed fine. He handed me a menu and returned with a thin slab of polished black marble dotted with appetizers. "Compliments of the house," he said. I was delighted. He placed the appetizers before me, bowed, and withdrew his hand. As he did, he brushed against the table's flower vase and upset it. "Don't worry, don't worry," I said. "It's not you; it must have been an earthquake." He stopped, appalled by what I'd said. When he realized I'd made a joke, he tried to change his face to match my tone. The result was a look of slack horror. As he sopped up the water, he said, "It's awful, isn't it?" "What is?" I asked. "That earthquake," he said. I nodded, but I had no idea what he meant.

The next morning, when I turned on the news, I understood: large parts of Mexico City were no longer standing. Thousands had been buried by the collapse; temporary morgues had been set up, but the authorities believed there were people still alive underneath the concrete. There were images of fire, buckled streets, shattered buildings, and open graves. " 'Who shall live and who shall die,' " I thought. " 'Who by fire and who by water; who by earthquake and who by plague.' Goddamn. It's getting closer and closer. You don't even have to go looking for it: you just turn on the tube; it's like an echo, you idiot. You've got an appointment with an undertaker who owns seven funeral homes and's working on an eighth. Why don't you ask him if he's heard the news? Maybe he'll see it as a business opportunity. Why don't you ask him if he has an opinion: can the Mexican funeral industry handle it? Is it ripe for a takeover? What are the investment opportunities south of the border?"

Feld didn't have any opinions about Mexico. "Is that so?" he said. "Haven't heard a thing." He showed up an hour late, wearing white chinos and driving a Mercedes SL. "Hi! Mike?

Danny Feld"—he extended his hand. "Hop in. I've got my gear in back, but—can you believe it?—I forgot my shoes. Do you have shoes? No? Okay. We'll go back to the house and get us some." Feld was a short, muscular man—blond hair, blue eyes, nearly bald, about my age. "Do you sail?" he asked. "Years ago, in Maine," I said. "I won't be much help." "That's all right; it'll be dandy. Here we are." We turned through the gate of a high brick wall, crunched up a peastone drive, and stopped in front of a huge, sleek, modern house, its façade broken by a dozen high, graceful arches that ran its entire length. "Come in and I'll get us some shoes," he said. Inside was all skylights, fountains, and atriums. There was art everywhere. Good art, bad art, prime stuff, also-rans, and would-bes. Except for a Rauschenberg, a few Lichtensteins, and a couple of Warhols, most of the two-dimensional stuff looked like it had been bought at art fairs. The sculpture was considerably better, nothing name-brand, no David Smiths, George Sugarmans, or Anthony Caros, but he had a Rickey knockoff gyrating in a courtyard beside a fountain. He came back carrying two pairs of tennis shoes. "Here we are!" he said. "Try these. How do you like the collection?" "Very nice," I said. "You obviously have a passion." "It's fun," he said. "When I like something, I buy it. Do they fit? Super. Let's go."

We drove to the marina, prepared the boat, motored past the breakwater, and then set sail for Fort Sumter and beyond, to the ocean. It was a clear day; the wind was steady, the harbor empty of sails. Once we were beyond it, Feld asked me to take the rudder; then he went below and came back with a cold bottle of Rhine white and two mugs. He poured us some, took back the helm, and as the boat rose and fell in a light chop, he told me his story. Two hours later, it was clear Feld didn't want to tell me about death. No, no. He wanted to tell me about his father and his own first wife. Mostly about his father, since he never would have married the woman if his old man hadn't insisted. His father, said Feld, confided nothing, controlled everything, and expected obedience. He acted that way when Feld was a boy; he acted that way when Feld was in high school; he acted that way when Feld was in college, and he didn't stop when Feld was his partner. The only thing that changed him was a stroke that left him deaf, dumb, and half paralyzed. When Feld

was a kid, the old man never told him what he did; he never came
home from the office and never let him press the buttons on the
office elevator. When Feld was a man, he never told him about
a loan, a deal, or a contract until it was six months cold. A con-
trolling son-of-a-bitch who never trusted his own flesh and blood.
By the time Feld got to his first wife, we'd finished the wine, and
I wanted to go over the side.

"Danny," I said, "do you mind if I interrupt? It's a terrible
thing that happened between you and your father, but, Danny,
it's a story I've heard before. Blood and money don't mix. A
family business is a time bomb, but it's what a lot of us have to
go through to get to where we are. I understand all that. I
sympathize. But, Danny, what you do is special; it's rare. A lot
of people wouldn't do it, even if the money was good. So—why
do you do it?" Feld didn't say anything for a while. I thought I
might have a chance to swim ashore. "Mike," he said, "no one's
talked to me that way for a long time. Not since college. So,
Mike, I'm going to level with you. I'm going to tell you the truth.
It's not the money. People call me in the middle of the day; they
call me in the middle of the night; they say to me, 'Danny,
something's happened. We need your help.' They say that to me
and, I swear to God, I drop whatever I'm doing and I go. I go.
My second wife, Rose Ann, she jokes, she says I jump into a
phone booth and come out wearing a cape. And it's true! It's
true! I become a Tower of Power. That's what I call it, a Tower
of Power. People *need* me, and I change. I take charge. I become
their doctor, their lawyer, their tax consultant, their psychiatrist,
their insurance broker, their therapist, all in one. I don't do this
for everyone, but for certain people, in their hour of need, the
sky's the limit, you understand?"

"Fine," I thought, "like father, like son." "I understand, Danny,
it's the helping that's important. But what do you do? What do
you do that's so special?" "Okay, okay, I'll give you an example.
A friend of mine, a wonderful person, a philanthropist, very
prominent, she gave a party at her country house. It was a party
for women only. She invited all her friends. She invited her
daughter. A beautiful girl, seventeen years old; wanted to be a
poet. Long blond hair. A beautiful girl. The party's over. It's late.
They've all had a little bit to drink. Everyone goes home. The

girl gets in her MG and ten minutes later she's dead. Went off
the road, into a ditch, and broke her neck. Such a tragedy. The
girl's mother calls me at home at seven o'clock in the morning.
She tells me what happened. I say to her, 'Veronica, don't worry.
I'll take charge.' I send a car to the hospital and we bring the
girl in. I'm waiting for her, along with my director of operations
and my chief embalmer. Except for some bruises, there're no
visible injuries. They go to work. At noon, when they're done,
I call the mother. 'Veronica,' I say, 'I want you to bring Betsy's
favorite clothes, her prettiest underwear, her nicest dress, and
all her cosmetics; I want you to come here with two or three of
your dearest, closest friends, and together we'll get her ready.'
And that's what they did. I had her laid out in a private room.
They came, and they combed her hair, and they put on her
lipstick, and they dressed her. They talked about her; they cried;
they held each other. They mourned her. They grieved. Mike!
You have no idea. Good grieving is so important. It's so important
and it's so hard to find. Then, when they were done, we had the
service. At her school, with all her friends. That was my idea.
Open casket. And, at the end of it, all her friends filed by and
tossed in mementos, little things that reminded them of her:
candles, records, roach clips, books, beer cans, whatever. Then
we closed the coffin and we buried her. Mike! It was so moving!
It was perfect."

Feld waited for me to say something. I don't know what did
it. Maybe it was the wine and the waves. Maybe it was the image
of a beer can being tossed into a coffin. Maybe it was that, plus
the doctor who'd seen the ghost in the snack-food section of his
supermarket, plus the little guy from the *Enquirer* looking for
Burt Reynolds, plus Skipper and the TV monitor surrounded by
prophylactics. Maybe it was all that and everything else I'd seen
and heard since I'd begun to ask people like Feld questions:
Hicks singing me his war song, the dead woman on her bed in
Florida, the bolt slamming into the head of the steer in Omaha.
Whatever it was, I looked back at Feld and I said, "Danny,
that was incredible. It was so creative. It was like the stage set
of an opera. I can just see the kids filing past. Very powerful stuff.
So I want to ask you something." Feld was beaming. "Shoot," he
said. "Danny, it's obvious that you're a man who loves art. And

that you have a certain flair for what you do. How many funerals do you handle a year?" "Twenty-five hundred," he said. "You do Protestant, Catholic, and Jewish?" "All faiths," he said. "And you do top to bottom, rich and poor, right?" "Right," he said. "Danny, I've got this idea for you. It wouldn't work for everyone. Just certain people, people like that woman, Veronica—people who call on you, people you know." "All right. I'm open. Let's hear it." "It might be a little far out, Danny. But it'd be unique. And right in line with how you think." "Okay. Go ahead." "Danny, do you know the work of George Segal, the sculptor?" "Yeah. The guy who does the plaster casts of people, right?" "Right," I said. "Now, Danny, here's the idea. Let's say you have a woman who's a terrific cook, okay? Famous for it, all right? And she dies. So, what do you do? You don't stick her in a box. What you do is stand her up behind a kitchen counter with a Cuisinart and a microwave. People come in, they see her, in death, as in life. You know what I mean?" Feld nodded. "Or some guy, he's a big stockbroker and he dies of a heart attack. So what do you do? You sit him down at a desk with a VDT in front of him hooked up to Dow Jones. You build the whole set. People come in. They see him, he's still in the harness, died with his boots on, you know?" Feld looked at me. "Joseph Hirshhorn, you ever heard of him?" he asked. "Sure," I said. "They named a museum after him in Washington. A famous collector." "Joseph Hirshhorn, when he died," said Danny, "they buried him with three telephones in his casket." "That's terrific," I said. "That's what I mean. Funeral art. The Romans did it, the Egyptians did it, the Chinese did it. Why not?" Feld's eyes narrowed and he didn't say anything for a while. "Let's head in," he said. "That's definitely an idea. Let me think about it. You're a very creative guy, Mike, you know that?" "Thanks, Danny." We sailed back to shore and he dropped me off at my inn. "Enjoyed it," he said, and drove off.

"If Feld plays it right, he could turn into the H & R Block of undertaking," I thought. "He could go on TV, sit at a desk with a Warhol in the background. 'Hello, I'm Daniel Feld, president of Feld Funeral Homes. Call us, day or night; we'll be there. Feld Cares.'" I walked into the same restaurant as the night before. The maître d' looked surprised. This time, there were no appetizers. The next morning, when I turned on the news, they were still burying the dead. Daylight shots of mourners standing in clouds of dust next to open graves; night shots of rescue workers in miners' hats, boots, and bandanas, clawing at piles of broken concrete. "Help is pouring in from all over the world," said the announcer. "The British have dispatched dogs specially trained to sniff out bodies after IRA bombings; the Israelis have sent special pneumatic devices used to lift huge concrete beams following PLO attacks; there are even firefighters and rescue squads from as far away as Florida and Texas lending a hand." "Great," I thought. "Everyone in the world has new inventions to find the dead. Maybe I ought to volunteer. 'I'm self-taught,' I could say, 'but it's in my blood.'" When the news was over, I called Phillip Lazar. "It's quiet now," he said. "Why don't you drop by?"

I drove past his funeral home twice without recognizing it. The House of Lazar appeared to be a gigantic columned residence, painted bone-white, built almost flush with the street, separated from the sidewalk only by a high, black, wrought-iron fence that ran around the perimeter nearly half a block long. The establishment's only identification was displayed on the face of a public clock, set on a cast-iron column, bolted to the sidewalk opposite its portico. "THE HOUSE OF LAZAR," it said in small black letters. Later, when I told Lazar how I'd missed the place, he laughed. "It's very common," he said. "Tourists think we're an inn. Once a month, someone wanders in and inquires about a room." He laughed again. "We're very gentle about it. First we tell them all we have are singles. If they press us, we apologize. 'They're too small and expensive for your needs,' we say. If they insist, we confess they're no better than coffins. That's when they look around and realize where they are." Lazar laughed again.

He was a tall, thin man in his late thirties, dark-eyed, dark-haired, loose-limbed but graceful, who often concluded a point by jerking his head up, back, and to the side, a habit perhaps retained from his youth when his hair had been long enough to fall into his eyes. He led me across the foyer to a corner where a panel hid a door that led to a dull little office he said belonged to his bookkeeper. We sat on green steel office chairs, facing each other across a table littered with invoices. I asked him how the firm had begun. "It was my great-grandfather," he said. "He was in the livery business. He had contracts to supply carriages, horses, and drivers to various funeral homes. One day, he noticed it was a good deal more profitable to carry mourners and the dead to and from the cemetery than to carry the living here and there on their errands. He began the business; my grandfather followed him. My father refused to have anything to do with it. He was determined to be a painter. He moved to New York and studied at the Art Students League. I was born in New York, but when I was ten, we moved to Paris. I went to a school run by a descendant of the Count of Monte Cristo. During the Algerian Civil War, the police came and took him away: he'd kept an arms cache for the OAS in the academy's basement. In the meantime, the business fell into my aunt's lap. She's eighty-five now, an extraordinary woman, a great collector, but—how shall I say?— she saw the merits of the business—but—it was the goose that laid the golden egg: we're not a prolific family; that is, there were never very many of us, so the business kept us quite comfortable. My aunt understood that, but she didn't have a head for figures. She lived on the grounds, in the residence next door" —I looked out the window and saw a huge stucco house with a rose garden behind it—"and turned the firm's management over to one of my grandfather's most trusted employees, who proceeded to embezzle a modest fortune before my aunt noticed anything was amiss. It took perhaps ten years. By then, I was twenty-five. My aunt told me she'd done her duty. Now it was my turn. I was interested in the poetry of Archilochus of Paros, but I came home and cleaned house. Fired nearly everyone. It was a bit messy. At one point my wife, who's a rather good watercolorist, actually had to come in and do some of the makeup." He laughed at that and jerked his head away with a smile. "I went back to school and got an MBA. It's like any other business: you have to know what your accountant's telling you."

"But it's not like any business," I said. "This is the House of Lazar. Four generations, a tradition." "It's a tradition; that's true," he said. "We serve the same families; perhaps every ten years, they call on us again. We serve them. We're expediters." "But what do you expedite?" I said. "You're not freight handlers, after all." "I concede the point," he said, nodding at me with a smile. "What we're responsible for, beyond the physical facts of simple removal, preparation, and deposition, is orchestrating the ritual of grief, the process of mourning, the rite of passage that begins at the moment of death. We help people understand that the person who was living is now a person who is dead. My motto is 'See, Touch, Feel, and Believe.' You *see* the dead; you *touch* the dead. The evidence of your senses impels you to *feel* grief. Grief, anger, sorrow, loss. Those *feelings*, provoked by the senses, lead you to the *belief* that what was is no longer. Without that belief, no one can resume their own life. The resumption of life is the goal of all mourning. Personally, I prefer Italian funerals. Weeping, screaming, women throwing themselves about, men kissing the lips and hands of the dead, people trying to jump into the grave, embracing the coffin, having to be restrained and carried away in a swoon. Then everyone returns home; they eat; they drink; they weep; they feast on food, they drink their tears; they acknowledge the death and then—they resume their lives." "This happens in Charleston?" I asked. He smiled again. "Not quite," he said. "Not at all. It's very understated, very understated, simple, decorous. The more money, the simpler. At times, in fact, pine coffins. There's even a tendency to cremation."

"What do you think of that?" I asked. He frowned. "It's a service we can provide, but I'm not in favor of it. The body should be present. The senses should be provoked. I think cremation is an extreme, as much an avoidance as hermetically sealed caskets. But, if the client wants it, we can provide it. Our business is stable; we conduct three hundred to four hundred funerals a year; we furnish price lists on request. We've been here a long time; we intend to be here in the future."

"Price lists?" I said. "Do you happen to have one?" He handed me one, a four-page, stapled Xerox that itemized and described costs for everything from "Minimum Professional Services" ($550) to "Funeral Merchandise" (caskets from $275 to $14,000), "Immediate Burials" ($625, "without any attendant rites or ceremonies"), "Direct cremations" ($625), and embalming ($230, "except in certain special cases, not required by law"). A Traditional Family Package, everything included, plus three limousines, ranged from $2,400 to $15,000. "As you can see," he said, "we believe that a well-informed client is a more satisfied client."

"Of course," I said. "But I must ask you something." "Please," he said.

"You're a man about my age," I said, "and I understand, even sympathize with your philosophy of emotional candor: repression is bad; expression is good. But isn't that as much a convention as Victorian prudery? The nineteenth century referred to a woman's 'limbs'; now we talk of her legs. Our grandfathers believed in discretion; we believe in spontaneity. Isn't this business of 'see, touch, feel, and believe' as much a social convention, a formula for behavior like jogging after work and a high-fiber, low-protein diet? The Victorians defined 'health' and 'sanity' one way; we define it another. Isn't it just one kind of 'good manners' replacing another, when, in fact, in spite of your well-intentioned prescription, death is still frightening, and grief is an emotion that can no more be anticipated or controlled than love or rage?"

"Well said," he replied, "and well taken. But when my father died, I learned my motto wasn't a cliché." "May I ask what happened?" I said. "Five years ago, my father was diagnosed as having cancer of the bowel. His prognosis was poor, but he held on. When his time came, I took him out of the hospital and drove him up to Provincetown, where he'd spent his summers, painting. I rented a cottage, found a nurse, and I and my mother and my wife and our children settled down to help him die. It lasted five days. It was very hard; it was very painful. But we were together, all of us. Everything I'd learned by doing what I do now, everything I'd learned about death and grief and mourning—I used it all. You might say I cashed in my chips. We helped him die and we helped each other live through it. It's still not over. I still feel his absence; my mother still feels the loss. I thought, when the time came, I'd be better prepared than I was, less affected by the sight of his body, less wrenched by it. I thought I'd become, not calloused, but—how shall I say it?—inured. Do you know that story about General de Gaulle?" he asked. "De Gaulle? No, I don't," I said. "At school," he said, "we were told that every morning, at breakfast, the general ate a bit of arsenic to enable him to withstand an attempt on his life. To survive poison, he experienced it. A little death every morning to live through the big one. I thought I was the same way. 'A body is a body; I've seen so many,' I thought. But the body of my father was my father's body. I was devastated. Then, like everyone else, I went on living." He looked up at the wall clock, clapped his hands, and stood up. "I hope I've answered your questions," he said. "More than I asked," I said. "Thank you." "Why don't you come back tomorrow," he said. "I want you to meet our chief embalmer. And"—he looked out the window toward his aunt's house—"I'll ask my aunt if she'll see you. She has an excellent collection; some of my father's canvases, some Klines, some Tony Smiths, quite a few others. I'll ask." "Thank you again," I said. "See you tomorrow."

I walked down the steps and turned down the street, not thinking where I was going. My car was parked nearby; the inn was some distance away; it didn't matter: I looked at the ground and kept walking. I walked until I noticed I was standing in a park, in a corridor formed by an avenue of live oaks hung with Spanish moss. Here and there were howitzers and mortars that hadn't been fired since the Civil War; nearby was a low stone wall, and beyond it was the sea. "Me and General de Gaulle," I thought. "I never would have guessed. That's why I've been wandering around, walking into pits and killing fields, asking people questions: I thought it was going to protect me from my father's death. Lazar's right: you can look at as many dead men as you like and listen to as many sad stories as you can bear, but they're always other people's stories and other people's bodies. Maybe, when your turn comes, you'll have some chips in your pocket. But it won't matter. When your father dies, the sky'll fall, and when you die, the universe'll end. Until then, you're nothing but a goddamn tourist."

I turned around and headed back for my car. By the time I returned to my inn, the evening news was on. The announcer said it had become a race against time. Rescuers were convinced there were people still alive in the rubble in Mexico City. Efforts had been shifted to the ruins of the General Hospital, where crews with special listening devices had heard faint cries. Arguments had broken out between French specialists and Mexican teams over the best methods to use. Crews were working through the night, hope against hope, fighting to reach those who were trapped. "My God," I thought, "buried alive in a hospital. One more day. One more day and I'll be out of here and done with this shit. No more bodies, no more graves. It's almost Yom Kippur. I'll go home, go to services, and ask to be forgiven. I definitely need to be forgiven. Otherwise, why am I doing this?" I closed my eyes and took a nap.

I woke up the next morning and called my parents. My mother answered the phone. "How are things?" I asked. "I don't want to call your father yet," she said. "He gets very emotional. I want to talk to you first." "What is it?" I asked. "I went to the eye doctor this week," she said. "I've never had a problem with my eyes. You know that. I went because your father's been pestering me. I needed some new reading glasses. I'd noticed it. My old ones weren't as good anymore. When I went in, I told him. He looked at my eyes. Then he gave me the biggest shock of my life. He said, 'You know, Sadie, you're going blind.' He said I had glaucoma. I told him I'd never heard that before. He told me to come back in two weeks. Can you imagine? I was just shocked. Hold on, here's your father." "Mom," I said, "wait, Mom." "Hello?" said my father. "Dad? It's Michael. How are you?" "What?" he said. "It's me. How are you?" "What?" he said. My mother took the phone. "He had a bad night. He just got up. He's a little groggy." "Mother," I said, "tell me exactly what the doctor told you." "I just did. I can't talk now. Goodbye." She hung up. "Wonderful," I thought. "My mother's going blind; my father doesn't know who I am, and I've got an appointment with an embalmer. This is it. After this, I'm leaving."

Gene Raymond met me at the door when I walked in. He had a gentle handshake and a low, quiet, raspy voice. His breath smelled of cigarettes and mouthwash: his eyes were gray. He was also nearly seven feet tall, with the face and white-haired mane of an old lion and the body of a circus strong man. He looked to be about sixty, but when I asked him, he ignored the question. He ignored so many of my questions at first and changed the subject so often that I felt like the fall guy in a silent film, rushing back and forth, trying to plug leaks that turned into geysers behind his back. Gene Raymond had a lot of opinions about embalming, opinions he volunteered, whether he was asked or not. First, I thought it was because he'd been a bachelor so long that he'd grown used to talking to himself. Then I thought it was because he'd been an embalmer for so many years that there was nothing else he knew how to talk about. Finally I realized he was so deaf he'd grown used to holding up both ends of a conversation at once. As soon as I understood that, I settled back and listened like a man eavesdropping on someone else's conversation. Occasionally, I'd break in, repeat myself two or three times, and get an answer out of him. Otherwise, it was an amiable monologue.

He was born, he said, in Arkansas, born poor. When he was a boy, a neighbor of his, "a nice old fella" who always gave him candy, came home one day, sat down on his porch, and asked his wife to bring him some ice "'cause his head was hurting something fierce." Then he keeled over and died. "Cerebral hemorrhage," said Raymond. They took him away and put him in a coffin. He looked "so old and bad and pasty" that Raymond decided "right then and there" to be an undertaker. "I wanted to make him more reposed," he said. I asked what he meant by that. "Pardon?" he said. "Reposed," I said. "What's reposed?" "What's what?" he said. That went on for a bit until he said, "Come on with me and I'll show you."

We walked across the foyer, up a short flight of steps, turned down a hall, and stopped in front of a massive set of sliding doors. Raymond drew them open, like Samson parting the columns of a pagan temple. We stepped into a dimly lit Victorian parlor. In front of us lay a man in a flag-draped coffin. Raymond turned up the lights. A sixty-five-year-old man, he said. Came back from World War II and "never did a stick of work since." He'd gone to the VA Hospital for a checkup. They'd done an angiogram and "that was that." Now the man lay dressed in a brown double-breasted suit he probably bought when he came back from the war, his hands folded just below his breastbone, his nose pointed straight up at the ceiling. "Did you do this?" I gestured. "Yes, sir," he said, nodding. The man's skin had the color of a Band-Aid. His lips were so flat and thin they looked as if they'd been painted on. They were lavender. "You try to make 'em look like they're at peace," said Raymond. "Like they're not suffering anymore." I nodded. The man looked like he'd been made by the same people who made Barbie dolls. "Very realistic," I thought. "Maybe this guy's Ken's Uncle Bill. Ken and Barbie go to Uncle Bill's funeral.

The Complete Set Includes: Uncle Bill's Body, his Coffin, and three Limousines, Barbie's Mourning Dress, and Ken's Dark Suit. Flowers and Flag, extra." "You do it right," said Raymond, "and you can keep a fellow out for maybe six weeks without him smelling. You put in too much fluid, and a man feels like a piece of wood and looks just like a balloon. What you need is a nice firm base for your makeup. Restoration's something else again. I worked ten hours on one fella, once. He'd gone into the back of a truck in a Volkswagen at fifty miles an hour. Automobile accidents are always like that: a lot of head and face work. You gotta join the fractures and fill in with your plaster of Paris; suture the cuts and seal 'em with your suture seal and your drying powder; fill in the cracks and build 'em up with your wax, then smooth it all down and do your cosmetizing. The only trouble was, I must not have used enough suture seal, 'cause when we lifted him up and put him in the casket, one side of his face fell off. There musta been fluid under the wax, so when we moved him, it cracked and the whole thing slid off. Took me five more hours to get him right." Raymond let out a long breath and a low whistle. "Boy howdy, I tell you," he said. "Most times, though, once you set the features, you just try to blend your cosmetics up into the hairline. Everyone's a little different, though. For instance"— he stood back and studied my face—"if I was working on you, once I got the fluid in, I'd come back and stipple in your beard a little, not to give you a five o'clock shadow, but just to get your coloring right." "You shave people?" I asked. "Sure do," he said. "My motto is, 'We aim to please, not to tease.' " He smiled. "What kind of stuff do you use for makeup?" I asked. "Any old thing," he said. "Some use Avon, some use Clairol. I like Mary Kay, myself. It's pretty good for the price." Raymond turned down the lights and motioned me to follow him out.

We walked back across the foyer, up another short flight of steps, and down another hall to a majestic mahogany staircase. The walls of the hall were covered with pale yellow flocked wallpaper and decorated with nineteenth-century engravings of Napoleon's funeral. On the wall opposite the staircase hung a gigantic gilded mirror, perhaps four feet wide and eighteen feet high. Above us was a crystal chandelier. For a brief part of our journey upward, before the staircase turned, we could see and assess our reflections in the mirror; later, on the way down, we could view our stately descent. "I been doing this nearly forty years," Raymond said, as we trudged upward. "Forty years, and as far as I'm concerned, when my time comes, I want to go up in flames. None of this waiting around. Four hours and you're done. They take you out, break up the big pieces, and put you in a jar. Otherwise, it'll take the worms twenty years to turn you into a puddle of ooze." At the top of the stairs, in front of us, was a conference room, furnished in the style of the First Empire. On the wall were two eighteenth-century oils of a man and a woman, their faces so decayed that not even Raymond could have restored them. "This is where we sit the clients to talk things over," he said.

To the left was a grand, brightly lit, carpeted space that may once have been a ballroom. "This is the showroom," said Raymond. There were dozens of coffins resting on draped biers, scattered in groups, displayed around the room. "Take your pick," said Raymond. There was a yellow one of welded steel with painted enamel plaques of pink roses fixed to its sides. There were several of solid bronze with cranks that closed their lids down into gaskets. They looked strong and sleek enough to be launched into space or fired out of the torpedo tubes of a submarine. There were quite a few made of oak, walnut, and maple that were substantial enough to serve as furniture in a law firm. There were several angular, wedge-shaped ones made of pressed wood covered with cotton brocade that reminded me of some I'd just seen on television laid out in a field beside a row of fresh, empty graves. Off to one side was a cabinet that displayed various urns and cylinders. Beside it was a door that led to a little room. "What's in there?" I asked. "For Jews," he said. I stepped in and saw four simple wooden coffins, two pine, two oak, the most elaborate decorated with a Star of David carved on its lid. "A lot of people prefer these, not just Jews," he said. "See"—he bent down and put his hand under one—"they got holes drilled in the bottom. That's the Jewish law. Speeds things up." I knew all about those holes: my father's sister, Molly, the one who had pawned everything to bring him to America after the First War, had lived into her nineties. Once a year, for fifteen years, my father would rush her into intensive care, her children would gather around her deathbed, and she'd wake up, look around, and ask them in Yiddish why they weren't at work. "Nu? You're so rich? Your family can live on air?" she'd say. Then, one day in February, her house burnt down. The firemen carried her out, but she'd inhaled too much smoke and she died. The Burial Society washed her body, wrapped her in a shroud, put her in one of those coffins with holes in the bottom, and we drove her out to the cemetery in a snowstorm. According to law, it didn't make any difference who buried her, as long as it happened within a day. The gravediggers had carved a hole in the frozen ground and set up the rigging to lower her. The rabbi said what he had to say, and the men began their work, but we stopped them. "We'll do it," we said. She'd been such a tough old lady; she'd used her impending death, year after year, to control her children and her children's children; she'd come back from the brink so often that this time we wanted to be sure. We lowered her down, but she wouldn't sink. Overnight, the grave had filled with ground water. Her coffin bobbed back and forth, bouncing against chunks of floating ice and frozen mud. We looked at each other. She was still afloat. We grabbed the gravediggers' shovels and started throwing dirt down on her. Lumps of clay hit the lid of her coffin, rebounded, then splashed in the water. Thunk-splash, thunk-splash, thunk-splash in the middle of a snowstorm. A nice, simple burial. "You've seen enough?" Raymond asked. "Oh, yeah," I said.

Raymond motioned me to follow him. We crossed the showroom, walked down the hallway past the Empire conference room with its two decayed portraits, until we reached a wooden door without a handle. The door faced the brightly lit showroom, but it was unmarked, in shadow, thirty feet away from it. Raymond pushed it open and I followed. The floor changed to painted wood; the wall to painted plaster. Fifteen feet in front of us was another wooden door. Raymond pushed it open, and then immediately opened another door, set in the wall to the right. That door revealed another immediately behind it. Raymond unlocked it and we were in the prep room. It was a high-ceilinged, windowless, brightly lit room perhaps twenty feet wide and twenty-five feet long, heavily air-conditioned, smelling slightly of formaldehyde. Its floor was tiled gray; its walls, tiled beige. There were three bodies—one man, two women. The man looked as if he'd been starved and then beaten to death; he lay on a gurney half covered by a white plastic sheet, the thickness and consistency of a kitchen garbage bag. One of the women had lost all her hair and one of her breasts; my guess was she'd died of cancer. The other one was a plump old matron who looked as if she'd died immediately after visiting the beautician. The women lay on the room's only two morgue tables, their heads and arms propped up by stirrup-shaped blocks of hard rubber, their legs apart, their feet pointed at the opposite wall. Against that wall, at the end of each of the tables, was a toilet whose valves could be set to flush continuously. Between the toilets was an old green wooden kitchen table on which sat a pump with two glass-domed reservoirs that could each hold two and a half gallons of embalming fluid. To the left, in one corner, was a large black freight elevator that ran to the ground floor. Propped against it was a shipping crate whose label read "Child's Casket/ Liner: Blue Velvet/ Cover: Blue Velvet." There were three fifty-gallon paper trash cans next to it, overflowing with wooden packing excelsior, plastic wraps, and empty quart bottles of embalming fluid. To the right along the wall was a zinc-topped counter littered with jars, bottles, glue guns, tacking irons, and chrome-plated tools that looked as if they'd been designed for a veterinary surgeon: there were pliers, L-shaped probes, tubes, scalpels, boxes of brads and wires, and catheters; here and there were bottles of nail polish and nail-polish remover, jars of pink wax, makeup base, massage cream, drying powder, lipstick, eyeliners, and rouge. On top of all this lay an old-fashioned ledger, opened to a double page filled with names and dates, each clumsily written in big block letters. Propped up against a quart bottle of cavity fluid was a color snapshot of a very pretty, radiantly happy, middle-aged blond woman wearing a white summer dress. Next to the picture was a small white cardboard box with a St. Jude medal on a chain in it. Next to that was a tube of Super Glue. Above the counter, fixed to the wall, were old glass-fronted wooden kitchen cabinets stocked with bottles of tissue restorative, cavity and embalming fluid, syringes, and balls of white string.

I pointed at the wrecked old man on the gurney. "What happened to him?" I gestured. "Him?" said Raymond. "Picked him up this morning. He was a removal from a state home for the insane." I pointed at the sores, cuts, and bruises that covered his hands and arms, his head, his back, and his buttocks. "Bedsores," said Raymond. "Old people's skin gets real tender. You got to be real careful with 'em. Same with children. A lotta people say they don't like to embalm children. They say it's too tragic. But that's not the reason. They just don't want to take the trouble. Kids have these little veins. You have to put the fluid in them very slow. People just don't want to take the time." I pointed at the snapshot on the counter. "Who's this?" I asked. Raymond nodded at the bald woman missing the breast. "That's her. Her husband brought in the picture and the St. Jude medal. Brought in a wig, too. I always like to have a picture to work from. Especially for someone who's been sick for a long time. You wouldn't recognize her, would you? We'll fix her up. She'll look better than she did when she was alive." "And her?" I pointed at the matron. "Died at home of a heart attack, I understand," he said. "Took care of herself, too. Nice-looking old lady. She ought to be pretty easy. I always like to start with the easy ones. Course, you never know about their plumbing until it's too late. You all set?" I nodded. Raymond rolled up his sleeves, slipped on an apron, pulled on a pair of latex surgical gloves, and took two bottles of fluid off the shelf of the kitchen cabinet over the counter.

He unscrewed one and offered it to me. "Sniff," he said. It smelled like cherry cough syrup and looked like Pepto-Bismol. "That's the embalming fluid. It's got lanolin and glycerin in it. Mix a bottle of this with a bottle of cavity fluid—your cavity fluid's got more formaldehyde in it—you mix 'em up, add two and a half gallons of water, and that'll do her. She's a next-day burial, so she'll be fine. If she were a five-day, I'd put another two and a half gallons in her. But she'll be fine." He poured the bottles into the glass reservoir of the machine, added water from a hose connected to the same plumbing fixture as the toilet, and then turned back to the old lady. Freshly dyed red hair, clear skin, no bruises or blemishes. He lifted one of her arms at the wrist, cupped his other hand under her elbow, and bent her arm back and forth until it was flexible. He did the same thing with the other. Then he bent her hands back and forth, at the wrists, clasped them, and set them down, just below her rib cage, at the midline. "A little massage cream," he said. He rubbed it into her cheeks and neck and forehead. Then he reached for what looked like a pair of pliers and threaded a wire with a brad at one end through its jaws. "What's that?" I pointed. "Needle injector," he said. "For her jaws." He pried open her mouth, peeled back her upper lip, positioned the needle injector, and, with a move that reminded me of the way cattlemen fix plastic tags to the ears of their stock, he shot the wire out through her upper palate. Then he peeled back her lower lip, moved aside her tongue, and did the same thing through her lower jaw. He twisted the wires together, clipped them, and pressed them down against her lower teeth. "Now the lips," he said. "If someone's got her eyes closed, you look at her lips: they tell the story. First, you got to find the weather line. See." He showed me her lower lip, one side rough, still colored with lipstick; one side smooth, still filmed with mucus. "That's the weather line; that tells you how she held her mouth." Since he'd peeled back her lips to wire her jaw, he'd disturbed things a bit. He patted her lips back in place, stepped back, looked, stuffed a little bit of cotton under her upper lip, and then stood back and looked again. "All right," he said. He reached for the Super Glue. "Sometimes, if they don't stay, you have to use this on 'em. For now, she's fine."

"Next we raise the vessels," he said. He cut open a V-shaped flap of skin on the left side of her neck close to her collarbone and exposed her carotid and jugular. "The carotid's the way in; the jugular's the way out." He took an L-shaped probe, slipped it under both blood vessels, and tugged them out and away from the connecting tissue. "Look like macaroni, don't they?" he said. He reached across to the counter and held up a long, stainless-steel tube with a thin metal rod in it. "This is your drain tube." He snipped open the jugular and slid the tube down it. Then he pumped the metal rod up and down like a plunger. This'll clear out the clots," he said. "Sometimes, though, you put two and a half gallons in, and you have lumps. Bumps and lumps. Then you have to open up the other side and put your fluid in there. That's what's called a two-point. If it's still clogged, you have to open up the axillaries in the armpits. You do both of those—

that's called a four-point. Then—if you have to open up the femorals, plus the axillaries, plus both carotids and jugulars, you got yourself a headache, and that's called a six-point. You only do a six-point if someone's gonna be out for a long time, or if the plumbing's shot. If nothing works, you call Roto-Rooter." He looked at me and laughed. "I'm just kidding. Here we go." He left the drain tube in the jugular, slipped an L-shaped metal catheter into the carotid, connected the catheter to a hose, and turned on the pump of the embalming machine. The machine hummed, and very soon a mixture of water, pink Pepto-Bismol, and blood was spurting out of the tube in the old lady's neck, and running down the table to a drain between her feet.

"We'll give her a while, and then we'll aspirate her," he said. I wanted to ask him what aspirating was, but I decided to wait and see. The smell of formaldehyde grew so strong my eyes began to water. Raymond leaned back and lit a cigarette. He picked up the snapshot of the blonde in the white dress and held it next to the face of the bald woman without a breast. "That cancer sure does take it out of you, don't it?" he said. He put down the snapshot, picked up the hose he'd used to fill the embalming machine, and ran water over the front of her, then turned her on her side, balanced her, and ran water over her back. "I always wash 'em first," he said. He found a sliver of soap on the counter, worked up a lather, and began to rub her down. By the time he'd washed, rinsed, and dried her, the reservoir of the embalming machine was almost empty. He turned it off, slipped the drain tube out of the old lady's jugular, pulled the catheter out of her carotid, disconnected it from the tube that ran to the machine, and tied off her blood vessels with some string. He reached over to the counter and picked up a polished metal tube. It was about two and a half feet long, and it had a sharp, hollow point at one end, rounded on the top, flat on the bottom, with three little holes like snouts drilled into the underside of its tip. At the other end were two fittings for hoses. He held it up in front of me. It looked like a lance. "This is what you call a trocar or an aspirator; it don't matter, it does the same thing." He connected one of the trocar's fittings to the hose he'd used to run fluid into the old lady. He connected another hose to the trocar's other fitting, and ran it over to the toilet at the end of the morgue table. He turned a valve on the toilet so that it flushed continuously, then reconnected the hose from the embalming machine to another valve, and flicked a switch. "Works like a suction pump now," he said.

The old woman lay on the morgue table with her eyes closed, her jaws set, her hands folded—looking, if anything, more self-satisfied and a bit rosier than she had before Raymond set her features and transfused her. Raymond held the trocar up in the air, its tip pointed at the ceiling. He stepped beside her, and with two fingers he pressed down on her belly, just below her rib cage, to the right of the midline. Then he stuck the trocar into that dimple like a spear. The sound of the machine changed from a hum to a rapid, steady thump-thump-thump-thump, and the contents of the old lady's intestines began to pump out of her, into the toilet. Raymond twisted and turned the trocar, pumping it up and down like a ramrod, rotating it, now in one direction, now in the other, puncturing the walls of her organs. "Sucks it all up," he said. "Otherwise, she'd bloat and push everything up, out her mouth and nose. You don't do this, you got yourself a real mess." The old lady's belly heaved and flummoxed. The pump ran, the toilet flushed, and suddenly I thought I was looking at a painting by Van Eyck, one of his triptychs of the Apocalypse, where sinners are tortured by devils with spears. The old lady was dead; I knew she was dead, but Raymond had done enough to make her look as if she were asleep, just enough so I thought I was watching a nightmare, her nightmare where she was asleep but awake, eyes closed, paralyzed as a giant probed her belly with a lance. But Raymond was no devil in hell, and the old lady never made a sound. When he finished, he turned off the machine, disconnected the suction hose, screwed a quart bottle of cavity fluid to it, upended it, and let it run into the old lady's belly. Then he drew out the trocar, wiped it with a paper towel, and screwed a gray plastic plug into the hole he'd made. "That's it," he said. My eyes were burning with tears from the formaldehyde. Just then, the door to the room slammed open and a black woman in a maid's white uniform said, "Mr. Gene! Mr. Phillip says to turn off the toilet immediately. There's a leak coming through the ceiling down below!" "Holy shit!" said Raymond and lunged for the shut-off valve on the toilet.

I backed out the door and walked down the grand staircase, wiping my eyes. Lazar was standing in the foyer with one hand on his hip. He looked upset but he was smiling. "You certainly picked an opportune moment for your visit," he said. He laughed at himself. "I spoke with my aunt this morning." He looked at his watch. "Why don't you drop by and visit her after lunch. See you later, okay?" I took the hint and walked out the door. I wasn't very hungry, so I walked until I found a park bench and sat and smoked a cigarette. It was noontime, and lovely women and well-dressed men strolled by. I looked at them and thought about the old lady, and felt like Savonarola. "A bonfire of vanities," I thought. "All those years of worrying about her figure; all her trips to the hairdresser, all her closets full of clothes, all her dinner parties, teas, and vacations, and she ends up with a spigot in her neck and a trocar in her belly. Damn!" I looked up at the tourists. I felt like a fool. "Talk about precious but useless knowledge. Even if they knew, they'd keep walking. The last time people like them even thought about the Last Judgment was the fifteenth century. Now it's just me and Van Eyck and Savonarola, and you know what happened to Savonarola. So smoke your cigarette, and shut up, and go off and talk to Lazar's aunt."

At the appointed hour, I walked through the side gate of the funeral home, across its parking lot, past a row of maroon Lincolns, to the house of Alice May Lazar Cummings, sister of the painter who'd studied with Hans Hofmann, and, as she soon told me, widow of a long-time member of the board of RCA. A black maid dressed in the same uniform as the woman who'd rushed into the prep room opened the door and invited me in. "Mrs. Cummings will see you in a moment," she said and left me. The house's front hall was paved with alternating squares of white and black marble that echoed as I walked. Along the left wall ran a twenty-foot long Jackson Pollock, a dancing network of red, blue, orange, and yellow tracks that bounced around like a transcription of the artist's nervous system. Above the hall table on the right were two small ink gouaches, one dynamite red, one ultraviolet blue, from Robert Motherwell's *Lyric Suite*, which arched like solar flares in their frames. Through the door to the front parlor, I could see, on the opposite wall, a grand and ominous Franz Kline, its thick jagged blacks cutting across a white ground like a traffic accident. I leaned through the door and saw a jade-green, cadmium-yellow, and red Hans Hofmann, and, resting on the mantel of the fireplace, I looked and thought I saw a Joseph Cornell box. I'd been in private rooms before whose walls were hung with Braques and Matisses, but never had I been in a private house that sheltered a Cornell. I forgot my manners and stepped into the room to see. I stood in front of the fireplace and took a breath: it was a Cornell, a rare beauty furnished with a bright paper parrot, two perches hung with spangled bracelets, a wooden ball, a chalkstone, and a moon.

The maid found me there. I was ashamed. "I'm sorry," I said. "I've just never seen a Cornell like this." The woman smiled. "Mrs. Cummings will see you now." I followed her through the parlor, to a dining room and then out a door, into a gigantic atrium that must have been added to the house long after it was built. The room was perhaps seventy feet long, two clear stories, perhaps twenty-four feet high. The left wall had once been the outer wall of the house; everything else was made of frosted glass and steel, like a gigantic greenhouse. There were date palms, banana trees, asparagus ferns, gardenias, and hanging geraniums. The floor was made of irregular blocks of gray granite. Far off, at one end, was a huge round white marble table with wicker chairs drawn up around it. In one of them, dressed in a rose-colored silk caftan, sat Alice May Lazar Cummings, drinking a demitasse while she looked at her mail through an illuminated magnifying glass. She glanced up as I was seated. "How do you do," she said, and offered me her hand. The woman was so old and frail, she had had so many face-lifts or had lived such a scant, provident, and elegant life, that the fine bones of her hand and the perfect bones of her face made her look like an animated Giacometti. "Cicely, bring Mr. Lesy a coffee, please," she said, and dismissed her maid. "My nephew tells me you're interested in the family business," she said, as she went back to her mail. "Well, I have very little to tell you. It's a business like any other: my grandfather started it, and my father carried it on, then it fell to me. Finally I relinquished it to marry my late husband. I'm sure Phillip has told you all this. It's all very tiresome. Do you have any interest in the arts?" "Yes," I said, and remarked on her Cornell. That began an hour of reminiscences about her brother the painter and Franz Kline and Robert Motherwell, his friends. The maid brought us one coffee after another, and we traded opinions about Motherwell's *Spanish Elegies* and Calder's *Stabiles*, and the early Jasper Johns. In the middle of a remark about some of Pollock's bad habits, the maid reappeared and announced: "The lady from the National Gallery is here." By then, Mrs. Cummings had finished her mail, which, I noticed, consisted of slitting open an envelope and then throwing the whole thing in the trash. "Nothing but junk, nothing but junk," she said. "Invitations, announcements, and appeals." She smiled. "I did enjoy our conversation. Please call if you have any more questions." She offered me her hand and I left.

"Very refreshing," I thought. "Not bad if you can manage it. Not a word about death. Except that she lives next door to it and ran the business to pay all the bills. How many funerals did the Pollock cost? How many for the Cornell? Art and death. Not a bad fertilizer. I always thought there was a connection, but nothing this obvious." I walked back to the funeral home and asked for Mr. Lazar. "Gone for the day," I was told. I walked across the foyer and down the hall to the grand staircase. Two maids walked past, carrying mops and pails of ammonia, still cleaning up from the disaster before lunch. I walked up the stairs and through the doors to the prep room. There was no one there but the bodies. The old man still lay on the gurney, but his hands had been folded and it looked as if he'd been washed. I put my hand on his shoulder. It felt cold and hard and smooth as an apple. Dead, definitely dead. I looked across at the old lady. Raymond had closed up the flap in her neck and patched it with wax: she looked as well-groomed and stolid as ever. It was the bald-headed woman who'd changed. She wore a chiffon summer gown, high heels, and a full head of blond hair. Her face was delicately colored, her features gently set, her mouth drawn in a faint smile. Raymond was a goddamn artist. She looked terrific. A little thin maybe, but that was fashionable. As far as the breast and the plug in her belly, no one could guess.

I stood back and looked at them all, then I said goodbye and walked out the door. I drove back to the inn, packed my bags, and left. I didn't think much of anything for a while. I just looked at the road and drove. I was headed home. Toward sunset, I thought about Gene. A real artist. Maybe not in the same league as Alexander Calder, but the man had some magic. He'd wired their jaws, flushed their plumbing, cleaned out their guts, filled in the holes, and fixed their faces. As good a job of taxidermy as I'd seen. Not art maybe, but better than some marlins and swordfish I'd seen over some bars. Which reminded me of something I hadn't done for a while. As soon as I saw a motel, I pulled off and checked in. Then I found the lounge and ordered a whisky. "See, touch, feel, and believe," I thought. It was over, but I didn't understand it. It was over, but I didn't feel a thing. Numb, maybe. But it wasn't right. "What did you expect?" I thought. "A glow, a sign, lights in the sky, pennies from heaven, the Three Kings knocking at your door, looking for a fourth? You lived through it, now go back home and wait." I stayed long enough to stop thinking, then I went back to my room. That night, what I dreamed I didn't remember.

The next morning, I woke up early and turned on the tube. They were broadcasting, live, an interview from Mexico City with a fireman from Dade County, Florida. He was standing in front of the ruins of the General Hospital, dressed in a slicker, wearing a helmet. Last night, he said, they'd found a five-day-old baby. The earthquake had happened four days ago, so the child must have been born and then buried. The mother was dead; the baby was alive; he'd sucked on her breast and lived. They'd also found a nurse and a doctor. They showed pictures of the doctor dragging himself out with his elbows, pulling himself onto a stretcher. They showed pictures of the baby being lifted out, wrapped up, and then rushed away. The fireman said they'd located the maternity ward. He said they could hear the babies crying and were trying to reach them. I stopped listening and started to shiver. Then I started to cry. "Born and then buried, born and then buried, born and then buried, and then born again. Born out of one womb, then born out of another; born out of life, then born out of death. Death and rebirth, just before the Day of Judgment, a living creature born from the grave. You wanted a sign? You got a sign. Now go home and wait."